SHIRDI SA

OTHER BOOKS IN THE SERIES

SPIRITUAL MASTERS

SHIRDI SAI BABA

His Divine Manifestations

Compiled by
Vinny Chitluri

HarperCollins *Publishers* India

Indus Source Books
Indian Spirit, Universal Wisdom

First published in 2016 by Indus Source Books

This edition co-published in India by
HarperCollins *Publishers* in 2019
A-75, Sector 57, Noida, Uttar Pradesh 201301, India
www.harpercollins.co.in

2 4 6 8 10 9 7 5 3 1

P-ISBN: 978-93-5302-690-5
E-ISBN: 978-93-5302-691-2

Printed and bound at
Thomson Press (India) Ltd

MIX
Paper
FSC FSC® C010615

This book is produced from independently certified FSC® paper to ensure
responsible forest management.

Contents

Preface

Years ago Baba had said, "I am immortal, know this truth; and forever get experiences of my immortality." Baba has kept his promise by appearing in the physical form before his devotees time and again, whenever the need has arisen. It is to provide succour, comfort and guidance that Baba appears before his devotees even to this day. This book narrates the experiences of those blessed devotees who have had the good fortune of having a divine vision of Baba either in his physical form, or in a dream, or by hearing his voice.

There are 108 *leelas* in this book, as 108 is a very auspicious number. The sum of 108 is 9, and the number 9 has profound astrological and mythological significance. Astrologically, there are *Navagrahas* or 9 planets, *Navratna* (nine gems) that influence human beings, and *Navadhanya* (nine grains) that appease the planets. The human body has *Nava Dwara* or 9 orifices. Spiritually, we celebrate *Nava-Ratri* the 9 days of the festival of the *Nava-Durga* or 9 Goddesses. There are the *Nava-Naths* or 9 sages of the *Nath Sampradya*, and *Nava-Narayana*, or nine forms of Lord Vishnu.

Most importantly for us Baba devotees, Baba stressed the importance of *Nava Vida Bhakti* or the nine modes of devotion. In chapter 21 of the *Shri Sai Satcharita*, Baba narrates the parable of the horse passing 9 lumps of manure to Ananthrao Patanker. The 9 lumps are symbolic of the *Nava Vida Bhakti*.

In chapter 12 of the *Shripada Shrivallabha Charitra* the meaning of the number 9 is described superbly. It says, "Paramatma is beyond this universe. When the number 9 is multiplied by any digit, the sum total will always be 9. The number 9 thus signifies the changeless Supreme Self," or the divine Lord Sainath.

In the *Shri Sai Satcharita*, chapter 3, ovi 3, Baba says, "If my *leelas* are recorded, then any sins committed through ignorance will be dissipated. And when they are listened to, with faith and devotion, the cares and troubles of worldly life will be forgotten."

I have tried to narrate some incredible *leelas* of Baba with the hope that the readers find answers to the trials and tribulations in their lives. By repeatedly reading them, they may find the spiritual gems embedded in them, which would be the "Light House" to help the devotees to navigate through their sea of troubles.

- Vinny Chitluri

Acknowledgements

I would like to thank Pavar Kaka for unhesitatingly giving me the photographs of Baba's devotees which are indeed very rare.

I am indebted to Sachin Kadam of Sanskruti Graphics for designing the cover of this book.

I would like to thank my dear friend Manjula for helping me in innumerable ways.

I owe a debt of gratitude to my dear friend Neha for undertaking the tedious task of editing the book, and helping me to put the material together.

And last but not the least I would like to thank the publishers, for bringing this book to you, the readers.

Mahadev Waman Sapatnekar and the Removal of Doubts

Mahadev W. Sapatneker   **Parvatibai Sapatneker**

It was at the insistence of his father that Mahadev Waman Sapatnekar, an attorney and a resident of Akkalkot, first visited Shirdi in 1913. At that point Sapatnekar was disillusioned and troubled by the turn of events in his life. He was a 33 year old widower, and had lost his wife and son to Diphtheria. He blamed God for this loss. Then he married Paravatibai, a young girl who was just 13 years old, but even after four years of marriage his wife was unable to conceive. Also, his wife suffered from terrible pain in her abdomen and trunk

Mahadev's father, Waman Sapatnekar, insisted that he go to Shirdi and seek Baba's blessings. Waman Sapatnekar had heard a glowing account of Baba's divinity from Shevde, who was Mahadev's friend and classmate. In chapter 48 of the *Shri Sai Satcharita*, Shevde's story is beautifully described. Shevde, a staunch devotee of Sai Baba was quite unprepared for a forthcoming examination, but was confident that he would pass as Baba had assured him of success.

In the bygone days, a son never questioned his father, but

implicitly followed his orders. Therefore, although Mahadev lacked faith in Baba, he did as his father advised, and along with his younger brother Panditrao, set out for Shirdi. Upon reaching Shirdi they went to the Dwarka Mai to pay obeisance to Baba. But when Mahadev bent down to touch Baba's feet, he roared "*Chal hut*" ("Go away") and shoved him with such force that his turban flew out of the Sanctum. Mahadev stayed at Shirdi for three days and whenever he went to meet Baba, he received the same "*Chal hut*" treatment. Mahadev felt humiliated and hurt, and returned home in a gloomy frame of mind.

Parvatibai has recounted those days: "When my husband went to Shirdi, I had a keen desire to accompany him. In those days a wife was subservient and couldn't speak to her husband openly, so I was left in my in-laws' home at Madhegaon. That night while I was sleeping beside my sister-in-law, I had this dream vision, wherein I saw a bright flash of light. At that moment I remembered that there was not a drop of water in the house, so I took a pitcher and went to the well nearby. The well was known as Lakkadsha's well. I was in a great hurry as the daughter-in-law was not supposed to go out of the house alone. I needed to fetch the water and return before my father-in-law returned from the court. There I saw a fakir standing next to the well. He approached me and said, 'My dear girl! Why get exhausted needlessly. I shall get your pitcher filled with pure water.' I was scared, as I suspected the fakir had some bad intentions. My fears were confirmed when he lifted his kafni and sat down to pass urine in front of me. I was petrified and ran home as fast as I could. However, he ran after me saying, 'Lassie! Don't run away, I have come to give you something.' On reaching home I closed the door securely, but the fakir came to the door and threw small pebbles through the slits in the door. 'Lassie! I have come to give you something', the fakir repeatedly said. I was about to shout when I got up sweating profusely with fright. When I realised that it was a dream, I woke my sister-in-law and asked her what the time was. However she jokingly said, 'Aren't you able to sleep? Aha!

Your husband has gone to Shirdi and you must be dreaming of him.'

The next morning I narrated the dream to my mother-in-law. My father-in-law overheard it, and inquired about it in great detail. He sternly told my husband to go to Shirdi and take me with him, as there was some divine message hidden in the dream. My husband was reluctant to revisit Shirdi and get insulted again. But my father-in-law insisted that he go, taking both me and his elder brother's wife, who didn't have a son till then.

Hence, we went to Shirdi; Baba was returning from Lendi Baugh at that time. I was stunned, as he was the same fakir that I had seen in my dream. Then looking at me he started yelling, 'Oh! Dear mother! My abdomen and trunk are aching terribly.'

I was baffled and concerned, and wanted to know what was wrong with him. The devotees explained that Baba often acted like this and relieved the devotee of the malady, by taking it upon himself. I however couldn't stop giggling at his perfect play acting of my symptoms. Two months later, the nagging pain in my abdomen and trunk disappeared, and I was filled with gratitude for Baba.

Later in the day, we went to have Baba's darshan in the Dwarka Mai. My husband went forward with the flowers and fruit offerings. Again Baba said, '*Chal hut*.' When my turn came, however, Baba allowed me to place my head at his feet, and made me sit near him. He then placed his palm in a container of *Udi* and with a little force placed his palm on my forehead and blessed me. He said, 'Take one, two, three, or four. How many do you want?' This was in regard to my barren state. Later I had 8 sons and 1 daughter, and Baba fulfilled his promise.

My husband was filled with remorse and repentance for having doubted Baba when Shevde spoke about Baba's benevolence. He decided to stay on at Shirdi until Baba forgave and blessed him. Once, he saw Baba seated alone in the Dwarka Mai, so he ran and clasped his feet, beseeching forgiveness. Baba placed his blessed hand on his head and

3

made him sit close by. Meanwhile a shepherdess came and started massaging Baba's feet. Looking at Sapatnekar, Baba said, 'This gentleman thinks I killed his son. Do I kill people's sons? Now I shall bring a son in his wife's womb.'

Filled with joy, my husband again fell at Baba's feet with tears gushing down his cheeks. He ran to where we were staying and excitedly narrated what had happened. He asked me to prepare *puran polis* (chapattis with a stuffing of Bengal gram cooked with jaggery) as an offering to Baba. However I had already prepared *shira* (semolina halva) as Bapu Sahib Jog had suggested. Then both of us went for the *arati*, and I handed my platter of *shira* to Jog. He kept it at the rear of the plates brought by various devotees. After the *arati*, Baba was given a plate filled with our offerings; but Baba pushed it aside and leaned over and pulled my plate towards him. With great relish he ate a handful of *shira* from my plate. The next day was Thursday and we saw the Chavadi procession."

Parvatibai narrates some unusual information about the Chavadi procession. She recalls, "Baba never sat in the palanquin. If devotees lifted him and put him inside, he disappeared and was seen walking at the back of palanquin. Baba often broke into a dance with great agility—he put one foot forward, then the other foot and danced in abandon. He rhythmically moved to the clash of the cymbals, his lithe body swaying like a reed. It was a sight that Lord Indra would have envied. Baba's face shone with a brilliant glow like Lord Panduranga."

The Sapatnekars were to leave Shirdi the next day. Before leaving, they went to seek permission from Baba. Mahadev told his wife, "I shall offer one rupee as *dakshina* to Baba. If he asks again I will happily give one more rupee. But if he asks for more money I will have to sell my gold ring and your bangles." To Mahadev's great surprise, Baba only asked for two rupees and repeated the exact same words that Sapatnekar had said to his wife in their room. Hearing this, the doubts that were still lurking in his mind disappeared and he was convinced about Baba's sanctity and omnipresence. Thus, Mahadev Sapatnekar became devoted to Baba.

The lessons that we can learn from this *leela* are:

1. Never ever doubt saints.
2. By shouting, "*Chal Hut*", Baba was removing Mahadev's bad karma and fructifying his '*sanchit* karma', then filling it with crystal clear water, which is his grace, mercy and blessing.
3. The passing of urine is symbolic of the removal of waste or impurities from Mahadev's wife.
4. The throwing of pebbles represents strong progeny. Baba says, "Take one, two, three, or four. How many do you want?" Thus she had eight sons and a daughter.
5. Sapatnekar used to think that Lord Datta didn't save his son. Since Baba and Datta are the same, Baba says, "He thinks I killed his son."

Ref.: *Shri Sai Leela Magazine*, Volume 65, No. 4, July 1986.

2

Parvatibai's Children and Mahadev's Faith

The story of Sapatnekar, his wife Parvatibai and his sons is exceedingly lengthy, so I have presented it as two *leela*s. I will now narrate how Baba's blessings came to fruition and the Sapatnekars had 8 sons and a daughter.

After the unforgettable visit to Shirdi, the very next year, that is in 1915, Parvatibai became pregnant and delivered a bonny, healthy baby boy. The child was christened Murlidhar, and when he was eight months old they took him to Shirdi. When Murlidhar was placed at Baba's feet, Baba picked him up, laid him in his lap, and cooed and spoke to him. In due course of time, Parvatibai had two more sons, named Bhaskar and Dinkar. Both were fortunate to have Baba's darshan. When Dinkar was about 3 months old, Parvatibai took him to Shirdi, and placed him at Baba's feet. Baba lifted the baby in his hands and threw him in the air with great force. However nothing untoward happened to Dinkar and he was caught by a devotee seated there. Dinkar says, "Because Baba threw me in the air while I was but a child, a transformation occurred and I became very spiritual from a very young age."

Parvatibai recalls, "After our first son Murlidhar was born, my husband's faith in Sai Baba became firm. In the years to come it developed stronger, so much so that when our second son Bhaskar died at the age of ten years, he did not blame Baba. On the other hand, he called all our children together and stood them before Baba's photograph and said, 'Baba! Take away all of them and I shall not mind as they are all yours. However, I shall not give up my faith in you.'"

Years later, Dinkar said, "My father was initially devoted

to Lord Datta, and used to go on a pilgrimage to Gangapur frequently. A year after the loss of his first son, Mahadev visited Gangapur. In a state of bereavement and anguish he jumped into the river with the intent of ending his wretched life. Lo! Lord Datta himself pulled him out of the river and asked him to go to Akkalkot. A few years later Sai Baba drew my father into his flock and made him into a staunch devotee. From this story it is crystal clear that the darshan and blessings of any saint are impossible without good karma and penance of past lives. Possibly Baba wanted to show my father that he and Lord Datta are the same. Baba wanted to push my father's original spirituality by removing his disappointment and sorrow of family life. Thus the '*Chal hut*' drama may have been Baba's secret method for removing all the negative energy that had enveloped my father's very being. This was Baba's unique method of drawing my father to him and guiding him on his spiritual path."

The Sapatnekars originally hailed from the village Sapatne, and hence were called Sapatnekars. Later they moved to Madhegaon. Practising law was their family profession, and even to this day it is followed by the members of this family. Mahadev became a well known Pleader at Akkalkot. He was an affluent landowner, with his own home and property. In 1961, some of his family members moved to Pune.

Parvatibai went to stay at Pune with her son Dinkar, as he had a paralytic stroke. She was 88 years old at that time and was not in good health. Parvatibai passed away on the 30th of October 1983, at 4 p.m. According to the Hindu calendar this was the same month when Baba took Maha Samadhi (10th day of Ashvin). Also like Baba, Parvatibai breathed her last after the 10th day had finished and *Ekadashi* had commenced. At the time of death, she was conscious till the last moment and left the world peacefully with a smile on her face.

Ref.: *Shri Sai Leela Magazine*, Volume 65, No 4, July 1986.

3

Gangubai's Persistence

Gangubai Aurangabadkar   **Sakharam Aurangabadkar**

In chapter 36 of the *Shri Sai Satcharita* the wonderful *leela* of
Gangubai and Sakharam Aurangabadkar is given. Although
Gangubai had been married for 27 years, she was unable to
conceive and bear children. Having heard of Baba's divinity
and compassionate *leela*s, she came to Shirdi along with her
step-son Vishvanath, to seek Baba's blessing. Gangubai sought
Shama's help, and through his intercession offered a coconut
to Baba. Then Baba said, "Do coconuts produce children?
How do you cultivate such superstitions?" However, Shama
was adamant that Baba bless her with a child. After a great deal
of persuasion, Baba finally blessed her saying, "She will get a
child, after twelve months." And so it came to pass.

A short biography of Sakharam Tatyaji Aurangabadkar and
his wife Gangubai is narrated by their grandson Dattatreya
Vasudev Aurangabadkar.

The Aurangabadkar's ancestral home was in Sholapur, and
they were "goldsmiths" by profession. Sakharam owned a
jewellery shop in Mangalwar Peth, and he was famous for
crafting "ready made" jewellery. During that time, clients

were unable to purchase exquisite jewellery. Hence they would come to Sakharam and explain to him the pattern and type of jewellery they desired to have made. Sakharam with his expertise, ingenuity and dexterity would create beautiful jewellery for them. He was respected for his righteousness and honesty. At that time there were no financial banks; so Sakharam also had a pawn-brokerage business. Thus his family was very affluent. In Sholapur he was fondly known as "Sakyha Hari", that is, Hari or the Lord who is my friend.

Dattatreya recalls: "My grandfather had a noble personality. He was tall and well built. He wore a 'pheta' (turban) and a coat on top of his *dhotar (dhoti)* and walked in a majestic manner. Sakharam was a pious person. At a young age he could recite the *Vishnusahasranaam* and every evening upon returning home he would sit on the swing and recite it with devotion.

At that time, it was a common practice for a man to remarry if his wife did not bear any children. Thus, Sakharam remarried and a son was born; and he was named Vishvanath. Gangubai was affluent, wore a lot of jewellery, and was well dressed. Nonetheless, she was extremely saddened by the fact that she was unable to conceive and everyone called her 'Vanjoti', a derogatory name for a barren woman. Society was very unkind to infertile women, and treated them as a curse to society. Consequently she was hurt and distraught, and was unable to enjoy her affluence.

So she sought refuge in God. There was a temple of Lord Ram in front of her home, and Gangubai spent most of her time praying in that temple. She observed numerous vows, like performing *Rudra Abhishek* to Lord Shiva during the holy month of *Shravan*. Gangubai would chant the thousand names of Lord Shiva while offering a thousand 'bilva patra' (Aegle Marmelos) on his *Shiva Linga*. At the end of that holy month she had a huge feast where everyone could come and dine.

On every *Purnima* (full moon) she had a *Satya Narayana Puja* performed in her home. Aurangabadkar's family deity was Renuka Devi, so Gangubai would climb to the top of Mahurgad at midnight. In the darkness of the night she would pick up the first stone that touched her hand and bring it home. She would apply ochre colour on it, and eyes, ears and a nose made of gold were fixed on it. Then the stone would be adorned with jewellery and worshipped as a Goddess. All these rituals are still conducted at their home even to this day.

Even after observing all these rituals, fasts, and vows, Gangubai was unable to conceive. As the Gods did not seem to come to Gangubai's aid she sought refuge in saints. Gangubai started visiting Humanabad, and did *seva* in Manik Prabhu's Sansthan. One day while she was sweeping the floor, she found two pearls. Gangubai immediately returned them to Manik Prabhu. However, Manik Prabhu did not accept them and asked her to keep them. Gangubai took them as a good omen, and returned to Sholapur. As Akkalkot is quite near Sholapur, Gangubai started visiting Swami Samartha. There also she performed a lot of *seva*. *Seva* done with devotion never goes in vain.

On one occasion, Das Ganu performed a *kirtan* in Sholapur, and she and her family attended it. This had a tremendous effect on her, and as Das Ganu spoke of Baba's divinity, his compassion for the downtrodden, and the numerous *leela*s that he performed for his devotees, she was filled with faith. After Das Ganu had finished the *kirtan* she met him and enquired about Baba. Das Ganu reassured her, 'You go to Shirdi and prostrate at his feet. Your desire will definitely be fulfilled.' Gangubai did not waste another moment and got permission from her husband to leave for Shirdi. Taking her step-son Vishwanath, she went to meet Baba.

At Shirdi she tried her level best to meet Baba and open her heart to him. This was especially difficult as there was always someone or the other present there. Then she sought Shama's help, and finally her wish was granted."

Gangubai and Vishvanath stayed in Shirdi for two months and her persistence paid off. Baba's promise came to fruition in 1911, and Sakharam and Gangubai were blessed with a baby boy. The baby was cute, with a rosy, fair complexion, but most importantly, he was a healthy baby. Gangubai basked in the joy

Ramkrishna Aurangabadkar   Vishvanath Aurangabadkar

of finally giving birth to a boy and everyone around her was happy for her. Sakharam had decided that the baby would be christened by Baba. Thus when the child was 5 months old they took the baby to Shirdi. Baba placed the baby in his lap and blessed him with the name "Rama Krishna" and as *dakshina* Sakharam gave Baba 500 Rupees. However, Baba didn't accept it and it was later used to construct a stable for Baba's favourite horse, Shyam Karana.

In 1915, Gangubai had another son named Vasudev, and a year later she passed away. Thus both her children were bereft of their mother's love, but as it was a large extended family, they were well cared for. Vishvanath's wife Mathurabai took good care of both the children.

The Sadguru surpasses the Kalpavriksha, or the wish-fulfilling divine tree, and Kamdhenu or the celestial cow of plenty, who bestows on the owner whatever he desires. Only after coming to Baba, did Gangubai conceive and have children. Thus the Sadguru is superior and excels the Kalpavriksha and Kamadhenu.

In chapter 36 of the Shri Sai Satcharita, ovi 149, Shama says, "Please look upon her graciously and put that coconut in the lap of her sari. By your blessings many sons and daughters will be born to her."

In ovi 150, Shama says, "Oh! We know the power and marvel of your words! So priceless are they that a long train of children will follow, on their own."

It was only by Shama's unshakeable faith in Baba, and Baba's word that she was blessed with children. Hence Baba's word is more powerful than the Kalpavriksha and Kamadhenu.

Ref.: *Shri Sai Leela Magazine,* Deepavali issue, 2010.

4

Bhau Rajaram Ambika's Transfer

Bhau Rajaram Ambika resided in Vaduz (Satara District) and worked in the Primary Health Center, in the Department of Primary Health and Immunization. One day, he received an order stating that he was being transferred to Nasik District. Bhau was quite unhappy about it, because in those days, transportation was limited. He would have to ride on a horse and the distance to be traversed was long. The officers in charge were British and a request for a stay or change was futile as they would not pay any heed to it. Now Bhau was in turmoil and didn't know what to do. Around that time he heard about Baba's divinity and benevolence, so he decided to visit Shirdi. Bhau thought he would tell all his problems to Baba, give him two *paise* as *dakshina*, and return after Baba had solved his problem.

Upon reaching Shirdi, he entered the Dwarka Mai and saw Baba seated in a corner. There was an earthen pot (*kolomba*) in front of him, in which someone had kept a few *bhakris* (unleavened bread made from Sorghum or Millet). Baba and two mongrel dogs were contentedly having their meal from it. Bhau was aghast to see this and he thought, "People pronounce him to be a great saint and here he is eating food with those slobbering dogs. Now that I have come here, I should prostrate and leave."

Baba turned and looked at Bhau and said, "Give me my two *paise* immediately." As Bhau was giving Baba the two *paise* he was thinking, "After all it seems Baba is really a great saint as he is omnipresent and knows that I had decided to give him two *paise* prior to leaving Vaduz." Almost as if Bhau's thoughts were spoken aloud Baba replied, "Whether I am a great saint, or I eat the scraps with slobbering dogs, how does it concern you? You came for *darshan* (pilgrimage to see a divine saint or a deity) and you had your *darshan* (auspicious viewing). Here, have a piece of *bhakri* and leave." As Baba said this, he took a piece of *bhakri* from his *kolomba* and threw it at Bhau. Bhau asked Baba, "Baba when should I come again to have your darshan?" Baba replied, "Why would you want to come again? Whatever darshan you want, have it right now."

Bhau had no choice, so he left. On his way back, he kept wondering why Baba didn't ask him to return. Upon joining his duty he found an order cancelling his transfer to Nasik, along with an order to return to Vaduz immediately.

Now he understood why Baba had asked, "Why would you want to return again?", as Baba had already granted his wish. Unfortunately Bhau does not state in which year he went to Shirdi.

Baba is omniscient, and knows what Bhau has come for. He is omnipresent and is even present in slobbering mongrels. Baba by his omnipotence, had cancelled Bhau's transfer orders.

"HE is the fear, cause of fear, and the destroyer of fear." Hence he is called "Bhutakrut Bhayanasana".

He knows all the "happenings" as he himself is the reason for it, and is the happening that is the action and the result.

Ref.: *Prasad*, Volume 33, No. 9, August 1979, narrated by Shashikant P. Ambika.

5

"Why Does He Ask for Money?" (Govind Vasudev Kanitker)

Around 1908, Shri Govind Vasudev Kanitker was a Judge in Yevola, Maharashtra. On his tour of duty he often visited Kopergaon and there his colleagues spoke about Baba's divinity, compassion and *leelas*. As his family was with him at the time, he decided to visit Shirdi along with his entire family. The very next day they crossed the Godavari and proceeded to Shirdi.

Kashibai Kanitker had heard that Baba collected money from the devotees and bought wood for his Dhuni from it. So prior to setting out she gave each child a coin to offer to Baba. They were a large group of people: Kanitker, his wife, his sister and 6 children. Together, they went to the Dwarka Mai, prostrated before Baba and placed the *dakshina* at his feet.

On that visit they stayed for 4 days, and were allotted rooms in the old Marathi *shala*, which quite a distance away from the Dwarka Mai. One day it was Baba's turn to sleep in the Chavadi, and he and Mhalsapati were chatting together. Then Baba wanted to smoke his chillum, so Mhalsapati filled it with tobacco and handed it to him. They shared the chillum and smoked it between them. Soon it was to be refilled, but the stone that was at the mouth piece (bit) was lost. Baba was enraged and soon a volley of abuses burst out of his mouth. Govind, who was seated nearby, was embarrassed and asked his wife and children to return to the *shala* where they were staying. A short while later Govind also retired for the night.

The Kanitkers were to leave the next day. That night while chit-chatting with some fellow devotees, Govind said, "Sai Baba may be a great Sadhu, but why does he need to ask people for money? This seems strange to me. Also Baba indiscriminately uses foul, abusive language regardless of who is seated before him. I cannot accept the fact that women hear his profane, vulgar abuses." His colleague who was seated next to him said, "For enlightened saints there is no concept of good and bad, as they are above it. They live life with utmost detachment and equanimity. Whether you sing their praises or abuse them, it has no effect on them." But Govind was adamant about his point of view. He said, "I don't agree with you. However, if he returns the exact amount of *dakshina* that we gave him thus far, I will appreciate him."

Kanitker visited as many saints and Sadhus as he possibly could, and he always sought advice from them on spiritual matters. He had also read a number of books on religious philosophy and tried to instil it in his life. As a matter of fact, Kanitker had got peace of mind at the mere *darshan* of Baba. However, Baba was silent; he didn't talk on any subject, nor did he give any spiritual advice, and this bothered Kanitker a lot. In that troubled state of mind the question of Baba demanding money from the devotees troubled him even more. Why did this saint need money? The next day, the Kanitkers were leaving, so they went to the Dwarka Mai to get permission from Baba. Then Baba returned the exact amount of money to each individual that they had given the previous day. And each time he repeated the same sentence that Kanitker had said the previous night. His wife Kashibai was very hurt by this and she said, "Why are you returning the money? It was meant to buy wood for Dhuni Mai."

Baba replied, "Why does he ask for money if he is a Sadhu?" Kanitker was exceedingly saddened by the turn of events, but what could he do. Carrying the money with them they returned home. Kashibai kept all the money on their prayer altar as a gift from Baba and worshipped it daily.

Kashibai Kanitker was devoted to Baba since the day she visited Shirdi, and continued to worship him her entire life. At one point in time, her youngest son fell ill, and was struggling for his life. She prayed to Baba to save his life and applied some of the *Udi* that Baba had given. Soon, her son started recovering.

Kashibai's youngest daughter Anubai was once seated in the balcony of their home and was watching the guards on duty, when a fakir came to beg alms. The fakir was tall and had a small green coloured handkerchief over his right shoulder. His head was covered with a white cloth that was tied like Baba's *shrivesh*. He asked the guard for some alms. The guard informed him that the *bajri* (sorghum) had finished, and the tin had yet to be refilled. Politely the guard asked him to come a little while later. The fakir laughed and went away. He returned about 20 minutes later and again asked for *bhiksha*. Again the guard informed him that the tin was empty. Then the fakir said, "There must be four or five grains of bajri in the tin, give them as *bhiksha*." The guard having no other choice took the tin and emptied it onto his green handkerchief. The fakir looked at the few grains of bajri and said, "This is plenty." Then he folded the handkerchief by placing one palm upon the other. A few moments later, he opened the green handkerchief and it was full of bajri. The fakir laughed, turned and vanished after taking a few steps.

Anubai ran downstairs and informed everyone about the miracle that had just taken place. Kashibai immediately sent the guard to search for the fakir, as she knew that he was Baba. But the fakir was not seen again. A year later Kashibai visited Shirdi and Baba told her he had come to her home.

Kashibai and her family visited Shirdi whenever they could. After her husband retired and they moved to Pune in 1909, they were unable to visit Shirdi. However Baba's blessings and the *Udi* that he had given them saw them through the ups and downs of life.

Through this *leela* Baba is teaching us the following:
1. Do not be judgemental about the doings of the Sadguru.
2. Baba/Sadguru does not want anything from us, as everything is his own creation.
3. If at all we give him any money or anything in kind, it is

only what we are taking from his treasury. So the question of "I" or Ego does not arise.

4. One should understand that Baba was demanding "*dakshina*" (money) to erase our "Ego Complex".

5. If at all he gives us the good sense or conscience to offer anything, even a few grains, the same will definitely be returned to us manifold.

Ref.: *Shri Sai Sagar Magazine*, Deepavali issue, 2008.

6

Kashibai Kanitker's Experiences

Kashibai Kanitker

Once, when Govind V. Kanitker was working in Yevola, he took his family to Shirdi. Prior to their departure from Yevola, Govind had hired a *tonga* for the to and fro journey from Shirdi. On that visit, Shama and his children accompanied them to the Dwarka Mai. As soon as Baba saw them, he turned to Govind and said, "Now where do you think you are going? You will go alone from here at 2 a.m." Kashibai realised that they would have to stay that night there. So they stayed in the old Marathi *shala*. Around midnight an officer from Yevola came to meet Govind, and handed him a telegram. The telegram was from his brother Chintu saying, "Mother is seriously ill," and asked him to come soon. As Govind had to leave, Kashibai packed his bags for him and he left at 2 a.m., exactly as Baba had said.

The next day, Kashibai packed her bags and got ready to leave. When they went to Baba to ask for permission to leave, he refused. So they sat in the Dwarka Mai. Baba said, "Time and again he promised to go and meet her, but procrastinated every single time. Now the telegram has come. Someone is sick, but the symptoms are present in someone else." Baba literally

19

said, "Who has the ailment, and who has the symptoms." No one could understand what Baba was saying or to whom. Kashibai returned to her room, and Baba sent a platter full of *burfis* so she could break her *ekadashi* fast with them.

When the Kanitkers returned to the Dwarka Mai, Baba was getting ready to prepare some *shira*. Baba said, "Would anyone like to eat *shira*?" Immediately, the thought cropped up in Kashibai's mind, "How to eat the *shira* prepared by a Muslim?" Concurrently Baba put both his hands over his ears and said, "Arre! I am not trying to desecrate or defile anyone's religious beliefs. It is good, and if anyone desires to eat the *shira* they may do so." Then Baba got up and washed the plates, wiped them, and filled the plates with piping hot *shira* from his *handi*. Thereafter Kashibai's sister and other family members, including her children, started eating the *shira*. After a while, Kashibai requested Baba for permission to leave, but he was silent. At that moment Dada Kelkar came to the Dwarka Mai. Pointing to Kashibai, Baba said, "She is my mother, and has come here from far away. She has observed the fast for *ekadashi*, so she and her family are hungry. Can't you prepare some *bhakri* and feed her and the children? Thus your soul will be satisfied." Hearing this, Dada Kelkar requested them to join him for lunch.

That day Kashibai received a letter from her husband saying that his mother was alright. However, his sister Gangu had severe labour pains, and had delivered a baby girl that night. Then Kashibai understood why Baba had said, "Someone is sick, but the symptoms are present in someone else."

In 1906, the Kanitkers visited Shirdi again. On that occasion Baba had wrapped his finger with a dirty, oily strip of cloth. Kashibai mentally wondered what had happened to Baba's finger. Simultaneously Baba said, "My finger got burnt, so I bandaged it." And he unwrapped the bandage and showed her his finger that had turned whitish in colour. Later she heard that Madhavnath Maharaj of Nasik had burnt his finger and Baba had taken the burns upon himself.

On that visit, the villagers claimed that there was a rabid dog in Shirdi, and they tried to kill it with steel rods and sticks. They chased it around the village, until finally the dog took refuge in the Dwarka Mai and sat behind Baba. The villagers cautioned Baba saying, "Baba, don't touch that dog; it is rabid and will bite you." Baba angrily drove the villagers away. The dog rested behind Baba for a short while and went away. Thereafter, it freely roamed about without any symptoms of rabies; nor did it attack or bite anyone.

Ref.: *Shri Sai Sagar*, Volume 12, No. 3, Deepavali issue, 2012.

7

How Baba Blessed Bhikaji

The magnitude of Baba's grace on Bhikaji Hari Risbood can be gauged from Baba's words: "*Arre!* Anna, I will come to stay in your home." This interesting *leela* is narrated by Bhikaji's grandson, Anil Narayan Risbood, who resides in Girgaon, Mumbai.

He relates: "My grandfather was a *Vaid* (Indian Shaman) and resided in Pean (District Raigad). As his financial condition was precarious, he often went to Mumbai to treat patients. He would usually go once a month and stay there for a week or so. On his visits to Mumbai, he heard about Baba's divinity, so in 1916 he decided to visit Shirdi, meet Baba and disclose his poverty stricken plight. Upon reaching Shirdi, he went to the Dwarka Mai to meet Baba, but at that time Baba was in a frightful rage. Bhikaji decided that he would prostrate before Baba later, when he had calmed down. So he returned to the *dharmashala* (pilgrim's inn), had his meal and went to sleep. A short while later, he dreamt of Baba, who said, "Have you come here to sleep? Or have you come here to meet me?" Bhikaji answered, "Deva! When I came to meet you, you were in a rage and I got frightened, so I left." Baba replied, "Did I call out your name and say anything to you?"

At that moment, Bhikaji woke up and immediately went to meet Baba, and prostrated before him. A few moments later, Baba spoke these amazing words: "Arre! Anna I will come to stay in your home, as your son. Remember this Anna, I should be named Shri Pada." At that time Bhikaji's wife was about 6 months pregnant. Satisfied, he returned home the next day.

Bhikaji's wife indeed delivered a baby boy, on a Thursday, around 7 a.m. When his wife was delivering the baby, Bhikaji was standing at the entrance of his home. Just then, a fakir passed by on the street. The fakir was attentively looking at his home, but Bhikaji didn't pay much attention to him. As Baba had predicted, a son was born, who was named Shri Pada. The child however had a unique birth mark on his neck. It looked like a three strand necklace; and in the centre, like a pendant, there was as a mark shaped like a *Tulsi* leaf.

Shri Pada grew up to be a charming lad. When he was about 5 years old his parents decided to perform his thread ceremony. That night Baba appeared in Bhikaji's dream and repeatedly said, "Now I am leaving, and I don't want anything from you." Bhikaji replied, "Did I come to invite you to my home? Then how does the question of your coming or going arise?" Probably Baba didn't approve of the idea of performing the thread ceremony as he is an *avatar* of Lord Dattatreya. The topic of performing Shri Pada's thread ceremony again arose when he was 8 years old, and his father decided to perform it sometime later.

One day, Shri Pada went into the forest; a thorn pierced his foot, and he developed Tetanus. The doctors treated him but without much improvement. That Thursday, very early in the morning, Bhikaji had a vivid dream wherein Baba said, "I am leaving now. I cannot stay any longer. Allah will bless you." Bhikaji jumped out of bed and went and stood at the entrance of his home. At that moment a fakir passed by, gazing intently at his home. He suddenly remembered that when Shri Pada was born this same fakir had walked by his home. Bhikaji ran to where Shri Pada was sleeping, but alas, he had passed away. The incomprehensible coincidence was that Shri Pada came into this world, and subsequently left it on a Thursday, at 7 a.m. At the time of his birth and passing away the same fakir walked by their home looking at the house with intense concentration. That fakir was never seen again by anyone, anywhere, thereafter.

Anil Narayan Risbood says, "Baba came to our home in the form of Shri Pada, and sanctified our house. And ever since he has been showering his grace and mercy on us."

Ref.: *Shri Sai Leela Magazine*, Volume 59, No. 9, December 1989.

8

How Baba Solved Bhau Sahib
Arnalkar's Crisis

Bhau Sahib Arnalkar was an advocate by profession, and resided in Mumbai. At that time his friends often visited Pandarpur, and hardly anyone knew about Baba. But as he was an advocate, he happened to meet Dabolkar and Dev Mamlatdar, and a close friendship developed. Around that time Dabolkar was gathering *leelas* and material to write the *Sat Charita*, and he along with Dev often visited Shirdi. Hence they often narrated Baba's wonderful *leelas* to Bhau Sahib. Consequently, he became devoted to Baba and was eager to visit Shirdi.

At that point in time most people thought that Baba was a Muslim Saint. However Arnalkar had no doubt that Baba was God Almighty, and hence a devotee could easily open his heart before his chosen deity. At that time Bhau had a financial crisis and he had no money for his daily expenses. Prior to commencing his journey, Bhau had made up his mind that he would go to Shirdi and seek refuge at the feet of his Lord. In his mind he rehearsed what he would say, and time and again he reassured himself thinking, "If a devotee does not tell his troubles and sorrows to God, then who will he tell them to?" With this firm resolve in his mind he set out to Shirdi.

Upon reaching Shirdi, he went to the Dwarka Mai and with utter devotion he prostrated before Baba. On this visit Bhau stayed in Shirdi for three days. He frequently went to the Dwarka Mai but on every occasion there were numerous devotees around Baba, and at no time was Baba alone. Consequently Bhau could not open his heart to him. Bhau was ashamed to tell Baba his problems in the presence of other devotees. On the 4th day Baba called him, made him sit close to him and said, "You should leave now. Don't you have any family or relatives?" Immediately Bhau placed his head on Baba's feet, and overcome by emotion, he was unable to speak. Now Bhau thought, "It is a custom in Shirdi that no one can stay a minute longer when Baba asks them to leave. But I had to tell Baba my problems and was unable to do so. Now I had better leave." Disappointed, he started walking towards the exit, when Baba called out to him. Baba asked him, "Bhau how much money do you have?" Bhau's spirits lifted and he thought, "Great! Baba himself has brought up the topic of money." Bhau told him that he had three rupees and some annas, and the money was sufficient for his return journey. Then Baba asked him to give him that entire sum of money, saying, "Give me that money. Arre! Even a fakir needs money." Quietly, Bhau handed the money to him. Baba said, "The tonga is outside waiting for you. Hurry up and go."

Disappointed, Bhau went to the waiting *tonga*. The driver was an acquaintance, so he made place for Bhau, although the *tonga* was full. The driver didn't take any fare from him as his *tonga* was filled with passengers. Soon, they reached the station. Now how was he to reach Mumbai? Travelling without a ticket was an offence. With these thoughts he was waiting on the platform, when the train for Mumbai arrived. From the bogie that was in front of him, someone called out, "*Vakil Sahib*, come into this bogie." The bogie was a 2nd class bogie, and like a robot, Bhau entered it. The person who had called out to him was an old friend of his, who was a Railway Officer. Bhau confessed that he did not have a ticket. His friend said, "When I am travelling with you to Mumbai why do you worry? By Baba's grace we have met after so many months." Together they had a comfortable journey and reached Mumbai.

Upon alighting from the train his friend went off somewhere. At the exit there was a Railway Officer checking the tickets, and he would not move away from the gate. Just then two rustic villagers entered the station, pushing the officer out of the way. They came straight to Bhau and handed him a bag that contained three hundred rupees in it. Then one of the men said, "*Vakil Sahib*, I had come here to meet this friend of mine. But by Baba's grace I met you here. After three days my case is scheduled to start, so please take this money, otherwise I would have to come all the way to Vasai, to give you the fees."

Bhau was speechless, as Baba had remedied his problem silently and appropriately.

Like the advocate Bhau Sahib Arnalkar, we also have crises in our spiritual journey to reach Baba. However he removes all the obstructions or obstacles from the path by taking away the root cause, and makes us penniless (taintless).

Once he makes us pure, he then makes the necessary arrangements for our progress. Our duty is to follow his orders like a robot.

Once we follow his orders he blesses us to manage the trigunas (the three subtle components) for our future progress and advancement.

Ref.: *Shri Sai Leela Magazine*, Volume 58, No. 7, October 1979.

9

How Daji Sahib Patwardhan's Doubts Were Removed

Around 1914 Baba's fame had spread far and wide. Within Maharastra he had innumerable devotees, as well as some sceptics. This is the *leela* of Daji Sahib Patwardhan who was a "doubting Thomas", and tells how he turned into an ardent devotee.

Daji's ancestors resided in Miraj (Sangli District) and were conferred the title of Sarkar, as they had a high political standing. They were affluent and owned vast acres of agricultural land. They had a huge *wada* where he and his entire family lived. Daji's grandfather Harbat Baba Patwardhan was a saintly person, and his family was spiritual, and devoted to Lord Ganesha. Daji was also utterly devoted to Lord Ganesha. Daji was a voracious reader, and he had read all the epics of the great saints of those times. However, he read them not with much devotion, but with an analytical mind, and he often wondered if the *leelas* therein really did happen. At that point in time a dear friend of his asked him to accompany him to Shirdi as he wished to meet the great saint Sai Baba.

Daji was disinclined to go, as he had heard that Baba was a Muslim fakir, who had numerous Hindu followers. These followers, according to what Daji had heard, were mostly Brahmins, and Baba had cast some magical spell on them and had drawn them towards him. He had heard that Baba stayed in a dilapidated mosque, begged alms, and had a Tulsi Vrindavan in the mosque. But what troubled him the most was that people actually believed that Baba had lit lamps with water, so he decided to see all this for himself. Daji decided that he would test Baba and prove that he was a charlatan. In May

1914, Daji set out to Shirdi. In those days it was not as easy to reach Shirdi as it is these days. It was a very long and tedious journey. From Miraj, Daji travelled by train to Pune, where he had to catch another train which took him to Manmad, and thence to Kopergaon. Daji got off at Kopergaon, and began the third leg of his journey by *tonga* to Shirdi. By that time Daji was thoroughly tired from his long, tedious journey and his clothes were dirty. He wished he could have a bath and put on a fresh set of clothes. With this thought in his mind he exited the railway station.

There was a huge well near the station, but it was very deep, about 60 ft deep. Daji looked into the well and the clear, cold water was very enticing. At that time Daji was a strong young man, 20 years old, and an expert swimmer. Without giving much thought to it, he jumped into the well. The villagers saw this and exclaimed, "The Brahmin jumped into the well and gave up his life." Daji found that he was sinking, and desperately thrashed his hands about. But the more he struggled, the deeper he sank. In desperation, he struggled to come up and take a breath, but to no avail. He now realised that he would soon lose his life as he was drowning.

At that very moment he thought of Baba and silently prayed, "Baba I came from such a far off place to test you, and you taught me a great lesson. Now without meeting you, you are sending me to heaven. I have recently got married, and I don't even have children yet. My wife will become a young widow; at least consider that and save my life. If you save my life I will worship you with devotion for the rest of my life." As soon as Daji said this, he found himself standing on a ledge of stone which prevented him from sinking deeper. Then taking the aid of the rim of the well he slowly came up. The villagers gathered there helped pull him to safety. Daji joined his hands together and thanked Baba for saving his life. Then he took a *tonga* and proceeded to Shirdi. As soon as Daji entered the Dwarka Mai, Baba greeted him, "Arre! Brahmin, at least now do you have faith?"

Daji went forward, prostrated before Baba and clasped his

feet. He became ardently devoted to Baba and from then on, Daji considered every day that he woke up in the morning as a gift from Baba.

Each and every one of us considers ourselves to be excellent and capable swimmers to cross the ocean of difficulties. But in reality we sink. However, only after praying and surrendering to the Sadguru will we be lifted by his grace and placed safely on the ledge.

Once we are saved, we should concentrate, to know the real "Self" and strive for "Self-realisation". That is why Baba addresses Bhau as "Brahmin".

Ref.: *Shri Sai Sagar Magazine*, Volume 3, No. 4, January–March 2013.

10

Baba Blesses Mrs. Pradhan

This is the story of a lady who had the courage, devotion and determination to visit Shirdi and meet Baba. Her story was narrated by Mangala Pradhan, a devotee residing in Thana. Unfortunately Mrs. Pradhan's first name is not mentioned; neither is the year that she visited Shirdi. That courageous lady was Mangala's husband's grandmother, so she will be referred to as Mrs. Pradhan.

Mrs. Pradhan resided in a village called Savarsai, in suburb of Pean, in the district of Raigad. She was eager to meet Baba, so she requested her husband to give her permission to go. He disapproved and said, "I will not give you a single pie, then how will you go?" The entire family protested, and forbade her to go.

Mangala's father-in-law recalled: "My mother lay low for a while, but in her mind she hatched a plan. She had no idea of how much money it would cost to get to Shirdi. However, she knew it would be a large sum, so she took all the jewelry that her parents had gifted her and pawned it. My mother had no idea where Shirdi was. But she was very stubborn and once she had decided to go, nothing could stop her. She discreetly made some enquiries, and learnt that it was near Ahmednagar and that was all she knew. But when a devotee yearns to see the Lord, everything falls in place. I was 13 years old at that time, and taking me along she undertook the back-breaking, long and tedious journey to Shirdi.

The first stretch of the journey was by bullock-cart, from Savarsai to Khopoli Karjat, a distance of about 100 miles. Then from Karjat we travelled by train and somehow reached Shirdi in one piece. However, during the journey my mother was filled with doubt, 'Shirdi is known to have frequent epidemics of cholera. If my son gets cholera what will I do?' Nonetheless we reached Shirdi and went to pay homage to Baba. As soon as my mother climbed the steps of the Dwarka Mai, Baba started shouting, 'Did anyone ask you to come here? Why did you come here after pawning your jewellery? Even after your husband forbade you to come here why did you come? Did I ask you to come here?' At that moment my mother recognised Baba's omnipresence, for he knew every detail that had taken place in her home. She was overcome with bliss and said, 'Baba what *seva* can I do for you?' Baba replied, 'Did your son contract cholera? Let it be. Arre! *Mai* near your front door you have a beautiful wood apple (Aegle marmelos) tree. Offer the leaves (*bilva patra*) to me.' Then Baba blessed us and gave us a fistful of *Udi*.

Following that pilgrimage to Shirdi my mother was changed for life. Till the end of her life she offered the leaves of that tree without fail to Baba's picture, and spent her time doing service to anyone in need. Wisely but sparingly, she gave Baba's *Udi* to sick people and to mothers who had difficulties during childbirth, with great success. Soon she became the favorite aunt (*kaku*) of the entire village.

Another blessing that Baba had bestowed on her was the gift of predicting. The villagers would come to her and ask her where they could find their lost cow or calf. *Kaku* would then pray to Baba and tell them exactly where they could find it. She also helped the farmers, shepherds and the downtrodden in any way that she could. Till the day that she died, she never failed to pray to the picture of Baba that he himself had given her, and to this day that picture is with us."

Finally, Mangala says, "After I heard this wonderful *leela*, I also started offering the leaves of that wood apple tree to Baba. And with pride I can say we still have and pray to the picture that Baba gave her."

Ref.: *Sai Prasad*, Deepavali issue, 1999.

11

Revering All Saints

Bapkar Maharaj, a saint from Bairaig, once visited Mumbai. His devotee named Nanasahib Pitkar met him, and entreated him to stay at his residence for a couple of days. However, Bapkar Maharaj repeatedly requested him to allow him to leave, as he wanted to visit Shirdi. He had written to his son, and asked him to be at Shirdi the next day. So it was very important for Bapkar Maharaj to be there. By that time Nanasahib and a lot of other devotees had come to have his *darshan*. Thus, he was unable to leave, as saints will go out of their way to fulfil the desires of their devotees.

Bapkar's son reached Shirdi as planned. As he didn't know anyone there he went to the Dwarka Mai and sat in a corner. Just prior to the Noon Arati, Baba caught sight of the young man seated in the corner. Baba, through his inner vision, came to know who that young man was, and sent Shama to bring the young man to the sanctum. Turning to the devotees seated there, Baba said, "This young man's father has attained great spiritual heights, and is a great saint. He was scheduled to come here today. But his devotees requested him to stay in Mumbai for another day, and he didn't want to disappoint them. So we should honour his son appropriately. Shama, today this young man will be seated on my *asan* and *arati* will be performed."

So that day all of Baba's devotees performed ritualistic worship and *arati* of that young man. Baba always treated the saints and sadhus that visited him with a lot of reverence. Thus, by example he also taught his devotees to have reverence for saints.

Ref.: *Sai Prasad Magazine*, Deepavali issue, 1993.

12

Baba Shows Tammaji the Right Path

When Tammaji, a resident of Shirdi, was a young lad his ambition was to become a renowned wrestler. But his parents were financially poor, and so they couldn't even provide Tammaji with adequate milk, let alone a high protein diet, which was necessary for such a rigorous activity like wrestling. Nevertheless Tammaji was determined to achieve his goal. He thought, "Baba gives so many of his devotees so much of money, I will go to him and ask him to help me."

He then went to Baba and told him of his desire to become a renowned wrestler. Baba patiently heard everything he had to say, and then said, "It is not good to be dependent on the money of saints and sadhus. You have some farmland; go and plough it carefully. In your farm there is a pot full of brass coins." Taking Baba's words literally, the next day Tammaji started tilling his field with great care. He was sure that with Baba's blessing he would be successful, and he gave up the idea of becoming a wrestler.

However, all this was easier said than done. Tammaji realised that he had very little land as loan sharks had confiscated most of their land. Most of the citizens thought that the British regime was fair to everyone, but Tammaji soon realised that the farmers who worked from dawn to dusk were in a very pitiable, poverty-stricken state. To add to this, the loan sharks took advantage of the illiteracy of the farmers and made then sign away huge portions of their farms. Thus, the loan sharks owned vast areas of farm lands and the farmers in turn worked for them, with very meagre income. However, Tammaji put his heart and soul in his work, and his farm yielded a good harvest. Subsequently, he rented another farm from the loan shark. His entire family worked day and night on that farm, which in turn yielded a bountiful harvest. With Baba's blessings, the water from the Godavari River also became available to the farmers, through the canals that ran close to Shirdi. Thus Tammaji's farms flourished and soon he was able to buy many more farms. Thereafter, he owned around 150 acres of farmland, and he and his family prospered and became affluent.

Tammaji says, "All this was possible because of Baba's blessings and I am eternally grateful to him for showing me the right path. I really don't know what would have happened to me and my family if I had not heeded his words."

Ref.: *Shirdi Che Mahan Sant Shri Sai Baba*, written by Pandurang Balaji Kavde

13

Saints Have No Caste, Creed or Religion

Shri Krishnaji Vishnu Ganpule was fortunate to have met Baba at a very young age. He was born in 1887 in an orthodox Brahmin family, which resided in Sangamnere. Krishnaji was at that time studying in the 1st standard in an English medium school. Once, the class was going on a picnic, and the teacher decided to go to Shirdi where they could have a wonderful time and also pay homage to Sai Baba. The teacher asked all the children to get permission from their parents. That evening Krishnaji came home and told his mother about the picnic. She readily gave her consent, but young Krishnaji said, "I don't want to go, as Baba is a Muslim." His mother told him that he ought to go as saints didn't belong to any caste, creed or religion. A few days later he put his name on the list as he had decided to go, or rather Baba wanted him to come to Shirdi.

The class arrived at Shirdi and his classmates prostrated before Baba. Krishnaji was the last student to do so. Baba said, "You are a high caste Brahmin and I am a lowly Muslim. So why are you prostrating before me?" That evening the class returned home except for Krishnaji, as Baba had detained him. Krishnaji stayed with Baba for 11 months, and just prior to his semester examination, Baba allowed him to return home. Krishnaji passed with flying colours. His mother Lakshmibai Vishnu Ganpule was a blessed soul who had the opportunity to give "*bhiksha*" to Baba. Both Krishnaji and Lakshmibai were utterly devoted to Baba, who took care of their every need, so that they led a comfortable life.

Ref.: *Sai Prasad Magazine*, Deepavali Issue, 1999

14

Baba Cures Gajanan Pradhan's Carbuncle

A chronic, painful swelling of the ankle brought Gajanan Ramchandra Pradhan to Shirdi in 1910. Gajanan was a young lad residing in Mumbai, and had developed a round swelling on his right ankle that year. He was checked and treated by a *vaid*, (Ayurvedic doctor) and then a *hakim*, (physician) without any relief. Gajanan religiously took all medicines, and drank the herbal brew that was prescribed. Every morning and night he applied a poultice to the swelling but instead of bursting, the carbuncle became hard and round. Soon the *vaid* and *hakim* gave up, and Gajanan was left with a very painful swollen ankle. As he lived in Mumbai, his parents got him checked by an allopathic doctor. The doctor prescribed some capsules for a week and told them that if Gajanan didn't improve within a week, he would surgically remove the carbuncle. However, the swelling steadily increased with every passing day. His mother (Mrs. Pradhan's first name is not mentioned) was very anxious about his deteriorating condition and was at her wit's end.

One evening, a friend of the family dropped by and he advised them to go and stay at Shirdi for a fortnight. He said, "There is a wondrous saint called Sai Baba living there, who has cured many people of their atypical and unusual diseases. So if you seek his help he will definitely cure Gajanan." Mrs. Pradhan decided to follow the friend's advice. The very next day Gajanan, his mother, and her younger brother Nana, set out to Shirdi. Upon reaching Shirdi they got a room in the *dharamshala*, (piligrim's inn) where Gajanan rested, while his mother and Nana scouted the village. They returned to their room with groceries and prepared the meal.

In the village there were numerous small temples and they went and sat there. They asked the villagers where they would find Baba, and learned that he stayed in the masjid. As they walked along they heard the *arati* and walked in that direction and soon entered the Dwarka Mai. There Baba being worshipped and his *arati* was being performed. After the *arati* Mrs. Pradhan and Nana went and prostrated at Baba's feet, and Baba blessed them saying, "Allah will bless you." They were filled with bliss. Upon returning to their room, they told Gajanan everything that took place. Ruefully he said, "When will I be able to meet Baba? That day will be the most important day of my life."

The next day they heard the bell of the Dwarka Mai ring and leaving Gajanan in the room they went to attend the noon *arati*. They reached just before the *arati* when Baba looked at them and said, "Which devotee staying at the *dharamshala* has not come for the *arati*?" Mrs. Pradhan told Baba that her son Gajanan was unable to attend the *arati*, as his ankle was very swollen and painful. So he was unable to walk. Baba shouted, "Go immediately and bring him for the *arati*." Mrs. Pradhan and Nana returned to their room, and helped Gajanan to limp all the way to the Dwarka Mai. When they reached there, the *arati* was over, and the devotees were prostrating at Baba's feet. Suddenly Baba picked up a stone and threw it on Gajanan's right ankle. Gajanan shrieked in pain and fell on the ground. However, the carbuncle had ruptured, and pus and blood flowed out of it. Mrs. Pradhan wiped it off with the leaves and flowers that were lying there, and applied *Udi* to the open wound. Soon the gaping wound healed and Gajanan was able to attend all the *arati*s. After receiving Baba's blessing they returned home.

A short while later Gajanan got a job in the railways. He was grateful to Baba for relieving him of his excruciating pain and thereafter he visited Shirdi twice or thrice a year till Baba's Maha Samadhi. Devotedly he worshipped Baba's picture at home. He also did *nithya parayan* (consecutively reading the *Charita* without any break) for about 8 hours daily. This practice he carried on till his death.

The reason for visiting Shirdi may be varied, but when Baba sets his sight on his devotee he will definitely draw him to his feet.

Ref.: *Sai Prasad Magazine*, Deepavali issue, 1999.

15

Dr. Inamdar's Spiritual Awakening

It is often said that it is not easy to attain the grace of a saint. One cannot go to the grocery shop or bazaar and get the grace of a saint. One has to have patience and devotion and when the time is right, the saint will shower his grace on the devotee. Dr. Inamdar was a blessed soul who, at a very young age, achieved *vairagya* (detachment) and was blessed by Baba. Unfortunately his complete name and where he resided is not known. His story is narrated by Rajani Burke, a devotee from Girgaon:

Dr. Inamdar had read and heard a glorious account of Baba's divinity. He thought, "I should seek refuge at the feet of such a divine saint, and if he blesses me then this human life will achieve its spiritual goal. So I should immediately go to Shirdi and meet Baba." So he went to Shirdi with the hope that one day Baba would glance at him compassionately, and initiate and uplift him spiritually. He stayed in Shirdi for a week; however, his restless mind gnawed at him. He thought, "How long ought I to stay here? Baba is not guiding me. Needlessly I am wasting my time here. I should find another saint who will quell my restlessness and guide me on the right path."

So the next day after taking permission to leave, the doctor went to Dhanoli, hoping to find Satam Maharaj. Fervently he hoped that Satam Maharaj would bestow peace and initiate him. At Dhanoli he inquired where he would find Satam Maharaj, and when could he meet him. But no one was able to help him, as Satam Maharaj rarely stayed at one place for long. The doctor stayed in Dhanoli for two days and again his restless mind bothered him. He went and sat atop a hill and thought, "How many more days am I going to waste here?"

Just then, Satam Maharaj appeared before him, softly singing this *abhang*: "You do not possess steadfast faith on one saint. Then how can he be pleased with you? Your restless mind flits about, in all directions. Then how can he give refuge to you? Your devotion lacks complete surrender, so inculcate devotion with mind and all your senses on one saint. Then definitely your spiritual goal will be achieved." Satam Maharaj blessed the doctor and asked him to return to Shirdi promptly.

Upon the doctor's return to Shirdi, Baba smiled and said, "God resides in everything that has a name. He is omnipresent." Dr. Inamdar was astounded that both saints had the same insight and said the same thing. That was the turning point for the doctor. From that moment on he became devoted to Baba. Steadily his faith became steadfast and one-pointed. As his faith increased, he developed total detachment, and his very being became filled with devotion to Baba. Baba blessed him and upon Baba's bidding he dedicated his life to him. Dr. Inamdar then wandered about all over Saurashtra, singing the glories of Sai Baba of Shirdi. He made Porbunder his home and was famous in Saurashtra as *Gongdi vale Baba'* (the sadhu with a sheep's blanket).

Ref.: *Sai Prasad Magazine*, Deepavali issue, 1991.

16

Value of Labour

It was the month of May in 1946, when Vasant Pradhan and his friend visited Shirdi. That evening there was a pleasant breeze and the heat of the day had tapered off. So both the friends walked through the village, hoping to find an aged villager who might have met Baba and could tell them some *leela* or interesting anecdote. They walked through the narrow alleys and soon found an aged Muslim gentleman. He was seated on a stone, smoking a *bidi*. Vasant said, "Baba, are you a resident of Shirdi?" The man nodded eagerly. Then Vasant requested him to tell them about Baba and any experience that he may have had. Unfortunately that elderly gentleman's name is not mentioned.

He said, "I used to sit near Baba and puff on his *chillum*. Every day I would go to his durbar and carefully listen to what he said. Baba had a strange way of talking—whenever he had something to tell a particular devotee, he would look at someone else and give his message or advice. Hence the person that he looked at was perplexed, but the devotee that it was meant for listened to it carefully and with concentration. Then he would fall at Baba's feet, and heed his advice.

Every day Baba would distribute vast amounts of money. He gave 5, 10, 50 and even 100 rupees to the devotees seated there. However, he never ever gave me any money. I owned a small farm and eked a living from it. One day, I accosted Baba and said, "Baba you liberally distribute money to all your devotees. I am exceedingly poor and yet you never give me a single pie." Where upon Baba said, "Arre! Why do you want money? Your farm has a pot of gold in it." The next day I carefully ploughed my field, put adequate manure in it and planted the seeds. Every day I worked diligently with Baba's words ringing in my ears. Time rolled on and I never did find the pot of gold; however by my hard labour, every time I had an abundant harvest. Soon I was able to buy three of the adjacent fields. Now I am quite affluent, and along the way I learned that by constantly remembering Baba and working diligently you are bound to be successful. Years later I told Baba that I still hadn't found the pot of gold. He laughed and said, "Continue trying." Thus Baba's words came true as I am now affluent and happy. Baba taught me that my hard labour and his grace can together yield a bountiful harvest."

Vasant also learned a lesson from this story. In chapter 19 of *Shri Sai Satcharita*, Hemadpanth writes: "You put forth your best effort and work hard; I am there with a cup of milk standing right behind you. And if you don't work hard don't expect me to be standing with a cup of milk."

Baba taught the illiterate and the literate devotee spiritual wisdom in such a simplified manner, that Baba was present in everything and is omnipresent.

Ref.: *Sai Prasad Magazine*, Deepavali issue, 1992.

17

Kashibai Kanitker's Visit to Shirdi

Kashibai was born in 1861, in a wealthy Brahmin family in the town of Ashte in Sangli district. At the age of 9 she was married to Govind Vasudev Kanitker who was 7 years older than her. She had no formal education, but on account of her husband's encouragement she learned to read and write. Kashibai soon mastered Marathi, Sanskrit and English. Kashibai was a prolific writer and received many accolades for both her fiction and non-fiction novels. She wrote the biography of Dr. Anandibai Joshi, the first lady doctor in India who received her education in the United States. It is read even to this day by scholars and aspiring doctors. Kashibai's talent was a gift from God, as no other member of her family had that kind of writing skill.

Kashibai was fortunate to visit Shirdi numerous times, and Baba loved and respected her a lot. In her autobiography, she has written about her frequent visits to Shirdi. In 1899 her daughter Krishnabai was unwell, as she had had a mishap. The bullock cart in which she was riding overturned and she sustained a head injury. The wound on her scalp failed to heal even after the best possible treatment was given. Following this, she had frequent bouts of headaches, dizziness and numerous other problems. In 1901 Krishnabai returned to Ahmednagar where her in-laws resided, and was treated there. Despite the treatment, her symptoms continued relentlessly. Then Krishnabai got treated in Mumbai, Pune and Alibaug, without any respite. So Kashibai and her family went to Ahmednagar to look after her.

One day Nana Sahib Chandorkar visited them. Nana said, "You have tried all kinds of doctors, taken her for treatment to renowned hospitals, but every modality of treatment has failed. Krishnabai has not improved a smidgen and is getting worse by the day. Now listen to what I have to say. Near Kopergaon there is a village named Shirdi where a wondrous saint called Sai Baba resides. I will give you a little *Udi* of his which is a 'cure-all'. This should be applied to her forehead and taken internally. She will definitely be rid of her problems. Thereafter do go and pay your respects to Baba." Chandorkar then gave a glowing account of Baba's divinity. However, Krishnabai's in-laws and Kashibai's family didn't believe in these things, thus they didn't use the *Udi* and didn't go to Shirdi.

A short while later, Kashibai's husband Govind got transferred to Dhule, where they stayed for a year. During this period they had quite forgotten Baba's name. The Kanitkers then moved to Malegaon, and then to Yevola, where Kashibai heard about Baba from the advocates that came from Ahmednagar to meet her husband. They spoke about Baba's compassion and divinity, and asked Govind to go and meet him. A few days later she found a picture of Baba lying on the table. No one had given them the picture, nor had anyone sent the picture by post to them. Nevertheless, the thought of going to Shirdi didn't occur to them.

Govind Kanitker then visited Kopergaon on his tour of duty and at that time they all visited Shirdi. Immediately after Govind Kanitker finished his work in Kopergaon, he was transferred to Rahata. As Rahata was the neighbouring village, they frequently visited Shirdi. Kashibai says, "These days where they have the Chavadi procession (South-facing Chavadi), that Chavadi was converted into a kitchen and we cooked our meals there. The Marathi school (now the Sai complex) was where we slept at night."

Kashibai says, "In those days Baba would accept no more than two paise as *dakshina*. With that money he purchased wood for his *Dhuni* throughout the day. He always paid the vendor 6 paise for it. Whether the vendor sold him 5 sticks of wood or the trunk of a huge tree, he would be paid no more than 6 paise. No matter how many times the cart came bringing wood, Baba never failed to purchase it, and the wood would be stacked against the rear wall of the Sabha Mandap."

In her autobiography, she writes about the incident of Baba returning the *dakshina* to her husband. "Prior to visiting Shirdi I had heard that Baba used the money given as *dakshina* to purchase fire-wood for his *Dhuni*. I liked the idea immensely as each devotee would receive a fistful of *Udi* from his *Dhuni*. So I had brought a large amount of change (coins) with me. Every day I gave everyone the same denomination of coins to offer to Baba. On the last day I ran out of change so I gave everyone a different denomination of coin to offer. My daughter Banutai came to receive her money and said, 'Mother why are you giving everyone different coins? Give everyone a coin of the same value.' I replied, 'I have run out of coins of the same denomination, and now there is no time to go and get change as it's getting late. Just give what you have in your hand, and go and sit in the cart. Besides, for the past 4 days didn't we give the same amount to Baba? That is enough.' Then my husband and his entourage went to meet Baba. First the sepoy, the bailiff, and other officers went and offered their respects and *dakshina*. Then my children and other relatives gave *dakshina*. Following them my husband prostrated at Baba's feet and gave him *dakshina*. Then Baba put his hand under the sack that he sat on and took out the money and returned all the money that was offered by the family. Thus my husband got proof of Baba's omnipresence, but I felt hurt and sad. So I said, 'Baba don't you want to buy wood for the *Dhuni*?' Then Baba repeated the same words that I had said to my daughter, 'Didn't you give me money for the past 4 days? That is enough.'" Thus, Kashibai also got an experience of Baba's omnipresence.

On Kashibai's first visit to Shirdi while they were travelling from Kopergaon, she thought, "How does one recognise a true saint? I am quite naive about this. And I don't know anything about this." Then she remembered when she was young, she along with her parents had gone to Akkalkot. There they met Swami Samarth and paid homage to him. So mentally she decided that if Baba was like Swami Samarth then she would have faith in him. Kashibai and her family then went to the Dwarka Mai and prostrated at Baba's feet. However her eldest son Madhavrao and her son-in-law Gangadhar Panth Dabholkar were late in coming. When they went to the Dwarka Mai, Baba had just returned from his *bhiksha* rounds and was seated near the railing. Just as they ascended the steps of the Dwarka Mai, both of them saw Swami Samartha seated there. A short while later they saw Baba seated there. Afterwards they narrated this wonderful experience to her. Thus Kashibai got the answer that she was looking for, though unfortunately she was unable to see this *leela*.

Thereafter Kashibai became ardently devoted to Baba and she frequently visited Shirdi and had wonderful experiences.

Ref.: *Shri Sai Sagar*, Volume 12, No. 3, Deepavali issue 2012

18

Gajanan Govind Dabolkar

Gajanan Govind Dabolkar was born on the 23rd of September 1903 in Bandra, Mumbai. His father was Govindrao, alias Anna Sahib, and his mother was Rukhmini Dabolkar. From very humble beginnings Gajanan's father rose to the level of a Magistrate. He became famous for writing the *Shri Sai Satcharita*, which he wrote with Baba's consent. Baba lovingly called him "Hemadpant". Hemadpant had one son, Gajanan, and five daughters.

Gajanan passed his Matriculation examination from the Aryan Education Society, Girgaon. In 1918 he joined Topiwala Medical College in Mumbai and in 1921 he successfully completed his course as a "Licensed Medical Practitioner". That same year, Gajanan was married to Lakshmibai, and over the years, they had three daughters and two sons. All his children were happily married and settled. Gajanan had a thriving medical practice till 1971, when he got a paralytic stroke. Although he recovered from the stroke, he was left with some residual muscular weakness, and so he retired from his profession.

How fortunate Gajanan was, to live his entire life in "Sai Nivas", the blessed house where Hemadpant spent hours writing the *Shri Sai Satcharita* on a low desk which is kept in a corner. Above the desk is a large casing that contains numerous rare photographs of Baba that were printed in the 1st edition of the *Shri Sai Satcharita*. On a small table the coins that Baba had given to Anna Sahib Dabolkar are kept, along with other memorabilia.

In chapter 40 and 41 of the *Shri Sai Satcharita* the story of the "Holi" dinner is beautifully described. It narrates how Baba appeared in a vision to Hemadpant, and subsequently came to have a meal at his house as promised, in the form of a bas-relief on the festival of Holi (festival of colours). Most importantly this well preserved bas-relief still hangs on the wall in their prayer room. This home is more like a place of pilgrimage, as it is filled with spiritual energy.

Gajanan recalls, "Once my father was getting ready to leave for Shirdi, when I was about fourteen years old. I was eager to accompany him, and I stubbornly insisted that he take me along; moreover I started weeping. My father finally agreed and I went with him to Shirdi; that was in the year 1914 that I first visited Shirdi. At that young age I was quite oblivious as to why we were going to Shirdi. Neither did I know anything about Baba's divinity. I was excited that we were travelling to a far off place by train, that we would be visiting another village so I would enjoy myself enormously. Upon reaching Shirdi, we alighted at Sathe Wada, as that was the only place for pilgrims to stay. It was a huge Wada as compared to the small mud huts in the village. After bathing we went to the Dwarka Mai, which was an old dilapidated mosque. There I saw an old fakir, seated near the railing. He was wearing a torn white *kafni*, which was rather dirty. His head was covered with a dirty white cloth that was knotted behind his left ear. I thought this must be Sai Baba. My father sat near his feet, and so did I. There were about 15–20 people seated in front of him, some were villagers, and both Hindus and Muslims were seated there. Some of them were rendering *seva* to him like massaging his feet, or lighting his *chillum* (clay pipe).

In the dilapidated courtyard below, some children were shouting 'Baba, Baba, Sai Baba' and were jumping about and playing. Baba picked up some '*pedas*' (milk confectionary) and threw them in their direction and they pushed and shoved each other to gather the goodies. The rest of the prasad he distributed to the devotees who were seated in front of him.

A short time later Baba held me by my hand and seated me close to him. Then with a great deal of love he called me 'Bapu' and hugged me. I was overwhelmed with emotion and I couldn't hold back my tears. I can never forget this in my life. After the *arati* that was performed by Megha, in a caring, gentle voice Baba bade everyone go home and have lunch. Baba said, 'Kaka, Nana, now go home. You must be hungry? Have your meal, then rest awhile. You may return after two or three hours, then all of us can sit together and talk about Allah.' The devotees assembled there were reluctant to go home even though their stomachs were rumbling with hunger. Who would want to leave the company of this kind, compassionate fakir?

Before the devotees returned home, Baba stood in front of his Dhuni Mai and gave every devotee a handful of warm *udi* (sacred ash) from his Dhuni. Then with his five fingers covered with *Udi* he placed them on their forehead with a certain amount of force so that the forehead was covered with *Udi*. At that moment I felt I was in heaven and tears of joy rolled down my cheeks. I can hardly describe what I felt. I can only thank my father for gifting me this precious experience."

Dr. Gajanan was fortunate to work in Baba's Sansthan as *Chitnis* (Secretary) many years later. Thus he was able to render *seva* to his Sadguru.

1. **Gajanan wept and stubbornly insisted that he be taken to Shirdi likewise we should be eager, yearn, and weep to meet our Sad Guru.**

2. **They alighted at Sathe Wada which was a well built cemented building as compared to the mud huts. Sathe Wada is symbolic of the soul residing in a body with all the faculties intact.**

3. **We are excited to stay in the materialistic world however when we surrender our 5; that is 1+4=5, or our 5 Indriyias, (senses) and Panch Maha Bhutas or the 5 subtle elements, then Baba will draw us close to him, and hug us and lovingly call us "Bapu".**

Ref: *Sai Leela Magazine* year 57, ank 2, May of 1978

19

Karandikar's Experience of Baba's Divinity

Narayan Neelkant Karandikar, alias Bapusahib, was born in 1893 in Pune. Till the age of fourteen he was surrounded by a highly spiritual atmosphere at home. His guru was Gopal Guru, who along with his mother and elder brother Vasudev Rao, influenced him to worship Swami Samarth. Every evening without fail they attended Swami Samarth's *arati* in Gopal Guru's ashram. In 1907 Gopal Guru took samadhi, so they sought spiritual guidance from his son Shri Abasahib Chitale, who not only guided them spiritually, but also brought about their meeting with numerous saints of that time. Some of the saints they met were Keskar Maharaj, Gondevalkar Maharaj, Narayan Maharaj, Baburao Bede, Gulvani Maharaj and of course Sai Baba of Shirdi.

Narayan Neelkant Karandikar emphatically says, "I reached the zenith of my spirituality only after I prostrated at Baba's feet. Merely by touching his feet I was elevated to a spiritual height that is impossible to attain by myriad of years of penance. That height was beyond the sun and the moon, because his divinity shone through every pore of his physical being.

During the period between 1914 and 1916, I frequently visited Shirdi. I was trained in classical music and had a good knowledge of music. I wished to sing in Baba's 'durbar' in the Dwarka Mai and I requested his permission. Baba replied, 'Not now. You have come for a couple of days, and you can sing when you stay for a week or so.'

Then I placed my head on his feet, and the sacredness of his feet enveloped my entire being. Gently I licked his feet as it felt as sacred as *tirth* (holy water). Immediately Baba said, 'Arre! What is this strange way of prostrating at my feet?'"

Ref.: *Sai Prasad Magazine*, Deepavali issue, 1999.

20

Dwarkanath and Kesarbai Are Fortunate to Meet Baba

Dwarkanath Janardhan Kwali was born on the auspicious day of Ram Navami exactly at 12 noon in 1889. He worked in the Department of Education in Ahmednagar. During that time Nana Sahib Chandorkar was also posted there and both of them became good friends. This was the period of the British regime, so every year they would get a week's vacation for Christmas. Oftentimes Chandorkar would utilise that time fruitfully by visiting Shirdi.

Once, Dwarkanath accompanied Chandorkar and together they went to Shirdi. They reached Shirdi at noon and went to the Dwarka Mai. At that time lunch was about to be served, and soon two rows were formed and all the devotees sat down. Chandorkar noticed that there was no clarified butter, and that day he was eager to have some. So he turned to Dwarkanath and said, "Dwarka go get some clarified butter from my personnel at the camp." Baba heard this and said, "If you don't have a particular article you ought not to borrow it from some other person. Don't go." The truth in Baba words had a tremendous effect on Dwarkanath and he followed it his entire life. Then everyone was served rice with lentil soup (*daal*) and the entire Dwarka Mai was filled with the aroma of fresh, delectable clarified butter that Baba had provided invisibly.

Ref.: *Sai Prasad Magazine*, Deepavali issue, 1991.

Baba was very fond of Kesarbai Jaikar, who was about 7 years old when she first visited Shirdi. She was the daughter of the famous Shyamrao Jaikar. She says, "It was during the winter when we visited Shirdi and it was bitterly cold. I was very fond of guavas and many vendors would come to the Dwarka Mai with their baskets of fruit. Unfortunately I had caught a cold and cough, and my grandfather was worried about it. Sternly he warned me not to eat guavas, and aggravate it. After the *arati* was over and the devotees had gone home, Baba called me. I ran up to him, and he put a guava in the pocket of my coat and handed another one to me. Then he said, 'Come on and eat them.'

Behind the stone on which Baba sat, there was a curtain made of sack cloth and I was curious about what was behind that curtain. Somehow Baba knew everything. In a very secretive voice he said, 'Go and sit behind that curtain and eat the guavas so that your grandfather doesn't see you. Otherwise he will get angry with you, as he thinks guavas will aggravate your cough.' With great delight I ran behind the curtain and chomped on the guavas. All the while I wondered how Baba knew what my grandfather had said to me in the room."

Ref.: *Sai Prasad Magazine*, Deepavali issue, 1999.

Baba Pulled the Tonga to Safety

Since 1910, Sadurao Navalkar frequently visited Shirdi. His son Baal Navalkar says, "When I was young I was scared of Baba, but soon the crowds from Mumbai started arriving and Baba would give all the children plenty of fruits and confectionery. My father was ardently devoted to Baba and Baba would tell him many things. At that time I didn't understand head nor tail of what Baba said. I do vividly remember my first visit to Shirdi. From Mumbai, we reached Kopergaon and we had to cross the river by *tonga*. I was seated next to my aunt, and midway across the river the *tonga* got stuck. The bundle that was in my aunt's hand fell in the river and started floating away. Desperate and afraid I clung to my aunt's neck and started sobbing as I knew we would drown. Instantaneously a tall *fakir* appeared there and said, "Don't be afraid. Nothing will happen to you." And expertly he pulled the *tonga* and led us to safety, to the other bank of the Godavari. When we reached Shirdi and went to the Dwarka Mai, I was astounded to find that *fakir* seated there. From that moment on I knew that he was my saviour."

Ref.: *Sai Prasad Magazine*, Deepavali issue, 1999.

Sainath and Venkatnath Are the Same

Shri Sai Baba and Shri Madhavnath Maharaj of the Nath Panth order (incarnations of Lord Shiva in the 8... century. Machhindranath was the first Guru) often communicated with each other telepathically. They would see each other mystically and know what the other saint was doing. Shri Yogiraj Venkatnath was chosen to be the successor to Shri Madhavnath. Once, when Madhavnath was with Venkatnath he suddenly remembered Shri Sainath. Then with utter love he said "Sai" and went into blissful samadhi for about an hour. When he regained normal consciousness, he informed Venkatnath that he had just gone and visited Shri Sainath. Venkatnath was filled with awe; that just by uttering the name "Sai", Madhavnath had blissful samadhi. At that point in time Venkatnath was about 11 years old and he asked Madhavnath, "Why can't I also meet Sai Baba?" Madhavnath said, "You" and was silent for awhile. Then he said, "Alright. If you desire to meet Sainath, then I will send you to Shirdi." One Thursday, Madhavnath sent Venkatnath along with a devotee to Shirdi.

They reached Shirdi and found Baba seated on a stone beneath the Neem tree. As soon as Baba saw Venkatnath, he stood up and welcomed him. At that time Baba's face radiated happiness and joy. He said, "This is my brother's son," and made Venkatnath sit next to him and fed him a piece of the *bhakri* that he was eating. Sainath, who is the Guru of Gurus, was happy to see him. This experience left an indelible impression on Venkatnath's young mind.

Venkatnath was Gopal M. Kolthe's guru, and once he narrated to Gopal his visit to Shirdi and his meeting with

Shri Sainath. Gopal was filled with awe upon hearing this wonderful experience and from the bottom of his soul, a deep attraction towards Baba developed. Subsequently he became utterly devoted to Baba. On one occasion while Gopal was going to meet a friend he saw a beautiful idol of Baba, and he immediately bought it. Instead of going to his friend's home, Gopal returned home with the idol. On his way back he thought, "His father is the beautiful sky above, his mother is this fertile mother earth, such a sublime God is coming to stay in my home." Gopal reverentially placed the idol at the altar of his prayer room, and devotion for Baba grew in his heart. He worshipped Baba with love and utter devotion. His every heartbeat chanted "Sai, Sai" and Gopal was filled with bliss.

One day, Gopal had an incredible dream: Gopal found himself in a huge temple. He was standing in front of a huge marble idol with a platform or altar in front of it. There were two tall lamps burning on either side of the idol. He climbed three steps and was on top of the altar and stood in front of the idol. He had a palm full of fragrant jasmines that he showered on Baba's foot. Then he took a *panch arati* (five wicks oil lamp) and waved it around Baba, and lay his head on Baba's foot. "Come to me, in Shirdi," he heard Baba say. At that moment he woke up, but he was not quite ready to come out of that sublime dream state. Baba's endearing voice rang in his ears, and he was thrilled that Baba had asked him to come to Shirdi. Gopal yearned to go to Shirdi but didn't know how. The very next day his cousin, who was a professor in a college in Ahmednagar, called and invited Gopal to his home. The professor wished to visit Shirdi and wanted Gopal to accompany him. Gopal learned that his beloved Shirdi was in the district of Ahmednagar, and not far from where the professor resided. Gopal couldn't wait to get to Shirdi, so the very next day he set out to meet his cousin. After a few days they were on their way to Shirdi. Gopal couldn't help idealising and savouring every passing scene and moment. Blissfully, he thought, "The birds flying by have brought a special message from Baba for me. The blue sky with the bright sun is proclaiming the divinity and splendour of Shri

Sainath. The cool breeze has definitely come from Shirdi, and is welcoming me." He says, "As we were approaching Shirdi my thoughts turned to the temple. What would Baba's temple look like? I couldn't contain my excitement. To me Shirdi was Lord Shiva's Kashi and Vaikunth of Lord Vishnu. With this thought in my mind I entered the holy village of Shirdi."

The street was lined with shops selling pictures of Baba, along with trinkets, ornaments and other novelties. Gopal entered the temple saying, *"Shri Sat-Chit-Anand Sainath Maharaj ki Jai."* Roughly translated: *Sat* is true/absolute being, *Chit* is true consciousness and *Anand* is true bliss; Hail to you, Lord Sainath.

Gopal looked at the magnificent idol of Baba and immense peace enveloped his entire being. This was his first visit to Shirdi, yet he felt he had been here, and seen this idol previously. Suddenly he remembered his dream, and Baba asking him to come to Shirdi. Now his dream was fulfilled. On his way to the temple Gopal had bought a ticket for *Abhishek* (ritualistic bathing of an idol), so he joined the rest of the devotees waiting there. Suddenly Gopal's number was called out, and with great reverence he climbed the steps of the Samadhi, and with adoration garlanded the idol with the beautiful garland he had brought along. Gopal bowed down and placed his forehead on Baba's foot. He had brought an *arati* that had 21 wicks drenched in clarified butter and with soul-deep reverence, he waved this around Baba. While he was performing Baba's *arati* a bright light akin to lightning exited Baba's statue and settled on his chest. He felt that his very heart and soul was illuminated, and waves of energy were passing through very cell of his body.

Gopal was quite content with his life, except that a few years ago he had developed severe hearing loss. Prior to performing the *arati* to Baba's idol he had requested Baba to heal his deafness. Gopal worked as the principal of a school and it was of utmost importance that he could hear and converse with the students, listen to their doubts and questions and answer them. On his very first visit to Shirdi, Gopal realised that he had regained much of his auditory range.

The next unforeseen event took place a few months later. Gopal's daughter, who worked as a nurse, asked him to come immediately to Ahmednagar, as a renowned surgeon was visiting their hospital and performing surgery on patients with hearing loss. Gopal knew that this was Baba's boon; he also knew that surgery didn't necessarily cure deafness. All the same, Gopal cast his burden on Baba and underwent surgery. And wonder of wonders, right after surgery he could hear perfectly. He knew that this was Baba's blessing.

Gopal was under the impression that Sainath and Venkatnath were different from each other. Venkatnath had narrated how Madhavnath had sent him to meet Baba when he was young. Hence, Sainath was the bigger Nath and Venkatnath the smaller. Once Gopal had a vivid dream, wherein Sainath and Venkatnath were seated next to each other and conversing. However, Venkatnath's turban was on Baba's head and his white kerchief was tied around Venkatnath's head. One morning when Gopal prostrated before Baba and sat to meditate, he gradually went into deep samadhi. He saw a large ocean in front of him. The waves were lashing at the coast line, but these waves were of a bright energy. One wave followed on the other in quick succession. Sainath had taken the form of Venkatnath and was shining like the setting sun. Gopal treasured this scene and locked it in his heart. A few months later, he went to Devgaon in the district of Aurangabad. In Devgaon there is a temple of Lord Venkatesha that was established by Madhavnath. Gopal thought that he would narrate the vision that he had during meditation and ask his Guru to explain it. He met Venkatnath, placed his head at his feet and sat down. Silently Venkatnath handed Gopal some photographs that a devotee from Mumbai had taken. There was one photograph that drew Gopal's attention. It was a photograph of Venkatnath wherein he looked like Sainath. This reminded him of the scene that he had seen during meditation, **and realised that both the saints were the same.** Gopal wanted that photograph and Venkatnath said, "Child, that photograph is for you. When you arrived here, the reason for your coming came to my mind so I placed the photographs in your hand. Child, if you take one step towards Lord Sainath he comes nearer to you by ten steps. If you talk about his glories he is definitely standing nearby listening to every word you say."

Baba cures our deafness, that is, both the physical and mental deafness, when we are willing and eager to hear his glories. This can happen only by the grace of the Sadguru or Baba.

Ref.: *Sai Prasad*, Volume 33, No. 9, August 1979.

23

Lighting Lamps without Oil

The sacred festival of Guru Purnima fell on the 24th of July 2002. Early in the morning, Megha Shrisa Kamath visited the Sai Baba Temple and offered fruits and confectionary to Baba. Then she went to Vijay Hazare's home and spent some quality time talking about Baba's *leelas*.

That night as usual Megha chanted Baba's name, and soon fell fast asleep. A short while later, Megha had this wonderful, life-changing dream. In the dream Megha saw Baba seated in his usual place in the sanctum sanctorum. Baba was sitting in his characteristic posture next to the railing with his left forearm resting on it. Megha ran up the steps of the Dwarka Mai and clasped Baba's feet and laid her head on them. Baba then placed his beatific hand on her head and blessed her, saying, "Allah Malik". He then applied some *Udi* on her forehead. Megha sat in front of Baba and asked him, "Baba why did you light the earthen lamps with water?"

Baba paused a while and said, "I had to light the lamps without oil for the welfare of all my devotees. My heart is over flowing with *maya*, love and compassion for each and every devotee. However, I am sorrowful to see that people are full of vicious tendencies. Unfortunately, it is wide spread and I see it in all four directions, and it hurts me." Immediately Megha asked, "Baba, what vicious tendencies?"

Shaking his head Baba answered, "A multitude of people pour oil in lamps and light them daily. They place them in their prayer room in front of God, outside their front door, and next to the *Tulsi Vrindavan* (Holy Basil plant in a container). Some do this ritual four times a day, while others keep an 'ever burning' lamp in their prayer room. Yet they are spiteful, malicious and inhuman to others. Their heart is devoid of empathy, humanity and love for other human beings. It is futile to light a lamp without love and compassion; it is akin to lighting a lamp without oil. So why light a lamp at all? Daily you light a lamp then go out and do deceitful acts, and conspire against others. You then spend huge amounts of money and offer incense, flowers and prasad to me, and make a show of your devotion. The person may be a man or a woman, they may be a brother and sister, a husband and wife, brothers, sisters, or any other relative, but the relationship is barren and devoid of love. Because they are 'blood relatives' and they are bound to them through karmic bonds the relationship is grudgingly maintained. Unfortunately a mother-in-law does not consider her daughter-in-law as her very own daughter. Or the elder brother's wife is devoid of love and sisterly affection towards the younger brother's wife. I perceive intense darkness in the deep recess of your mind and heart. Indeed a few of you are straightforward, humane and compassionate, and it is extremely hard for you to survive in this world. If your heart and mind is devoid of love, do not bother to light a lamp. I feel a person should light a lamp if his heart is pure and free of ill will towards others, and then it will dispel the darkness. And the real lamp will be ignited. Neither my *Udi* nor meditation will help if you are bereft of goodwill towards others. Only when you embrace love and compassion will the darkness disappear. I am saddened by the intense darkness that I see all around me. My child, you questioned me about lighting lamps with water, so I told you this. It will benefit all of you if you tell as many devotees as you can about what I said, and make them aware of it. Even if they don't read my *leelas*, my *Charita* or perform my *aratis*, it is alright as long as they embrace my message and change their callous ways. My dear child will you do this for me?" After saying this Baba with tears in his eyes placed his hand on Megha's head and blessed her. At that very moment she woke up and realised that she was dreaming. From that moment it has become a mission in her life to give every devotee that she meets Baba's special message.

Baba in his characteristic way helps us to clear the darkness

created by our own karmas. Through this *leela* he is giving
us the message that each one of us has to do *sadhana* to light
our *Atman-Jyoth*, that is "Self-realisation".

Ref.: *Sai Prasad*, Deepavali vissesh ank, 2002.

24

How Baba Pulled Vishkanta into his Flock

Professor R. Vishkanta, a resident of Bangalore, was fortunate to be blessed by Baba when he was just seven years old. The Professor states, "Way back in 1944, when I was seven years old, my father passed away under tragic circumstances on June 30th. After the eleventh day rituals were performed, I went to school on the twelfth day. I returned home at about 12:15 p.m. My mother was in the kitchen preparing lunch for us. As lunch was not yet prepared, I started playing in the corridor of our home. Our home was situated at the rear end of a huge plot of land. Suddenly I saw a young lad of about nine years standing at the front gate. He was very handsome, with a light complexion. He was wearing a white *kafni* and had a cloth tied around his head. At that time neither my mother nor I knew anything about Sai Baba. Possibly Baba thought that I would be scared if he appeared as an old man wearing a *kafni*, hence he appeared as a young lad.

The young lad approached me and said in a very pleasant voice, 'I would like to meet your mother.' This he said in Kannada, the local language of Bangalore. At that time we were residing in Gandhinagar. In those days, needy boys would come to our home at lunch time and my mother provided them with a nutritious, satisfying meal. They were referred to as *Vaarda Anna* which means 'he who comes once a week for a meal'. I thought the lad was one of these boys, so holding him by his hand, I dragged him all along the corridor and stopped a few feet away from the kitchen. Then I shouted, 'Amma (mother), someone has come to meet you.' This young boy was standing on my left side and had placed his right hand on my left shoulder. His foot was crossed at the right ankle and was resting on top of his left foot. (He was standing exactly as Baba is seen standing in the photograph on his way to Lendi Baugh.)

On hearing me call out to her, my mother had come out of the kitchen. In dismay she said, 'Oh! You have come on a very wrong day. I have nothing to give you at this moment. But if you can wait till the meal is cooked then I will surely feed you.' My mother was full of anguish and despair because after my father passed away the creditors from whom my grandfather had borrowed money had seized everything that we owned. We were virtually left with nothing except the clothes on our back. In a very pleasing voice, the young lad (Baba) said, 'Amma! That is why I have come. I know you are in deep trouble.' Then he handed my mother a small photograph of Baba in his *Abhaya Hasta* pose (with his right hand raised in a blessing posture). He then said, 'This is Sai Baba of Shirdi. Worship him and all your troubles will cease.' He then patted me on my shoulder and left.

Unfortunately, that photograph got lost when we moved from the affluent Gandhinagar to a less affluent neighbourhood in Malleswaram. In reality, without our knowledge Baba had drawn us close to him, as we had moved to our new home that was very close to Baba's temple."

These are Baba's words: "My man, even if he is in another country or thousands of miles away, I shall bring him to me by tying a rope to his legs." (Ovi 15, chapter 28, *Shri Sai Satcharita*). Just as a small boy would draw a sparrow to himself by tying a string to its leg and pulling it, so also Baba drew his devotees to himself in a similar manner.

Once you are drawn into his flock, worship him earnestly by placing him in your heart. Then all your troubles will cease, and when troubles persistently crop up Baba will pull you out of them in his incomparable way.

Ref.: As narrated by Professor R. Vishakanta in 2015.

25

Baba Grants Vishkanta the Gift of Life

Life is never a bed of roses, and after Prof. Vishakanta's father passed away, life was extremely difficult. His mother was unable to make both ends meet.

Prof. Vishkanta recalls, "The following years were riddled with hardship. Poverty was killing us. My mother who fed so many poor Brahmin boys was unable to provide a square meal for her children. More often than not we had to go to bed hungry. I had two elder brothers, and one elder and one younger sister. On one occasion my eldest sister made us sit and explained our plight. She said, 'Now we are in deep trouble because of father's death. Promise me that come what may, even if we may have to hungry for long periods of time, we will never ever beg.' At that time I was only eight years old. I decided to take up some job, and I started working in a printing press that belonged to my father's friend. The owner, knowing our plight, gave me the job against his will, as I would not accept alms.

My job was to sort out ten thousand lined sheets per week, and to discard the sheets that didn't have straight lines. For this I was paid one Rupee per week. Whenever I came home and handed the Rupee to my mother, she would cry. My mother, who used to live like a queen with numerous servants to serve her, was now cooking food in different homes as and when opportunities arose. However, I continued my education, and graduated from school and joined college.

When I was in the 2nd year of college, my health was in shambles. The food deprivation and the state of near starvation had taken its toll on my health. Due to hyperacidity my intestines were riddled with multiple ulcers; which was confirmed in the X-rays. I was admitted in the Government Victoria Hospital where they treated me for a few days. In the hospital I was fortunate to receive two square meals. However, the doctor in charge asked the superintendent to discharge me, saying, 'Why kill the poor boy in this hell? Let him go home and die peacefully.'

When I overheard this, my spirit was completely shattered, and I was sent home.

The doctor had prescribed some antacids and sedatives upon my discharge. My family was not of much help to me; and I felt I was more of a liability rather than an asset to them. In utter desperation I decided to end this wretched life. Over the week I collected a handful of sedatives from various pharmacies. Then I wrote a letter stating: 'To Whom It May Concern, I am ending my life and no one is responsible for my action.' Then I swallowed the entire lot of sedatives late one night.

My mother, who used to get up very early in the morning, came to my room to check on me and tried to awaken me. Then she saw the letter that I had written and it dawned on her what had happened. Hence she started shaking me vigorously and started sobbing. As all this was taking place I was 'out of my body' and looking down at my mother. In vain I was trying to tell her that I was fine and happy now. But she couldn't see or hear me. But what surprised me the most was that an old man who resembled Sai Baba was standing there. I could clearly see that he was not at all pleased; in fact he was quite vexed with what I had done. However, the ambulance was called and my body was put in it and taken to the hospital. Since the link between my body and the soul was not severed, I could perceive the pain of being dragged along with the body. In the Operation Theatre of the hospital my body was laid on a table, while I was sitting on the top of a steel cupboard and gazing down at everyone. But most importantly, Baba had come along and was standing next to the cupboard, very close to me or my soul. The doctor and his assistants first cleaned out my stomach. Then using a defibrillator, they gave me electric shocks on my chest. At that moment Baba, who was standing next to me, thumped me on my back and commanded, 'Get in at once.' I was sucked into my body and slowly woke up. I was kept in the hospital for observation, and in the afternoon the doctor discharged me.

After this hoary experience, everything started improving. I and all my siblings are well educated and well settled. But most importantly, we all are ardent devotees of Baba."

Baba unequivocally disapproved of any devotee contemplating suicide. In chapter 26 of the Shri Sai Satcharita, the story of Ambedkar is given, who was fed up of his wretched and destitute life, and decided to end his life in Shirdi. However, at that juncture Sagun Meru Naik came to him and gave him Swami Samarth's Charitra. Ambedkar read it and did not follow through on his plan.

We are given this body and are responsible for all the happenings, good or bad. We have to undergo the cycle and clear the debt in this life only. Otherwise it will be carried forward to our next life. We cannot escape the cycle of Karma. Obey his order and be blessed.

Ref.: As narrated by Prof. R. Vishakanta in November 2014.

26

Baba Saves the Professor's Life Again

Every night, prior to retiring for the day, Prof. R. Vishakanta has the habit of placing 4-5 almonds in a little bowl of water, so that when he wakes in the morning they are plump and delicious. These almonds are then offered to Baba and later he has them as prasad. On the 26th of May 2014 he soaked the almonds and went to sleep. On the fateful day of 26th May after cleaning the prayer room, he put the almonds in his mouth and started munching on them, and choked. The Professor states, "I was eating the almonds, when suddenly a piece of almond lodged in my trachea and immediately closed it. I was unable to breathe and no air was entering into the lungs. Neither could I cough it out. My eyes were bulging and slowly life was ebbing out of me. Somehow I managed to reach the front door and open it wide. My thought was that in case I died, people in our apartment complex or even the guard may be able to see the dead body lying on the floor, as I was alone at home. Slowly I went back to the prayer room and prostrated myself with my face down. I said, "Baba if you want to take me to your feet, I am submitting myself. It is up to you to decide 'life or death', and closed my eyes. Then suddenly from the front door a sweet aroma blew in. I knew that Baba had come. Whenever Baba comes, just prior to it a whiff of pleasant aroma comes and then Baba materialises in one form or the other. Suddenly, someone gave me a very hard blow on my back, and with that the bit of almond flew out of my mouth. Slowly, I was able to breathe. I immediately looked around to see who had hit me, but there was no one there, except for the smiling photograph of Baba in my prayer room. Thus, Baba gave me another chance to serve him. Thank you Baba."

Baba says, if you chant my name "Sai, Sai," constantly, I

will draw you out of the jaws of death (*Shri Sai Satcharita*, chapter 3).

We should offer ourselves in total surrender; and allow Baba to decide 'life or death'. He will decide the best course of action for us. Receive the same as prasad from him, as he knows what is best for us.

Ref.: As narrated by Prof. R. Vishakanta in November 2014.

27

How Baba Helped Pujari Write his Biography

R. Shri Pujari was a biographer, and over the years he had written the biographies of six saints. The foremost thought in his mind was, "Now which Saint's biography should I write?" While he was contemplating this, three dear friends of his suggested that he write Baba's biography. However, Pujari was disinclined to do so; the reason being that he had never read Baba's *Charita*, nor had he ever seen it. Around sixteen years ago, Pujari had visited Shirdi, but was sorely disappointed by what he saw. He was dismayed by the fact that most of the devotees visited Shirdi for some materialistic favour from Baba. Because of this there was a sort of barricade in his mind regarding this saint. At that time, one of his friends gifted him with a copy of *Shri Sai Satcharita* and requested him write Baba's biography.

Pujari started reading the *Charita*, which he found extremely difficult to do. He recalls, "I was astounded to find that the *Charitra* was a store house of profound spiritual and philosophic truths. Most of the *ovis* (verses) had double meanings. And I was at my wits end trying to decipher its deep spiritual meaning." However, he read and wrote the first four chapters. Pujari then discontinued writing as he felt it was an impossible task to understand it.

While Pujari was in this predicament, one night he had a vivid dream. In the dream he saw Baba, who placed a handful of candied sugar in his palm. This candied sugar was for him. Then Baba gave him a handful of 'sakarpali' (a confectionary made of refined wheat flour and sugar) which was to be distributed as *prasad*. Following this dream, the turmoil

69

in his heart was pacified. Pujari now felt confident that he could complete the reading of the *Charita*, and understand it. Therefore he concentrated on it and continued writing.

A few days later, Pujari had another dream. Pujari says, "In this dream a Muslim gentleman was standing next to me. This man behaved like an old friend and put his arm around my shoulder. Then both of us strolled about for some time, and finally reached a huge building. We entered a large hall and it looked like the hall of the *Prasadalaya* (dining hall) in Shirdi. While we were in the hall, another person walked up to the Muslim gentleman and asked him who I was. However the Muslim gentleman didn't reply. Instead, he pulled out a small diary from his breast pocket, and opened it. On the page in bold letters was written, 'Pujari the Principal is my best friend.'

In August of that year, Pujari visited Shirdi. Upon his return he had another wonderful dream. In that dream he saw an ascetic seated cross-legged on a platform that was at a considerable height. Pujari then climbed on the platform and prostrated before the ascetic. The ascetic then blessed him and gave him a *peda* (confectionary made of condensed milk and sugar). Pujari prostrated again. And this time the Sadhu gave him a tender Banana flower.

Pujari continued writing the *Charitra* with zeal and enthusiasm. Soon, he had written 58 chapters of his version of Baba's *Charita*. One morning when awoke he was surprised to see that the rear end of his pen was broken. Drop by drop, the ink was leaking and falling on the floor. Nonetheless he picked up the pen and started writing as the nib was intact. But he was unable to write anything to his satisfaction, so he tore up that page. Try as he may, the words just didn't seem right. Pujari tried writing after composing himself, but in vain. On the sixth attempt he gave up, and started reviewing what he had written. To his utter delight he realised that the 58th chapter of his book had the description of Baba's Maha Samadhi.

After editing his book he sent it for publication in the Sai Leela Magazine. Two chapters of his book were printed in each issue of the Sai Leela Magazine, and in the October issue the

57th and 58th chapters were printed. Surprisingly, Baba had taken *Maha Niryan* on October 15th 1918, and the 57th and 58th chapter of his book described Baba's Maha Niryan.

Baba has earmarked each one of us for a particular job. He confirms the same in various ways and gets it done in the way he wants. No job is bigger or smaller in nature, and all are equal. We should pray to him to bestow the enthuism and zeal to perform it in the best possible manner. We should put forth our sincere efforts, with equanimity, and without an iota of ego.

Ref.: *Sai Sagar Magazine*, Deepavali Visesah Ank, 2003.

28

How Baba Summoned Dr. Patil

The next two *leela*s are about Dr. Sharmila Patil.

Since childhood, Dr. Sharmila Patil, a resident of Malad, Mumbai, was devoted to Lord Ganesha (Ganapati). Her mother devotedly worshipped Lord Ganesha, and Sharmila followed in her footsteps. From 1984 to 1996, she went to Siddhi Vinayak Temple every Tuesday without fail.

One day when Shramila was in second year of medical school, she happened to watch the film, *Shirdi Ke Sai Baba* on the television. The movie had such a profound effect on her that she started sobbing. That night Baba appeared in her dream and said, "Bring your sister along and come to my temple in Worli."

Sharmila states, "I was thrilled by this dream. I felt wonderful as Baba had spoken to me. At that time I knew nothing about Baba except that he was a great saint who had taken Maha Samadhi. Neither was I aware of Baba's unique method of drawing his devotees into his flock. I thought saints were those blessed souls who had intense faith and devotion in God, and God was pleased with them. Before long I wondered if Baba's message was meant for my sister. Nevertheless, I was determined to take my sister along with me to His temple. But where was this Baba temple in Worli? Then I remembered that a friend of mine lived in Worli. So my sister and I went to her home and asked her about this temple. My friend's mother directed us to the temple, and we finally reached there. In that temple there was a huge idol of Baba 'sitting on the stone'. My heart was filled with reverence as I joined my hands together and bowed to him. Then we offered a garland and a coconut and returned home. However, I continued my worship of Lord Ganesha."

A few years after Sharmila had this dream, an aunt gifted her an English *Shri Sai Satcharita* and asked her to read it. Sharmila accepted it with all the good intentions of reading it, but was unable to do so as she was rather busy.

In 1990, Sharmila got married, and went to her in-laws' home. To her utter dismay, Sharmila found that they had no prayer room, nor were they of a religious frame of mind. Her husband, though not an atheist, believed that there was some "higher power", and performed no ritualistic worship of any deity. Nor did he have faith in *sadhu*s and saints. After their marriage they were to go on a pilgrimage to "Ashta Vinayak" (eight self-manifested idols of Ganapati), but they were unable to go for some reason or the other. Four years later, in December of 1994 they booked a tour of Ashta Vinayak through a travel agency. There were two options in the package—Ashta Vinayak and Bhima Shankar, or Ashta Vinayak and Shirdi. Sharmila and her husband chose the Bhima Shankar tour, but they were unable to get leave on those dates. Quite disappointed, Sharmila and her husband took the Shirdi tour. On the day of the tour, Sharmila stood in front of Baba's picture and asked him to forgive her as she preferred to go to Bhima Shankar. "Baba I will try my level best to keep you in my heart, and cherish you for the rest of my life. But, Baba if I waver I will need you to help me," said Sharmila. Their pilgrimage to Shirdi was indescribably peaceful.

Upon her return, Sharmila started reading the *Charita* in earnest. What she read had a tremendous effect on her, and the *leela*s astounded her. The spiritual philosophy gave her a new insight on life, and she wished the book wouldn't end.

Baba in his unique way draws us into his flock. Baba's directive is not solely for Sharmila, but for all of us: "Worshipping deities, in whatever form they are worshipped, is equivalent to worshipping Baba". Be devoted with sincerity to your chosen diety and it will definitely reach Baba.

Ref.: *Sai prasad Magazine*, Deepavali issue, 1998.

29

A Medical Marvel

The year was 1995, and Sharmila was dejected and distraught as she was unable to conceive. She and her husband had consulted a renowned doctor in the field of infertility. They had all their tests and work-up done and they were being treated by this doctor, but it didn't work out.

One evening, Sharmila was all alone at home, and she was overcome with grief. She could not hold back her tears, and soon she was sobbing. With a heavy heart Sharmila thought, "For the past four years we have been trying to have a baby. Faithfully we have followed the instructions given by the doctor, and taken the medicines as prescribed. I have never missed a single appointment, only to be disappointed again and again. Now only God can help me. Sai Baba is so merciful, but will he shower his mercy on me? Will he accept me into his flock? Will he take away this problem, and make me happy?"

With these thoughts in her mind, she fell asleep. Late that night she had this wonderful dream. In the dream, Sharmila had gone to a Ganapati Temple, and she couldn't believe what she saw. Instead of a Ganapati idol, she saw Baba standing there. He was wearing a white *kafni* and in his hand was his *satka*. With sheer compassion in his eyes, he was looking at her. Then with immense love he stretched out both his hands and beckoned her to come to him. And there ended the dream.

The next morning, she stood in front of Baba's picture, and thanked him for accepting her into his flock. Then she remembered Baba's words, "If you take one step towards me I will take ten steps towards you." Subsequent to this dream, Sharmila started reading the *Charita* with eagerness and devotion. She also tried to find out more about this wonderful God. Sharmila read all the *Sai Leela* magazines that she could

74

get, and any other literature that she could find.

With renewed vigour and enthusiasm she kept her appointment with her doctor during her fertile period that month. But the disappointment that she had faced over the years caught up with her and she made up her mind that this would be her last attempt to conceive. Sharmila then cast all her burdens on Baba's shoulders and had her sonogram done. With great anticipation, Sharmila went to get the result. Her doctor shook her head and said, "Sorry! Sharmila, this month you had an 'anovulatory cycle'. So it is futile to try any further."

Filled with remorse, Sharmila thought, "Baba to conceive I need only one single egg. But this month the ovary has not ripened and released an egg. Now I am not going to worry as I have left my destiny in your hands. Baba I am going to stop all my attempts to conceive right here and now."

With Baba even the impossible is possible. And that very month Sharmila got pregnant. "This is a medical marvel. Indeed science has advanced tremendously and impressively. With this advanced technology the physician and radiologist can see very minute things that are happening inside the body. Nevertheless, it is unable to see Baba's blessing. So I thanked Baba from the bottom of my heart." Sharmila's faith had increased by leaps and bounds. She started chanting Baba's name regularly and reading at least a chapter of the *Charita* daily.

What was beyond the bounds of possibility, Baba made possible.

Ref.: *Sai Prasad Magazine,* Deepavali issue, 1998.

30

Dr. Patil's Faith Strengthens

Baba answered Sharmila's prayers and all her pregnancy tests were positive. Surprisingly, she had no discomfort like morning sickness, pica (perverted appetite) or swelling of her feet.

Late one evening, there was a shutdown of electricity. Sharmila was alone at home as her husband had not returned from his clinic. Soon she started feeling restless, so she pulled her chair next to the window and sat down. As usual, Sharmila was mentally chanting Baba's name; and before long she fell fast asleep. Then she had this reassuring dream.

"My Baba had come to my home. Though I couldn't see his face clearly, but I knew it was him, as he wore a long white *kafni*. Without a moment's hesitation I ran and fell at his feet. Tears were copiously flowing from my eyes onto his feet. However Baba's feet felt cold to me. Baba then said, 'Everything will be alright.' There my dream ended. Now I was sure that my pregnancy would be alright and I would have an uncomplicated delivery. After all, my Baba had come to my home and had reassured me."

And so it came to pass. Although this was her first baby, Sharmila's labour pains lasted only a few hours. Moreover, she had an uncomplicated delivery, and Baba blessed her with a baby boy. A week after Sharmila and her son came home, she again dreamt of Baba. In the dream, she was sitting on the floor with her son in her lap. Baba sat in front of her; his forearm was resting on a railing. He then raised his hands and said, "Nothing will happen to your child. He will be fine." Thereafter Sharmila stopped worrying about her son.

From then on, if her son had any ailment, her first line of treatment was to give him *Udi* mixed in water, and needless to say her child recovered. Although Sharmila was a physician, and physicians tend to frown on other modalities of treatment other than what they practice, Sharmila considered *Udi* as '*Sanjivani*' or the only life-giving elixir on earth.

With tears of gratitude in her eyes Sharmila recalls, "There are innumerable instances when my son was growing up that Baba came to my aid. I am not a 'great' devotee, nor do I qualify as a good devotee of Baba, as I am unable to assimilate his teachings like '*Nava Vida Bhakti*' into my life and daily routine. Nonetheless, whenever I find time I read his *Charita*, and the *Sai Leela* magazine. I do chant his name but it is not sustained. Time and again I marvel at Baba's unconditional compassion, for he comes running to the aid of devotees like me without fail. I am still incapable of understanding this magnificent God, consequently I sing the hymn '*Ananta tula te kase re stavave*': Thou art eternal, how shall I praise thee? Thou art eternal, how shall I do obeisance to thee? Even the thousand-tongued Adisesh (the snake on whom Lord Vishnu reclines) gets exhausted in singing your praises. Therefore, I only 'salute' you with eight-fold prostrations, Shri Sainatha."

Tumcha mee bhar vahina sarvatha
Navha hai anathyia vachan majhe

Roughly translated, this means: **"I will carry the burden of your life forever, till eternity. Or this promise of mine will be untrue".**

Ref.: *Sai Prasad Magazine*, Deepavali issue, 1998.

31

Dhananjay Junerkar Gets Darshan

Numerous friends, relatives and devotees told Dhananjay Junerkar that they had the "divine vision" of Baba in this or that form. Dhananjay says, "I too yearned to meet Baba. However I was doubtful if I would be able to recognise him if I met him in any other form. So I firmly decided in my mind that if Baba wanted to appear before me then he should appear like the photograph that I prayed to, because I knew that I didn't have that spiritual sight to recognise him. Otherwise, he need not appear before me at all. And my desire was fulfilled by Baba two years ago.

One Tuesday evening I met my friend Annu Dixit, who asked me if I would like to accompany him to Ozar. Ozar is famous as it is one of the Ashta Vinayak or Lord Ganesha temples. I had not planned to do anything that evening, so I readily agreed to accompany him. I realised that I had a single five Rupee bill in my pocket. Before I could say anything to Annu, he suggested that we could go there on his motorcycle. Hence the question of spending any money didn't arise. Then we set out to Ozar. Upon entering the temple there was a long queue. So I stood in a corner and worshipped Lord Ganapati. After receiving prasad we exited the temple.

Annu went to get his motorbike which was parked some distance away. I waited for him to return just outside the gate. There I saw a few beggars seated in a row. One of them attracted my attention. He was a young man with a dark black beard; his forehead had a *kumkum tika* (vermilion mark) on it. He had a *sirvesh* (head gear) tied exactly as Baba did, and was wearing a long *kafni*. He sat peacefully without begging. His eyes shone brilliantly, and face had a divine lustre to it. Before I knew it, I had taken the five Rupee bill from my pocket and handed it to him. He laughed and accepted the money without saying a single word. My hair stood on end and I felt I was in a trance. At that very moment Annu turned up with his motorbike. In a confused state I sat on the pillion and he drove a short distance; when I asked him to turn around and go back to the temple. We reached the gate where the beggars were seated, but Baba was not there. Then I narrated what had happened, but he didn't believe me.

I was elated that Baba had appeared to me in his natural, tangible form. However I had one regret: that I didn't recognise him. On the other hand, I am glad that I gave him everything that I had, that is, the five rupee bill. I am sure that Baba will take care of all my requirements in life."

Baba definitely answers our prayers, but it is our responsibility to do *sadhana* or spiritual practices to develop the internal eye to identify him when he manifests in front of us.

Ref.: *Sai Prasad Magazine,* Deepavali issue, 1998.

32

How Baba Protected Ambakar

A.G. Ambakar, a resident of Dombivili, Mumbai, is devoted to Baba. He strongly feels that this universe cannot function without Baba's grace. That you are able to breathe is due to his benevolence. Each breath that you take is because of Him. Yet we are filled with false arrogance. When we are unable to fully know ourselves, then how can we comprehend the greatness of Baba? Just hand over your life to Baba and then you will realise what he will do for you.

On Bhau Beej (two days after Deepavali) of 1995, terrorists had planted a bomb in one of the bogies (cars) of the Mumbai-Ambarnath train that exploded at Kalyan Station. On that day Ambakar was working the night shift at the S.T. Depot (State Transportation Department) which was close to the railway station. That night at around 11 p.m. his friend and colleague suggested that they go out and have a meal. Thus they went to a restaurant, and Baba saved then from injury and death. They had hardly started their meal when they heard the loud, earth shattering sound of the explosion. Shortly after that they heard the sirens of the police vans and the fire brigade. It was then that Ambakar realised that there was an explosion in the Ambarnath train. The impact of the explosion had not spared the building where he worked, although it was quite some distance away. The glass panes of the windows were shattered and there was debris all around. But by Baba's grace, no one was hurt in his building. Upon completing his night shift, while returning home he saw the devastation caused by the explosion. The bogie was a mangled mass of soot-covered steel.

The next evening, he was apprehensive of travelling by the train. Ambakar's mind was in turmoil as he had seen the devastation caused by the explosion. Nevertheless he lit an incense stick in front of Baba, applied *Udi* to his forehead and set out. On the way, Ambakar decided that he would board the train to Kalyan and would avoid the Ambarnath train. He reached the Dombivili station and the Kalyan train arrived, but he was still a bit frightened. He finally boarded the train and it so happened that the bogie was empty. Ambakar looked around and on the rack opposite to him he saw bundles that were tied in a cotton sheet. His heart skipped a beat as he thought, "If those two bundles are filled with explosives, I won't reach Kalyan as I will be blown to smithereens." So he decided to go to the rear end of the bogie.

At that very moment he heard Baba's voice loud and clear.

"Arre! Vedya. Maranala bheethose. Wha re! Kuthe bhi gelas tari theye yenarach! Thithese ubha raha."

Roughly translated, it means: "Oh! You Fool. You are afraid of death. No matter where you go death will definitely come. Just stay where you are."

Hearing Baba say this Ambakar was overwhelmed. He thought of how much concern Baba had for him, and his mind lost its fear. Ambakar said to himself, "Fool. Death is waiting behind your back. Death is inevitable no matter where you are. But Baba is in front of you, *so chant his name. Baba will help you cross this ocean of materialistic life and will give you the strength to walk on the path to salvation."*

In chapter 27, ovi 85 to 91 of the Shri Sai Satcharita, Baba himself extols the power and significance of chanting his name (*naam*) and it is given below as he said it to Shama:

"*Naam* can smash mountains of sins. *Naam* can sever the bondage of the physical body. *Naam* can eradicate and destroy millions of evil passions.

Chanting the *Naam* can break the neck of death itself; it avoids the pull of the birth-death cycle.

Naam when chanted with conscious effort is excellent. Chanted without conscious effort is not bad either. Even if it comes to the lips unexpectedly it will reveal its power.

There is no other means easier than the *Naam* to purify the

81

heart. It is the adornment of the tongue. *Naam* **nourishes the spiritual life."**

Ref.: *Shri Sai Sagar Magazine*, Ramnavami Edition, March–April 2000.

33

Baba Removes Evil Spells

Around August of 1983, Sulochana M. Joshi, a resident of Nagpur, started having menstrual problems. At first the bleeding was not significant, but it occurred at frequent intervals with excruciating pain in her pelvic area. Sulochana consulted a Homeopathic doctor and took the pills as advised. As she was devoted to Baba, she also took *Udi* mixed in water along with the pills.

The festival of Rakhi Purnima (full moon day in August) happened to be a few days later, but Sulochana felt very weak and could not participate in the festivities. Thereafter, her health started gradually going downhill. In spite of taking the pill regularly as prescribed, she didn't benefit at all from the treatment. Instead of improving, she started bleeding profusely and for a longer period of time. Sulochana's husband then consulted the allopathic family doctor, who checked her and prescribed some multi-vitamins along with iron, a good diet, and complete bed rest. Now Sulochana was at her wits' end, as her condition started deteriorating further. She felt as if her life force was sucked out of her, and she was unable even to stand up. So she just curled up and lay on the bed. As there was no other female relative to help her, the responsibility of doing the household chores fell on her husband. Sulochana's husband would get up at the crack of dawn and help her with her toiletries, then make breakfast. He also had to get their two sons ready for school and then go to work. This cycle of household chores and looking after his wife and children went on endlessly.

Then in early 1984, her husband consulted an acclaimed homeopathic doctor who was considered a specialist in the field of gynaecology. He enthusiastically treated her, but to

83

no avail. Sulochana felt "as if someone was sucking up all her energy", and every day she felt weaker than the day before. To add to her problems the doctor informed her that she was hypertensive, hence he changed her medication and diet. The doctor also advised her to consult a gynaecologist. As that was the only remaining option, her husband had her checked up by a famous gynaecologist who advised Sulochana to have numerous blood tests, and X-Rays of her pelvis. The doctor also did an internal pelvic examination and took a biopsy from the uterus. With bated breath Sulochana waited for the results. Her doctor informed her that the tests were normal and she did not have any malignancy or tumours of the uterus. Sulochana sighed with relief, but her life was in shambles. Her husband had spent a great deal of time and money on her illness. He had to bear the brunt of it all, without any succour.

One day in utter desperation Sulochana cried out in front of Baba's photograph. "Baba you are the ocean of benevolence; then why are you not helping me to recover? Baba I have never stopped taking *Udi*, nor have I failed to chant your name then why have you deserted me? Baba please stop this incessant bleeding; if not, give me death." Sulochana knew that her husband would soon collapse under the pressure of looking after her, taking care of their two young sons and then going to work.

It was now almost a year since Sulochana's problems started; and she wondered if she ought to have her uterus removed. However, the very thought of surgery frightened her to death. As she lay in bed, Sulochana thought, "Baba what am I to do? My husband is spending huge amounts of money on my treatment and special diet. What sin have I committed to suffer like this? Why have you become so hard hearted? If you won't alleviate my suffering, grant me death instead." Then Sulochana opened the *Satcharita* and the words "Allah bhala karega" appeared before her. Immediately she felt reassured and slept soundly that night.

The next day a lady along with her family visited her. The lady said, "Yesterday I had this vivid dream of Sai Baba. In that dream he clearly instructed me to go to your home and tell you that you will recover soon. Baba emphatically asked me to tell you that in the top shelf of your cupboard you have this particular sari that you should get rid of immediately. He said, 'Ask her to burn that sari at once and everything will be alright.'" Sulochana immediately followed Baba's order and from that very moment she felt better. Needless to say, from that very day the "evil spell" that was causing havoc in her life ceased, and since then she has been healthy.

Steadfast and unswerving faith in Baba removes all kinds of "evil spells" and affords protection. By Baba's grace all of us can have an armour of protection against evil spells and sorcery by His name.

Ref.: *Shri Sai Leela Magazine,* Volume 6, No. 6, September, 1984.

34

Baba Takes Care of His Devotees

This *leela* was narrated by a devotee who wishes to remain anonymous; and calls herself Sai's sister. The *leela* is about her younger brother Sai, and she will be referred to as Sister. Her family resided in Dombivili, Mumbai, and was devoted to Lord Dattatreya and Shri Sai Baba.

Sister recalls, "Ours was a large, happy family. I had six brothers and three sisters. Every Thursday my parents performed *arati* in the evening, and then distributed prasad of some confectionary. When Sai was a young child he was often sick with high fever. At that time my mother would place an onion on his head and tie a thin white towel around his head. All the siblings would point at him and say, 'Look, Sai Baba has come.'

One day when Sai was about three years old, our maid had given him some *bhel* (a savory of puffed rice, peanuts and deep fried gram flour noodles) as a treat. His elder brother teasingly said that he would eat up all his *bhel*. Sai started crying, immediately stuffed a fistful of *bhel* in his mouth, and choked on it. This resulted in a severe bout of coughing, followed by vomiting. My mother was unaware that a small piece of peanut had lodged in his lung. Thus a few days later he came down with a cough, cold and fever. Sai received treatment for it and seemed better a few days later. From then on Sai had frequent bouts of cough accompanied with fever. This went on for more than a year, and he received treatment from various doctors. Once a doctor gave Sai an emetic (an agent that induces vomiting) and in his vomit a piece of peanut was found. Immediately an X-ray of his chest was taken, and the foreign body was identified in his right lung. The doctor advised my mother to have it immediately removed surgically.

The very thought of surgery on such a little boy frightened us immensely, and all of us fervently prayed to Baba for Sai's recovery. Baba came running to our aid.

My aunt, who worked as a nurse in St. George Hospital, informed us that a renowned team of pulmonary surgeons were to visit their hospital a week later. She also promised to present Sai's case before the team. The team reviewed the case and Sai's surgery was scheduled the next day. That night Sai dreamt of Baba, who came and placed his hand on his head and said, '*Chirenjeeve Bhava.*' The next morning Sai narrated the dream to my mother. Then he questioned her, '*Ayi*, what does *Chirenjeve Bhava* mean?' My mother with tears in her eyes said, 'Sai, Baba has blessed you with a long, healthy life. Now you need not be afraid, everything will be fine as Baba is there to take care of you.'

True to his word, the surgery was successful, and when Sai regained consciousness he smiled at the doctor. Sai never had any respiratory problems thereafter, although his lung was removed.

Sai completed his medical schooling in India and went to America. There he did his post-graduatation in paediatrics, and is the Director of a children's hospital. His wife and both his sons are also in the medical profession. But the most wonderful part of this miracle is that at the age of fifty-two he started playing tennis. And when you watch him play tennis it is impossible to guess that he has only one lung."

Every word that Baba utters is true. His blessings never go in vain. The only prerequisite is unconditional and unquestioning faith in him.

Ref.: *Shri Sai Sagar Magazine*, Ramnavami Edition, March–April, 2000.

35

Baba Heals Jyothi Babar through a Dream

Like a tornado, Swine Flu was sweeping across Maharashtra in the month of August and September of 2009. The virulent outbreak had gripped Pune and Mumbai, quickly reaching the magnitude of an epidemic.

At that time, Jyothi Naren Babar, a resident of Mumbai, was suffering from flu-like symptoms of fever, cough and cold. Jyothi was a teacher in a school called *Amchi Shala* in Chembur. Although she was miserably sick, Jyothi somehow continued to attend school. It was rather difficult for her as she had to look after her two sons aged seventeen and eleven, as well as her husband Naren, who worked as a manager in the Times of India newspaper. There was no one to help her. Joythi's mother Maya Savant resided in Sindudurg in Ratnagiri, and was unable to be with her.

Since she had fallen ill, Jyothi had been treated by Dr. Shedge and Dr. Anita Patil, with very little improvement. On the following visit her doctor got an X-ray of her chest done. When Jyothi revisited her doctor to get the result of the X-ray, Dr. Patil sat Jyothi down and said, "There is a small knot in your lung. Further work up ought to be done for it." When Jyothi heard what her doctor said, she felt as if the very earth under her feet had opened wide and she had fallen into a gaping hole.

At that juncture, two of the children in Jyothi's school were admitted in hospital with Swine Flu. Now Jyothi and her husband were extremely anxious and worried. Panic stricken, she hoped that she was not infected by the H1N1 virus. However, as both of them were devoted to Baba, they sought refuge in him and cast their burden on his compassionate shoulders. That evening Joythi and her husband decided to take a second opinion. Thus they consulted Dr. Shashank Joshi who had graduated from medical school with honors in medicine. Dr. Joshi re-evaluated her X-rays, and after examining her suggested a CAT scan of her lungs, as a round nodule was definitely visible.

On the 14th of September, Jyothi had the scan done. That night Jyothi did not get a wink of sleep. She brooded over her problem. "What if the nodule is malignant? Then who will look after my family, if I die? Will I have to undergo surgery? Will I ever recover from this, and regain my health?" Her mind kept churning these thoughts over and over again. Finally she fell asleep and at around 3 a.m., Jyothi had this dramatic dream.

Jyothi saw a small cave; and in that cave both her mother and she were standing. Suddenly Baba appeared, stomping his feet, and entered the cave. He seemed exceedingly angry, as his face was red, and he rolled his eyes around. Baba had a *mor pisari* (a wand made of peacock feathers) in his hand. He passed that wand up and down Jyothi's entire body and loudly proclaimed, "Now that I have come I will take it with me." Simultaneously as he said this, a round bright light exited from Jyothi's body, and she woke up.

Early next morning she narrated her dream to Naren, and he was delighted that Baba had taken her nodule away. However it is natural for human beings to be frightened of the unknown. That evening they were to get the result of the CAT scan. Naren prayed to Baba the entire day. The doctor in utter amazement said, "I cannot believe my eyes, but your scan is normal. There isn't even a smidgen of suspicion of a nodule. Your lungs are absolutely clear." Upon leaving the doctor's office Naren called Jyothi's mother. "*Ayi*, Baba has taken away the nodule from Jyothi's lung. That round nodule that was clearly visible on the X-ray is not visible on the scan, and Jyothi's lungs are normal. *Ayi*, even the doctor couldn't believe it." Then both of them thanked Baba from the bottom of their hearts for coming to their aid so promptly and taking away the nodule.

In chapter 7 of the *Shri Sai Satcharita*, the *leela* of Baba

taking the bubonic plague of Balwant Khaparde upon himself is given. Balwant was running a high temperature. His mother became restless, as there was an outbreak of plague. She wished to return with her son to Amravati, and came to seek permission from Baba.

Ovi 106: Gently Baba said, "The sky is overcast, but it will rain, bringing forth the harvest; and the clouds will melt away."

Ovi 107: "Why be afraid?" So saying he lifted his *kafni* and showed the inflamed buboes to everyone. Baba had taken upon himself four egg-sized buboes, and added, "Look! I have to take upon myself the suffering of my devotees."

For the sake of his devotees the Sadguru takes on himself, the karmas of his devotees.

Ref.: *Shri Sai Sagar Magazine*, Deepavali Ank, 2010.

36

Baba Visits Dinesh's Shop

Every year during the holy festival of Guru Purnima, Dinesh B. Nikam, a devotee from Pune, went on a pilgrimage to Shirdi without fail. However in the year 2009 his mother had undergone major surgery, hence he was unable to go. That year Dinesh decided that he should stay at home and take care of her. Nevertheless, he felt a twinge of disappointment because of his inability to visit Shirdi.

A few days after Guru Purnima, Dinesh, who was a tailor by profession, had gone to his shop to complete the backlog of orders. He was rather busy that day. That afternoon he was at his table, engrossed in marking and cutting the material that lay in front of him. A fakir entered his shop and stood near his table. Dinesh continued his work without paying much attention to him. As a matter of fact, Dinesh was annoyed with the *fakir* for having the audacity to enter his shop without his permission. Seeing his unresponsive behaviour the fakir said, "Why are you not looking at me?" Without glancing at him, Dinesh replied, "If you want a rupee or two just take it and leave." The fakir's entire conversation was in Hindi, while Dinesh replied to him in Marathi. Then the fakir said, *"Tu mujhe kya dega? Mujhe pehchana nahi kya?"* Roughly translated, it means: "What will you be able to give Me? You still have not recognised me." Dinesh was unable to reply to the audacious words. The fakir continued, "Why didn't you come to the Shirdi Durbar this year?"

Flabbergasted at what he said, Dinesh was speechless. In utter confusion, he thought, "It is my practice to go to Shirdi and attend Baba's durbar every year at Guru Purnima. I know this for sure, but how on earth was this fakir aware that I didn't go to Shirdi this year?" The fakir then said, "Now have you recognised me? At least have a look at me now."

Finally Dinesh looked up. In front of him stood a fakir wearing a long white *kafni*, with a white cloth tied around his head. Dinesh was astounded that he looked exactly like Sai Baba. As Dinesh was speechless, the fakir said, "Now give me a piece of paper." Immediately, Dinesh handed him a piece of paper, and started searching for a pen, when the fakir said, "I do not require a pen." Then he proceeded to write something on the paper with his finger. He handed the paper to Dinesh and said, "Preserve this paper, and keep it with you at all times." Then the fakir strode out of his shop. However, all this while Dinesh seemed to be in a trance.

A short while later Dinesh thought, "This is not an ordinary fakir. Without taking a single rupee from me he reminded me that I had not gone to Shirdi this year. I should have at least offered him a cup of tea." Immediately he called a small boy who worked in his shop and sent him in search of the fakir. A short time later the boy returned and informed him that the fakir couldn't be found anywhere. There were numerous shops adjacent to his shop, so Dinesh went looking for him there. However the fakir had not stopped at any of the other shops, and was never seen thereafter in that locality. Then it dawned on him that the fakir was none other than Baba himself.

With delight Dinesh thought, "There are millions of devotees who visit Shirdi during the festivals. Some devotees make it a routine to visit Shirdi every month. Others visit Shirdi on every Purnima and if they fail to go, no one notices it. There are hundreds upon thousands of devotees that visit Shirdi from time to time; and yet Baba noticed that a devotee like me failed to come to his Durbar on this Guru Purnima. He came to my shop and made me aware that he knows each and every thing. **If you love Baba with your heart and soul, Baba also reciprocates with the same intensity. You and I may forget him, but from this experience I can say with conviction that Baba will never forget you."**

Ref.: *Shri Sai Sagar Magazine*, Deepavali Ank, 2010.

37

Baba Saves Krishnarao's Family

Around 1956, Subash's father, Krishnarao Saptharushi, a resident of Pune, bought a new car. As he was an ardent devotee of Baba, he decided to first visit Shirdi in his new car and have the car blessed there. It is a tradition in India to have a new vehicle blessed.

That Thursday, Krishnarao along with his family set out to Shirdi and reached there by noon. In those days Shirdi was a quiet little village, and today's colossal crowds were absent. Upon reaching Shirdi, Krishnarao parked his car near the Samadhi Mandir, and went inside to pray. Then they went to all the holy sites in Shirdi and returned to their car. The priest then performed *puja* of the new vehicle. By then it was late in the evening. As soon as the priest had completed the ritualistic worship of the car, Subash's father was eager to return to Pune as he had some important business to take care of.

It was a practice in those days to not leave Shirdi on a Thursday; numerous devotees follow this practice even today. Krishnarao's son Subash says, "When the villagers saw that my father was ready to leave Shirdi, they asked my father to stay overnight and leave the next day. Most probably out of respect for the villagers, my father stayed and we attended the *Sej Arati*. As soon as the *arati* was over my father was in a hurry to leave. At that time the priest from the Samadhi Mandir requested him not to leave as it was Thursday. He said, "Bhau, do not leave today. If you have urgent business that you need to attend to, at least leave a few minutes after midnight; then it will technically be Friday." Not heeding his advice, my father bundled us in the car and drove off. Soon we were on the road; it was pitch dark, as there were no street lights. Except for the light thrown on the road by the headlights of the car, you couldn't see anything else. It was difficult to make out where the road ended and the fields started. There were fields on either side of the road, and the eerie sounds of nocturnal creatures were loud and frightening in the still night. There was hardly any traffic on the road, when the headlights from our car suddenly went out. With a thud, our car came to a screeching halt in someone's field. My father tried in vain to turn on the headlights and to start the car, but his attempts proved futile. Then he got out of the car and went on the road to flag down any passing vehicle for help. A truck or two did pass by, but sped away without stopping. Krishnarao stood on that road for an appallingly long time hoping that someone would stop and help him. He regretted his decision of leaving Shirdi when so many people had forewarned him not to go, so he joined his hands together and begged Baba to forgive him and to help him get out of this predicament.

At that very moment Krishnarao saw a military truck approaching; he waved out to it and it stopped. A sepoy got out and inquired what the problem was. Upon hearing what had happened, he went to the truck and brought a huge flashlight and both of them returned to where the car had stalled. The sepoy (soldier) then opened the hood of the car and looked in. Probably there was nothing wrong with the car, as he returned to the driver's seat and turned the key in the ignition. Lo! The car started, and the lights turned on.

The sepoy gasped and shouted, "Sahib you are extremely fortunate, or you would have driven your car into this well and all of you would have lost your lives!"

In the light thrown from the headlights, we could clearly see that the car had stalled just a foot away from a huge open well. That well was at ground level and didn't have an embankment. When I saw that, my heart leapt into my throat as I envisioned a watery grave for all of us. Swiftly the sepoy reversed the car and brought it on the road. Krishnarao thanked him from the bottom of his heart for his timely help. Then he asked the sepoy, "Sir, can you tell me where we are at present?" The sepoy laughed and said, "Sahib you are at the boundary of Shirdi."

Then he jumped into the military vehicle and drove off. It was then that my father realised that Baba had come as the sepoy and helped him.

Krishnarao then looked at his wristwatch. It was five minutes after midnight. Again he joined his hands together and begged Baba for forgiveness; then thanked him for coming to his aid. Thereafter, the car ran smoothly and they reached home safely."

About a year later Krishnarao dreamt of Baba. In the dream, Baba stood in front of him and angrily said, "You have hung me precariously. Shall I hang you too like that?" Immediately Krishnarao awoke, and he thought, "What have I done now for Baba to say this to me?" The next morning he noticed that the nail on which Baba's picture was hung in the prayer room was loose and the picture could fall at any moment. That morning he got a carpenter to securely fix the nail in the wall, and attach an ornate wooden strip below the picture for support.

Baba warns Krishnarao through the villagers and the priest of the impending catastrophe. Our body is the carrier of our *Jeev-Atman* (soul); therefore, this carrier should be respected by doing sadhana, and Baba will definitely protect us from falling into the well. Baba will defend us against all the karmas just as military personnel protect the borders.

Ref.: *Shri Sai Sagar Magazine*, Deepavali Ank, 2010.

The Power of Udi

Shri Mule was a famous advocate residing in Nasik. Both he and his wife were ardently devoted to Baba. Mule had performed numerous spiritual practices; besides meditation and yoga, he also kept numerous fasts. Mule's fasts were very severe, as he fasted for days, weeks and sometimes months. He only drank milk and ate seasonal fruits for long periods of time. Nevertheless, he was very fit and active and had a bright aura around him. His face shone with extraordinary brightness.

One day, a huge serpent entered his house while his wife was alone at home. Mule had gone to court, and there was no other male in the house. Mrs. Mule saw the serpent and fervently prayed to Baba. The snake went into a corner of the room and sat there coiled up. With great courage, Mrs. Mule went into her prayer room and brought the box of *Udi* with her. Then she bowed to Baba and went near the corner where the snake sat coiled up, and addressed the snake: "Oh, *Nag Devta*, (serpent deity) this is Baba's *Udi*. I expect you to respect it. I am drawing a *Laxman rekha* (a line that Sita was forbidden to cross in the Ramayana) and you ought not to cross it." Then she drew a long line with the *Udi*.

Amazingly, the snake did not dare to cross that line of *Udi*. Then she went about calmly doing her chores. When her husband returned from court, he called a *mantric* (person well versed in *mantras*) and the snake was taken out of their home.

The power of *Udi* cannot be described by words. By applying *Udi* on your forehead and taking it internally it prevents the serpent of your ego from showing its fangs. And importantly, your Kundalini will awaken and open and listen to your Atman.

Ref.: *Shri Sai Leela Magazine*, Volume 58, May 1978.

How Baba Blessed Kulkarni

B.V. Kulkarni, a resident of Kolhapur, is absolutely certain that Baba has blessed him and given him the essence for his spiritual advancement. One day, as per his usual practice, Kulkarni awoke at 5 a.m. but that morning he crawled back into bed and soon fell fast asleep.

A while later he dreamt of Baba. In that dream he saw a well-illuminated huge hall, wherein there was an ornate throne. On that throne, Baba was seated. He had on a green shawl that was exquisitely embroidered with golden threads. Baba had a golden crown on his head that was studded with diamonds. He was dressed in the splendour that Baba's idol in the Samadhi Mandir is dressed prior to the *arati*. But he sat on the throne cross-legged (lotus position in yoga).

A short distance from the throne, some devotees were leaving and some were entering the hall. However Kulkarni and his wife were standing before him with their hands folded. Kulkarni prostrated before Baba and sat on the floor, and said, "Baba if you sit on the throne cross-legged, then how can I massage your feet?" Immediately Baba stretched out his feet, and Kulkarni started gently massaging Baba's feet. He was astounded that Baba's feet were so soft. Kulkarni remembered that he had read *Khaparde's Diary*, in which Khaparde said, "Although Baba was advanced in age, his feet were exceptionally soft."

He thought, "Even today, that is after 70 years, Baba's feet are so soft." He then looked at Baba and said, "Baba how fortunate I am, that I am able to massage your feet with my hands in this life. Baba this is unfeasible, as I was born 4 years after your Maha Samadhi. However, your *leela*s are mind boggling and I am fortunate to be a part of it. Let your grace always be with me, Lord."

Then Kulkarni said, "Even a person like Chandorkar..." Baba interrupted him and said, "Arre! Chandorkar was a remarkably good person."

Kulkarni said, "Baba, in your *Charita* the importance and greatness of 'Charan-savahan' or messaging the feet is..." Again, Baba interrupted Kulkarni and said, "Isn't the *Charita* an excellent book? You do read it?"

Kulkarni then told Baba that he read it daily. At that moment he realised that he had lied, because that day for some reason he was unable to read it. Baba continued, "This *pothi* is outstanding and exceptional so make it your daily routine to read it without fail."

At that moment Kulkarni was aroused from his sleep. He lay there for a long time as he was overcome by love and emotions, and was sobbing. He couldn't control his sobbing, and hearing it, his sons woke up. Together they performed Baba's *arati*. And this is how Baba blessed him.

Prayers to serve our Sadguru with a pure heart will definitely reach him, and will allow us to serve him in the desired manner.

Ref.: *Shri Sai Leela Magazine*, Volume 67, No. 8–9, November and December 1988.

40

Baba Solves Devyani's Problems

For the past 30 years, Devyani C. Joshi and her family had venerated Baba. Moreover, through thick and thin Baba was always there to solve their problems.

Devyani's husband Chandrashekar was an advocate, and they also ran a milk distribution business. However, for the past year they had a lot of financial problems. Even though her husband worked at his legal practice and the milk distribution hadn't closed, they were unable to make both ends meet. Devyani was extremely troubled by this and didn't know what to do. As they lived in Pune, she and her husband would go to the Swargate Baba *Mutt* for the evening *arati*. One Thursday, both of them went there and spoke to Shri Lombar about their problem. Shri Lombar is an ardent devotee of Baba, and the chairman of the *Mutt*. Numerous devotees seek his guidance and help for spiritual and worldly problems. When Shri Lombar heard their problem, he gave them *Udi* and asked Chandrashekar to meditate on Baba and tell him their problems every night before going to sleep.

Chandrashekar did as advised and the next Thursday he dreamt of Baba. In the dream, Chandrashekar found himself at the entrance of the Dwarka Mai and Baba was standing at the door. Baba looked at him compassionately and asked him to light lamps at the main door. Then he pointed out the spots where the lamps were to be placed.

The next day both Chandrashekar and his wife went to Shirdi. That evening they lit numerous lamps in all the spots that Baba had indicated. The miracle of the lamps was that although it was gusty and raining, the lamps were not extinguished, and they continued to burn all night. They stayed at Shirdi for two days and returned home. In the following week, many buyers who had withheld payment for the milk came and delivered the payment to Devyani. Devyani also got a few new job offers, thus a lot of money started rolling in.

Jaana yethe aihae sahayia sarvatha
Mange je je thyiasa te te labhae

Roughly translated, this means: "Know that they who seek my help will receive it abundantly. And they shall receive whatever they ask for."

Baba says, "I give my devotees whatever they want, so they will begin to want what I want to give them."

Ref.: *Shri Sai Leela Magazine*, Volume 67, No. 8–9, November and December 1988.

41

Neela's Vision

In the summer of 1960, Neela Upadhya, a resident of Ahmadabad, had this wonderful experience. Her entire family had gathered together in Ahmednagar where her parents lived, to spend their summer vacation. One day her family decided to visit Shirdi, but they were unwilling to take Neela along as her baby was just 3 months old. The reason for this was that in those days Shirdi had very few amenities. However, Neela was determined to go with them. They had to travel by the State Transport bus to Shirdi, as no other mode of transportation was available. When they set out it was unbearably hot and humid, and the bus was jam packed. Nonetheless, Neela got in with her baby and immediately someone vacated their seat for her. Her tiny baby gave her no trouble at all, nor did she cry on the way to Shirdi. They got a room in the Samadhi Mandir, and the members of her family went to visit the holy sites leaving her with her baby.

That night, possibly there was no electricity, so they had placed two huge lanterns in front of the rooms. The insects hovering around the lanterns were bothering her, so she spread a mat at some distance away for herself and the baby. Neela thought, "When my baby is sound asleep I will then go and have darshan of Baba." However, before long she fell fast asleep. A short time later she had this dream.

In the dream, she saw an old man wearing a white *kafni* that came up to his knees. He had a white cloth tied around his head, and his eyes shone with a brilliant lustre. Stealthily he came and stood at her feet. She said, "Who are you?" and she woke up. Neela looked around for that person, but no one was there. However, the identity of the man was at the top of her mind. Then she became fully aware that it was Baba himself.

Neela was overcome by emotion and tears rolled down her cheeks. With a twinge of regret she thought, "Arre! That was indeed Baba, but I was unable to comprehend it. And foolishly I didn't prostrate at his feet. I am extremely lucky that Baba gave me a visitation in his physical form."

On the other hand, her mind was making her doubt what she had experienced. She thought, "Did Baba really come to see me? Or was I mistaken?" Neela then resolutely made up her mind that Baba had come and blessed her. Neela would never ever forget the divine form of Baba that she saw.

In chapter 28 of the *Shri Sai Satcharita* Baba tells Megha, "No door is necessary for my entry. I have neither shape nor size. And I am everywhere." (Ovi 199)

"Casting his burden on me, he who truly becomes one with me, of him I become the controller, regulating his body functions." (Ovi 200)

Ref.: *Shri Sai Leela Magazine*, Volume 62, No. 5, August 1986.

42

Udi as Panacea

Neela and her family stayed for two days in Shirdi on that visit in 1960. When Neela had left for Shirdi she had severe pain in her knee joints. She had collected some *Udi* from the Dwarka Mai and brought it to her room. Then she mixed some in water and took it internally, and rubbed some on her joints.

After taking permission to leave from Baba in the Dwarka Mai they returned home. At home Neela was busy looking after her little baby, and doing her household chores. A week after returning home she remembered that her knee joints were hurting before she left for Shirdi. However she had no problem now, as the *Udi* had taken care of it.

When she had reached home, Neela carefully poured the *Udi* in a bottle and kept it a cupboard. Neela said to herself, "This is Baba's precious *Udi* and I should preserve it carefully. This sacred *Udi* is a symbol of Baba himself; besides it is the panacea for all illnesses. Hence if I keep it in this cupboard no one will meddle with it."

One day Neela was looking for something so she opened the cupboard. At that time she had quite forgotten that she had kept the *Udi* there in a bottle. There were a number of bottles and they looked the same to her. Neela opened one bottle and what happened next left her flabbergasted.

Neela declares, "When I opened the bottle I was astounded to see that perfectly round smoke rings were arising from the surface of the *Udi* to the mouth of the bottle. For a moment I thought I am imagining this. Then I thought that I might have shaken the bottle and agitated the *Udi*, and thus the *Udi* was giving me the impression of smoke rings. So I put my finger right in the centre of the ring and touched the *Udi* and it felt hot. O! Baba you have blessed me by giving me hot *Udi* from your Dhuni." Then the smoke rings disappeared and the *Udi* settled down. Immediately she took the *Udi* bottle and kept it in her prayer room.

Ref.: *Shri Sai Leela Magazine*, Volume 62, No. 5, August 1986.

43

The Power of Prayer

The idea that power is inherent in prayer is an accepted one. The power of prayer is quite simply the power of God who hears and answers the prayer. Numerous devotees undertake vows and pledges to give up eating rice or drinking their favorite beverage until their wish is fulfilled. If prayers and vows are undertaken for villages and towns struck by disasters like floods or cyclones, Baba will definitely fulfil these vows. These vows are of an unselfish nature and are born out of goodwill towards the unfortunate. The two *leelas* given below illustrate this point well.

My friend Manjula was transferred to the Internal Audit Department of United India Insurance Company recently. Hence her job entailed her to visit various cities and towns for the audit. On the 7th of September 2014, her team was scheduled to visit Jammu. At that time it had been raining incessantly and the cities of Srinagar and Jammu were flooded. It continued raining ceaselessly. On the 6th of September I was watching the news, and I was horrified to see the devastation caused by the flood. That evening I sent a message to Manjula informing her that Jammu was flooded. I also added that she should watch the news before leaving for Jammu. Manjula was at the Malleswaram Baba temple when she received my message. I spoke to her at night and advised her not to go.

Early next morning, I went to Lendi Baugh as usual to do *pradikshina*s, and while doing them I felt apprehensive about Manjula's trip. I prayed to Baba for her safety, and took a vow: "Baba please take care of Manjula and her team as they are going to Jammu, and bring them back to Bangalore safely. When they return home safely, I promise to light a candle for you in Lendi Baugh daily for a week." This was a miniscule vow that I had undertaken, but at that time I could not think of anything else.

On the 7th, the team did leave for Jammu as their team leader was determined to go. That morning Manjula was feeling uneasy about the trip, so she asked Baba what she should do, via chits. Baba asked to read the 51st chapter of *Shri Pada Shri Vallabha Charita*, which provides protection from drowning and other perils, and write that chapter on a sheet of paper. So Manjula wrote the chapter and carrying it with her as a mantle of protection, set out.

They reached Jammu at 2 p.m. and heard that all the bridges were submerged under water since 10 a.m. that morning. The Indian Army was directing traffic and helping the citizens there, as the water level had risen to the height of the third floor of the buildings. The River Tavi had flooded way beyond the dangerous level. People were standing and praying to the river to recede peacefully. When the team set out for their office, they were surprised to see that the water had receded and the Army was allowing the traffic to cross the bridges. Thus Manjula and her team were able to complete their assignment and return to Bangalore safely. Here I took a vow for my friend and her team, and Baba granted it. However, not only did Manjula and her team return home safely, but the entire populace of Jammu was able to return to their homes as the River Tavi had receded. This indeed was due to the combined prayers of innumerable people, who like me may have taken numerous vows.

The second *leela* shows how collective prayers and vows saved the life of the member of a bhajan group. My friend Nagraj narrated this *leela* to me. Years ago Mr. Kamath and his wife Vandana had started a bhajan group in Bangalore. Every Sunday they would perform bhajans and soon they formed a large group. Nagraj and his friend Tej Kumar used to attend the bhajans regularly. It so happened that once Tej Kumar met with a major accident and was rushed to hospital in a critical condition. He had a severe head injury; however the neuro-surgeon was doubtful about his survival. The entire bhajan group was anxiously waiting outside to help in any way they could. They decided to seek refuge in Baba. They went to Vandana's home and collectively prayed for his recovery.

Nagraj says, "It was rather late at that time, and Vandana had already performed *Sej Arati*, so we removed the mosquito net and literally awoke Baba. Then all of us prayed for Tej's recovery. Finally all the group members took some vow for him. Each member took a different vow, like walking barefoot from Kopergaon to Shirdi, or doing 108 *pradikshinas* of the Samadhi Mandir, and the *parayan* of the *Charita* and so forth.

The doctor took Tej to the Operation Theatre, and started the surgery. As there was profuse internal bleeding, the Surgeon required 4–5 bottles of blood. It was rather difficult to arrange for the blood as Tej's blood group was B Negative, which is a rare blood group. Then Baba's miracle started unfolding. A Muslim gentleman who was standing in front of the hospital came on his own accord and donated his blood, which was B Negative. The surgery was successful and Tej was out of danger. We were hopeful that he would recover without any brain damage. However, we were told that Tej would be hospitalised for a long period of time.

One day, Tej dreamt of Baba. In his dream Tej had gone to the Samadhi Mandir which looked very different from the present Samadhi Mandir. There was just a samadhi and it looked like the photograph of the samadhi that is in the Museum. That is, there was a samadhi without Baba's idol above it, and Baba himself was sitting inside the samadhi. Tej approached the samadhi and seeing a *jholi* slung on Baba's shoulder said, "Baba what do you have in your *jholi*?" Baba smiled and said, 'Just as you devotees read my *Charita*, I keep the *Charita* of each and every devotee of mine in my *jholi*. I take it out time and again and look at it.'"

Tej recovered fully without any neurological deficit, and is leading a happy life. From this *leela* it is evident that the vows taken and collective prayers for Tej brought him back from death's door.

Society has given a lot to us, and we can return to society

in a befitting manner. At least we can pray for the wellbeing of the entire society.

Vamanrao Pai prayed for the welfare of people in this universe. He asked God to give them a good virtuous character. He also asked God to give them good health, and to bless and protect them.

We can perform service to the needy and the less fortunate. Baba not only approves but gives us a lot of strength both mentally and physically to perform the service perfectly.

Ref.: As narrated by Nagraj in 2004.

44

Asavari's Devotion

Asavari Vaikul was a renowned *Lavani* singer who resided in Mumbai. *Lavani* is a traditional song and dance of Maharashtra. Although she was known as the "Empress of Lavani", Asavari devotedly gave numerous programmes singing devotional songs of Baba. Her performance left the devotees gathered there spellbound, as she sang from her soul and was quite oblivious of her surroundings. Asavari was blessed with a melodious voice, and her ardent devotion to Baba was evident from her rendition. Happily, Asavari returned home after her program was over, prostrated before Baba's picture, and then went to sleep.

In the wee hours of the morning, she dreamt of Baba. Asavari found herself in the Dwarka Mai and Baba was seated in his usual place next to the railing. He was wearing a white *kafni* and a white cloth was tied around his head. However, his forehead was marked with a sandal wood *tripunda* (three horizontal lines of Lord Shiva). He was sitting in his Dwarka Mai pose and his *chillum* and *satka* lay on the floor next to him. He was looking intently at Dhuni Mai. Asavari climbed the steps and stood there for a moment. Baba turned his head and looked at her; he was all alone. Then he beckoned her to come in. Baba smiled and said, "My child come in." Happily Asavari went and sat at his feet. With glee, Baba stroked her head and said, "My child, keep singing my songs with devotion as you do. Sing them for your entire life. *Allah* will bless you." Asavari was overwhelmed by what Baba said, and she had a lump in her throat. She knew not what to say. Baba was looking with utter empathy at her, and Asavari started sobbing. Those tears were of happiness. Baba pulled her close to him as if she was a small child, and stroked her head. Then he said, "Why do you cry? What do you want from me?" Asavari was silent for a long time. Finally she said, "Baba let me be contented and happy. I don't want anything else." In a pleasant voice Baba replied, "*Allah Malik. Allah Malik.*" Instantaneously, Baba disappeared. Asavari screamed "Baba!" in her sleep and woke up. She looked at Baba's picture on the wall in front of her and mentally thanked him.

Asavari recalls, "Baba approved of my singing his devotional songs, and doing *kirtan*. In fact, he stressed the importance of the first stage of *Nava Vida Bhakti* that is *Bhajan, Kirtan* and *Chintan*. He did not give importance to other modes of devotion. I am certain by doing this we will receive a hundred fold blessings from him. Thus he gave me the key to his treasury. This is the reason it is written in the *Shri Sai Satcharita,* chapter 3, ovi 12: 'Whosoever hears my *Charita,* narrates my *Charita,* and sings my *Charita* in any which way, but with love and devotion, I will never forsake him. He who sings my praises, my *leelas,* and describes my divinity, I will stand behind him, by the side of him and surround him on all four sides with my grace."'

In chapter 21 of the Shri Sai Satcharita, the story of Anantrao Patankar, who had read numerous Theosophical texts, but didn't have peace of mind, is described. Baba narrates the parable of the merchant who astutely collected the 9 nodules of dung that the horse passed. Following this his mind became peaceful and steady. The 9 nodules of dung are the 9 modes of devotion. The first three, that is, *shravan* (hearing the attributes, excellences or wonderous achievements of saints, as read or recited); *kirtan* (reciting); and *smaran* (calling to mind and meditating upon the names and perfection of the Lord) are the first steps on the ladder of devotion. Baba himself explicitly approves of Asavari's singing of his devotional songs.

Ref.: *Shri Sai Leela Magazine,* Volume 63, No. 8–9, November 1984.

45

Janardan's Guest

This *leela* is narrated by Janardan Ramchandra Adkar, who is the grandson of Madhavrao Adkar of the "Arati Sai Baba" fame. He is the son of Ramchandra Madhavrao Adkar, a centenarian who celebrated his 100th birthday on 13th April 2014, and was blessed by Baba.

During July 1980 to August 1984, Janardan Ramchandra Adkar was a senior officer in a bank. At that time, he was transferred to Shivni. Shivni is a village in a rural area, in the town of Pandurna in district of Chincholi-bad, in the state of Madhya Pradesh.

Janardan's parents were very concerned as this posting was to a different state that was miles away from home, and his son Sagar was only 2 months old. In those days, there were very few facilities like telephones in remote villages. The only method of communication was through letters, which took a long time to reach. Under these circumstances his parents were naturally concerned.

On 13th October 1980, Janardan dreamt of Baba. In the dream, Baba was standing in front of him with his *bhiksha-patra* (bowl for receiving alms) in his hand. However, at that very moment his son Sagar started crying, and Janardan got up. Early next morning, he narrated his dream to his wife, who said, "Today is Dussera, why can't we serve a meal to some Brahmin?" Janardan liked her suggestion very much, so he decided to invite their neighbour Kishore Kondalkar. Upon hearing the reason for the invitation, Kishore happily agreed to come. Around 1 p.m. they finished their meal, and sat on their sofa chatting and chewing betel nut.

At that time the main door was closed. Suddenly, a stranger, about 60 years old, opened the door and entered the room.

He was tall, and had a short beard and moustache. He was wearing a white *dhoti*, and a long white shirt. As Janardan didn't recognise him, he presumed that he was a villager who had come to discuss some banking problem. In remote villages, the home of the officer is right next to the bank, and villagers often drop in to consult the officer about matters related to banking and loans. Hence, the following conversation took place. In this conversation, the stranger will be refered to as "Guest".

Janardan: "Can I help you with any banking matters?"

Guest: "I want to have lunch."

Janardan: "Please come and have a seat."

Janardan then went into the kitchen and told his wife to serve the guest a full meal. Immediately, his wife placed a low seat for the honoured guest and served him the meal. Since it was Dussera, his wife had prepared *basundi* (flavoured condensed milk). Janardan was fascinated to see that his guest mixed the *basundi* in the rice and ate it, as this was rather unusal. After he had a hearty meal Janardan requested him to be seated on the couch. Then the conversation continued.

Janardan: "What is your name?"

Guest: "My name is Bhagvan (God)."

Janardan: "And your last name?"

Guest: "My last name is Garfade."

As there were numerous families with this last name, Janardan said, "You must be having a lot of relatives in Shivni."

Guest: "Of what use are they to me?"

Janardan: "What made you want to visit my home?"

Guest: "My heart told me to."

Janardan: "Is there anything else I can do for you?"

Guest: "You can give me 12 *annas*."

Then Janardan asked him why he needed 12 *annas*. The guest told him that he had walked from Pandurna, and if he got the money he would board a bus to Chincholi-bad. Janardan happily gave him the money, and the guest accepted it and left. However, he didn't proceed in the direction of the bus stand, but went into the village.

A few months later, Janardan met Digarse Babu, who

happened to reside in Chincholi-bad, and during the course of conversation Janardan asked him if he knew Bhagvan Garfade. Then he told Digarse about his dream, and the guest arriving for a meal at the appropriate time. Digarse was intrigued by this story and told Janardan about the saint of Chincholi-bad. "Just outside the village of Chincholi-bad there is a magnificient Banyan tree. That tree must be very ancient, as the aerial roots of the tree have anchored themselves in the ground, and as a result the diameter of the tree is humongous. Under that tree no less than 5000 men on horseback can stand comfortably. During the period that Sai Baba was in Shirdi, there was a Sufi saint living there, his name was Sheikh Farid, who could be seen hanging from that tree in an inverted positon. He has his tomb there and every year they celebrate *Urs* in the month of February. However the food served that day is totally vegetarian in Hindu style. It is claimed that he came from Girad, a village in Maharashtra. I have a strong feeling that Baba came for *bhiksha* to your home in the form of that Sufi saint."

Janardan was not surprised, as Baba could appear in any nook or corner of the world, in any form that he chose.

Ref.: *Shri Sai Sagar Magazine*, Volume 5, No. 4, January–March 2015.

46

Minal's Dream

This *leela* is narrated by Minal V. Dalvi, a devotee residing in Pune, and is about the trials and tribulations that her parents had to face in finding a suitable groom for her sister, Madhuri.

Madhuri was born in 1980, and when she was about 3 months old her parents took her to Shirdi. The priest in the Samadhi Mandir took the tiny baby and placed her in Baba's lap (on the idol in Samadhi Mandir). This heart-warming action of the priest confirmed their belief that Baba would stand beside Madhuri through thick and thin. Her father told his wife, "She is Baba's child and Baba will look after her welfare; we don't have to worry."

Madhuri was studying in college when her parents decided to find a suitable groom for her. They contacted friends and relatives about a prospective groom. However, they faced innumerable problems, of which the main problem was Madhuri's horoscope. Every family that the Dalvis contacted refused marriage. In the meantime, Madhuri got a job as a teacher in Pune itself. However, when a suitable groom was found, Madhuri refused to marry him as he lived away from Pune, and she was unwilling to give up her job. Everyone persuaded her to give up her job, as many suitable grooms resided outside Pune.

The Dalvis, as a last resort, quite unwillingly sought the help of an astrologer. Minal recalls, "I was quite horrified that an astrologer was consulted. I didn't believe in astrology, zodiac signs and planetary movements. I only believed in Baba and that Baba would come to her aid. I kept remembering what Baba said to Savitribai Tendulkar in chapter 29 of the *Shri Sai Satcharita*. Her son Bapu was to appear for his medical examinations; however because an astrologer had predicted failure, he had decided not to appear that year. Then Baba said, 'Ask him to appear in the examination and he will be successful. Ask him to roll up the horoscope and keep it aside. And do not rely on astrologers and palmists.' I was very disturbed by the turn of events. I thought, at this juncture, my parents should have *saburi* (patience) and not turn to superstitions and charlatans."

The next problem that cropped up was that if Madhuri's father didn't present the horoscope to the prospective groom's parents they would ask many questions. If they insisted, her father would give them Madhuri's horoscope and then they would say, "Gosh! Her horoscope is terrible and inauspicious. She is a '*Manglik*' (fault of planet Mars) or she has *Kaal Sarpa Yog* (a combination of *kala* i.e., time, *sarpa* i.e., serpent) which is considered very harmful for the groom's parents. The effects of these bring ill-health and even death to the groom's father, and numerous misfortunes."

Since a very young age, Minal considered Baba to be her doting grandfather. She therefore stood in front of his picture and said, "Baba isn't this superstition? Only you and you alone can find a suitable groom for Madhuri. And if you don't, I will leave you and go to Gajanan Maharaj, or to Swami Samartha. So you better do something and fast." After she had bullied Baba thusly she fell asleep chanting his name.

That night, she dreamt that she was outside the Sabha Mandap of the Dwarka Mai. There a woman was sweeping the street and her tiny baby was crying. Minal told the lady that she was going inside to meet Baba, and she would take her baby along with her, as Baba would definitely play with the child. The lady handed her child to Minal, who entered the Dwarka Mai. She saw Baba seated serenely on his stone, and he smiled at her. Minal then handed the child to Baba, and gave him a box of *peda*s, saying, "Baba the date for Madhuri's wedding is finalised." At that time the child had stopped crying and was contentedly lying in Baba's lap, sucking his thumb. Surprised to see this, Minal said, "Baba you know this child from numerous past lives, right?" Baba didn't reply, but started playing with the child. Then he got up and went to the *chuli* (hearth) and in a small pot heated some milk. Minal impulsively said, "Baba I don't know your *aratis*." Instead of answering directly, he replied, "Wait a bit. Mhalsapati will soon come here. Jesus you are Yashodha's Krishna, and Mother Mary is my Bayja Mai."

Minal relates: "At that time I thought this must be a line from the *arati*. Baba then played with the child again, while I waited for Mhalsapati to arrive. At that very moment my mother woke me up. But I was impatient to know what would happen next, so I closed my eyes and slept. As luck would have it, my dream continued. Baba said, 'Child, take my *Udi* and then go. Child, now 5 lives are yet to be lived.' Hearing these words I got up startled, and became wide awake."

Minal lay there thinking of the deeper meaning of this dream. There were a lot of questions like, "What did Baba really look like in his true form? How did I give *pedas* to Baba when Madhuri's wedding date was not yet fixed? Who was the child in my dream? What did Baba mean by 5 lives are yet to be lived?"

A year later Minal met Mugdha Divadkar, a great devotee who had written a great deal on Baba and asked her to decipher her dream. Mugdha said, "Any spiritual practice you do for Baba never goes in vain. The child is symbolic of ignorance—you told Baba that you didn't know the *arati*. Milk represents the knowledge that Baba will bestow on you."

In the mean time, Minal and her family prayed earnestly, read the *Shri Sai Satcharita*, and chanted Baba's name. The following year, Madhuri got married to a highly educated man who worked in Pune. Thus she didn't have to leave Pune, and the wedding was celebrated on a grand scale, without any difficulty. Thus Minal's dream came true.

Ref.: *Shri Sai Sagar,* Volume 5, No. 4, January–March 2015.

47

Kaumudhi's Grandpa and the Concept of Rinanubandh

Often we think, "I have done so much for my kith and kin, and today when I need them the most, they give flimsy excuses and they are not there for me." This is a wonderful *leela* about karmic cycles, and *rinanubandh* in the present life.

For 15 days Kaumudhi had been running a high temperature, and the fever had taken its toll on her. She felt extremely weak and was unable to get out of bed. It was around 10 a.m. in the morning and Kaumudhi was waiting for her younger brother, Chandu, who was a doctor, to arrive. She was the eldest among her siblings, and had two younger brothers and two younger sisters.

Kaumudhi lay curled up on her bed and her entire life of self sacrifices unfolded like a movie in front of her eyes. She was only 15 years old when her mother passed away, and just 2 months later her father also died. The responsibility of taking care of her siblings fell on her young shoulders. For the next 20 years life became drudgery, but Kaumudhi faced the tribulations with a smile on her face. When she was 19 years old she took up the job of a teacher in a high school. Every morning Kaumudhi got up at 5 a.m., cooked lunch for all her siblings, and went to college so that she could get her Master's degree. She then returned home and served lunch to her siblings, had a bite herself, then attended her job as a teacher. Kaumudhi taught in the school and returned home around 6 p.m.; then she cooked dinner for her siblings. She supervised their studies and home work, and finally corrected her class work. After all her chores were done, she finally crept into bed around 11 p.m. Thus, with her meagre pay as a teacher,

Kaumudhi managed to put food on the table, and educated her siblings, though this was not an easy task.

Both her sisters, Sushma and Pratima, were well educated, and had graduated from college. Kaumudhi had found suitable spouses for them and now they were married and settled. Both Sushma and Pratima had two children each. Kaumudhi had looked after them during their pregnancies, and had paid all the hospital bills for their deliveries. Kaumudhi realised that her brothers, Chandu and Nandu, were bright and intelligent kids, and she encouraged them to study hard. Hence Chandu had graduated from medical college and was now working in a famous hospital in Mumbai. Nandu had become an engineer and was also working in a multi-national company in Mumbai.

When she had written to all her siblings and informed them about her illness, she had expected all of them to come running to her aid. However, just the opposite happened. Nandu had to attend his brother-in-law's house-warming function in Aurangabad and was unable to come. Shushma informed Kaumudhi that she was unable to come as her sister-in-law had morning sickness, and she had to look after her. Pratima was going on a trip with her family to Delhi, thus was unable to come. Each of them wrote to Kaumudhi, how much they regretted their inability to be with her at this time. Now only Chandu was left. "He is a doctor who cares for people; surely he will come to take care of his sister," thought Kaumudhi. Finally she received a letter from Chandu. Even before opening it, she instinctively knew that he wouldn't come. Nonetheless, she opened the letter and read it. He had written that a friend of his was to have a major operation; hence it was not possible for him to come. He asked Kaumudhi to forgive him. However, he suggested that she should hire a maid who could look after her, and he would send Kaumudhi the money so she could pay the maid her wages. Chandu's letter was the last straw. The floodgate of tears opened, and she sobbed inconsolably.

She thought, "Will a hired maid tend to my needs like my own brother and sister? If I had to get a maid would I have written to all of you about my illness? Today I have learned that you have to stand all by yourself as no one will stand beside you in time of need. Like a mother I looked after all of you, fulfilled all your desires, and never allowed you to do any chores. Although I had the intelligence and good qualities, I did not get married, for your sake, and this is what I got in return. Today I have learned that kith and kin are mere names and no one really cares." Kaumudhi then sobbed her heart out, and threw herself on her bed.

At that very moment there was a knock on her door. Kaumudhi dejectedly thought, "Now who has come to trouble me?" Somehow she managed to open the door. An old gentleman in a torn white *kafni*, but with a blissful expression on his face stood in front of her. Unwittingly she said, "Please come," and she moved aside to let him inside her home. The old man entered, and closed the door behind him. Gently holding Kaumudhi's hand, he led her to her bed. His soft touch had a life-changing effect on her. She didn't feel like taking her hand away from his. With compassion and love he patted her hand, and spoke to her softly. "Child, I am very hungry, your Shantabai had prepared soft fluffy rice. Bring me a plate of rice along with some lemon pickle."

Kaumudhi wondered, "How does he know that the rice was cooked, and that my maid Shantabai had cooked it?" Nevertheless she brought a plate full of rice and served it to him. "Grandpa, you must be very hungry. But today I have nothing else to serve you; neither do I have the strength to prepare anything else for you. This fever is just not leaving me."

He replied, "Kaumudhi, don't be upset about it. Today I desire to eat rice. And I will happily eat it." Then he sat down and contentedly ate it. "Child, there is still some rice left. Serve it to me and bring some water to drink along with it." In a daze, Kaumudhi quietly went into the kitchen and brought the remaining rice and a *lota* (drinking utensil) full of water and gave it to him. He kept aside some water in the cup, then quietly ate the entire rice, and drank the water. Then he sat beside Kaumudhi and gently passed his hand over her back. He took out a packet of *Udi* from the pocket of his *kafni*, emptied the *Udi* into the cup filled with water and handed it to Kaumudhi saying, "Child drink this and your fever will flee from your body. And don't worry."

Kaumudhi drank it without giving it a second thought. Grandpa laughed heartily as he watched her drink the water. Then he caressed her cheek, and said, "Child, this is not our first meeting, and I know you since you were little. Years ago your parents, along with you and your siblings, came to meet me. At that time your mother entrusted all her children to my care. Subsequently your parents passed away. Then you grew into a responsible and capable young lady. You got educated, and started working, and simultaneously you dutifully took care of your siblings. You gave all of them a good education, and got both your sisters married. And just like your name Kaumudhi (moonlight) you spread cool, gentle, caring, moonlight upon your siblings and everyone around you. I have been watching all this from a distance, and as I promised your mother, I have been taking care of you. Finally all your siblings attained success and moved away from you and today you are alone. Then how is it possible for me to be away from you? If you feel deserted and alone then of what use am I? So I came to meet you on my own accord. Now you don't have to worry anymore. In your previous lives your siblings took good care of you, and in this life you have repaid that debt and become free. So do not think 'I did so much for them and all of them have forgotten me', and be hurt. Don't say 'I did this and that' and be filled with conceit. Just as you did kind caring acts for your siblings, in one of your previous lives you did the same for a very special person. This person is Sadanand Ranade, and he will come looking for you of his own accord. He, like his name, is full of happiness and bliss. He is perfect for you and he will make you very happy and you shall not want for anything; but don't turn him away. I assure you, you will not regret accepting his hand in marriage. My words are never untrue, have complete faith in what I say. You served me rice today, but do not eat rice for the next 5 days. Only drink fluids, like hot tea, hot water, and butter milk. Here is a packet of my *Udi*, apply some on your forehead and also have some mixed in water."

Grandpa then placed his five fingers in the packet of *Udi* and applied it to Kaumudhi's forehead with a little pressure. Again he gently patted her back and got up to leave. Prior to leaving he said, "I have to leave now. Kaumudhi, you will become alright in a few days. And you will be very contented and happy in life. If at all you feel the need to talk to me just call my name and I will be there right beside you." Grandpa had reached the door and was about to exit, when Kaumudhi said, "By what name shall I call you?" Grandpa laughed and put his hand into the pocket of his *kafni* and took out a fistful of Bakul flowers (Mimiesops Elengi) and threw them in Kaumudhi's direction and vanished. Kaumudhi eagerly looked at the floor and saw that the flowers had taken on the shape of the name "SAI BABA". Simultaneously Kaumudhi's room was lit up by a brilliant light and a sweet aroma filled her room.

With tears in her eyes she looked at the name of her grandpa and said, "How lucky I am! Even though I never prayed to you, nor was I devoted to you; yet you came running to my aid. Now I know that I am not alone, nor will I ever be alone. I don't have to worry about anything, as I am sure you are right behind me. Henceforth I will adhere to all that you said to me, and try not to let pride creep into my life. I will wait for the life partner that you have chosen for me and welcome him into my life. From this very moment, Baba, I will seat you on the throne of my heart, and remember you always. I will start chanting your name from today, as I am now completely healed mentally and physically."

Ref.: Narrated by Usha P. Adhikari, in *Shri Sai Leela Magazine*, Volume 59, No. 2, May 1980.

48

How Baba Helped Shantaram, Physically and Spiritually

Shantaram A. Naik was born in Madkai, Goa (Ponda District), and his father was a farmer. Upon completing his education, he got a job in the Government regime, and soon rose to the post of an officer. As luck would have it, he sustained an injury to his right hand. Shantaram had his hand checked by several specialists who subjected him to various forms of treatment, but to no avail. Finally he decided to go to Mumbai and have his hand treated there. At that point in time Goa was not a part of the Indian State, so Shantaram had to get a visa to enter India. He tried his best to procure a visa, but failed to do so. Finally he decided to enter India illegally. Shantaram thus boarded a small boat which brought him to Karvar and thence to Mumbai. At sea he faced a lot of difficulties, but by Baba's grace he somehow reached Mumbai. In Mumbai, Shantaram stayed at Byculla with a Christian friend, who immediately got him checked by a surgeon. The surgeon told him that his arm would have to be amputated. Shantaram was now in turmoil and didn't know what to do. In utter anguish, he lay on his bed and tossed and turned about.

When he finally fell asleep, Baba appeared in his dream and asked him to come to Shirdi. The very next day he decided to visit Shirdi, but he didn't know how to get there. After asking a few friends, he went to Dadar and boarded the train for Shirdi at 3 p.m. on the 18th of August, 1957. Shantaram reached Kopergaon at 2 a.m. and he was the only passenger to disembark there. A few passengers were sleeping on the platform. Now Shantaram was frightened as it was the first time he was going to Shirdi and he had no idea how to get there. In fact, he knew nothing at all. Bewildered, Shantaram went and stood near a pillar and prayed to Baba for help. At that very moment, an old man brought his *tonga* and stopped in front of him. He spoke in Hindi and said, "You want to go to Shirdi, isn't it? Come sit, let's go." The road was deserted and Shantaram was fearful, but within 5 minutes they reached Shirdi. The old man stopped the *tonga*, and looking towards the temple spire, he pointed the way to Shantaram. Then Shantaram asked him the fare. Without saying a word he showed him two fingers making a "V" sign. Shantaram gave him two rupees. Then Shantaram stooped to get his bag and when he looked up, the old man and the *tonga* had disappeared.

Astounded, Shantaram walked towards the temple. Many questions arose in his mind. Was it possible for a *tonga* to traverse 10 miles in a span of 5 minutes? Why did he ask for two rupees? That was a large amount in those days. How could the old man and his *tonga* disappear? But with Baba everything is possible. For instance, in chapter 33 of the *Shri Sai Satcharita* the Jamner miracle has been described, where Baba becomes the *tonga* driver who takes Ramgir Bua to Jamner, leaves him there and disappears.

Shantaram went to the Samadhi Mandir, but the doors were closed, so he sat there and waited for them to open. Then he dozed off, and had a dream in which he saw some scenes of Shirdi of bygone days. He woke up, attended the *Kakad Arati*, and offered flowers to Baba. Shantaram begged Baba to have mercy on him and prevent his right arm from being amputated. Then he returned to Mumbai.

Two days later, Shantaram and his friend went to the same doctor for a checkup. However this time the doctor informed him that amputation would not be necessary, but he would have to undergo a major surgery. Consequently, he would only be able to write with that hand. After carefully thinking it over, Shantaram agreed to have the surgery performed. The operation was a success and after two months his bandages were removed. The doctor handed a piece of paper and a pen to Shantaram, and the first words he wrote were "Sai Baba". At that moment Shantaram's heart was filled with love and joy. After completing his medical treatment, Shantaram returned to Goa, and went back to work.

The incident of the old man and his *tonga* disappearing lingered in Shantaram's mind. With every passing day his faith in Baba grew stronger and he started chanting Baba's name with devotion. He found profound solace in chanting Baba's name. Now he was well on the path of devotion. Shantaram voraciously read books on devotion; he also attended *kirtans* and *pravachans* (spiritual talks). Each step he took helped him on his spiritual path. One night he again dreamt of the scenes of bygone Shirdi, and the dream recurred the next night too.

Shantaram decided to visit Shirdi again, so he came to Mumbai and took the train to Kopergaon. He reached Kopergaon around 2 p.m. this time, and he again remembered the scene of the old man and his *tonga* disappearing. Shantaram had mixed feelings—happiness that Baba had come as a *tonga* driver for him, and sadness that he had been unable to recognise him and fall at his feet.

Upon his return home, Shantaram undertook innumerable pilgrimages to various holy shrines. He also read a lot of books on religion and spirituality. For a long period of time Shantaram was overcome by a sort of restlessness, thus he would go from one deity to another. He was unable to have one-pointed concentration on any deity. Then Baba appeared in his dream and said, "Arre! Why are you wandering from one forest to another? Why are you reading all these books? Do not read too many books."

From that moment, Shantaram stopped wandering about, and curtailed his reading. He followed Baba's instructions and sat at home and started doing Baba's *manas puja*, that is, mentally worshipping Baba with all rituals, as one would do externally. Over time, he had numerous visions of Baba, and many other experiences. The next *leela* shares some of Shantaram's later experiences.

Ref.: *Prasad*, Volume 33, No. 9, August 1979.

49

How Baba's Temple Was Built in Madkai

As mentioned in the previous *leela*, Shantaram A. Naik hailed from Madkai, Goa (Ponda District). Here, he built a small temple of Baba. Let us read how this happened.

Early one morning, he had a dream of a small temple that was being constructed. He saw himself inside the temple worshipping Baba's idol with all rituals like a priest. The next morning he had the same dream, but in this dream Baba was standing in place of the idol and Shantaram was standing in front of Baba. Baba was looking at him with absolute benevolence. At that moment Shantaram was entreating Baba, "Baba when I construct this temple of yours, please ensure that I don't have to beg for financial aid from other people." From that time onwards Shantaram started putting away a fixed sum of money from his wages.

A few years later, Shantaram had a dream wherein he again saw a small temple being constructed. This time, he was helping the workers. Inspired by this dream, he went in search for the place that he had seen in his dream vision. Surprisingly after much search he found that such a place existed in Madkai, the town where he was born. Excited, Shantaram immediately made inquires about the plot of land and requested the owner to sell it to him. The owner readily agreed and in this way the land came into his possession.

Soon thereafter, he saw another vision of the temple. This time, Shantaram got an architect to draw up a plan according to the temple that he had seen in his dream. With this plan of the layout in hand, he went to Shirdi and placed it on Baba's Samadhi. Shantaram prayed to Baba: "Baba I can beg for anything from you without hesitation. However, when I start building your temple, please ensure that I do not have to spread out my hands and beg from other people to give me donations." Saying this, he returned home.

On 22nd January 1976 he commenced the work of the temple. On 8th July 1978 Baba appeared in his dream and said, "Henceforth become the slave of only one." At first, Shantaram couldn't understand what Baba was trying to convey to him. Finally he understood that Baba meant that he should serve Him and Him alone. So he decided to take early retirement and live on his pension; but since he was just 45 years old and had served for only 22 years, he was not eligible for pension. However, in September '78, a new law was passed that any individual with 20 years of service was eligible for pension. He was very glad to learn of this and immediately retired from his post.

In January 1979 the temple was completed, and a small idol and *padukas* of Baba were consecrated and placed in it. Following this, Shantaram devoted his entire time to doing various rituals and worship in the temple. This is how Baba blessed him and granted his desire to build a temple.

Ref.: *Prasad*, Volume 33, No. 9, August 1979.

50

Baba Gives "Proof" to Ram Bhau

Around 1954, Ram Bhau Kakade, a devotee from Pune was suffering from pain in his abdomen. His doctor suspected that he had pleurisy and had prescribed antibiotics along with bed rest. Ram Bhau was devoted to Swami Samarth and Sai Baba. One afternoon as he lay on his bed, his thoughts turned to the raw materials that constitute our food. He thought, "The food that we ingest must be having an effect on our mind and body, so we should be aware where we get our food supplies from and who we purchase it from. We should also be careful how we bring it home and who brings it for us. Moreover, we should pay attention to who cooks the food and how they cook it. We should think about all these factors, as the food ingested must be having a profound influence on our mental and physical well being."

Ram Bhau was mulling over this when Baba appeared before him and said, "Arre! Get your food supplies from Narayan," and vanished. There was a grocer called Narayan, whose shop was close to his home. Thereafter Ram Bhau started getting his groceries from his shop as advised by Baba. He started feeling better and regained his health.

It was Ram Bhau's routine to get up every morning and spend his time in meditation. In 1960 he had this wonderful experience. It was around 4 a.m. when Ram Bhau was meditating. At that time he had an auspicious visitation of Swami Samarth. Ram Bhau couldn't believe what he saw. He wondered whether it was a dream. He pinched himself to ensure that he was awake; and indeed he was fully awake. Then Swami Samarth started talking to Ram Bhau. He still couldn't believe it. At that moment Baba appeared there and said, "Arre! You still have doubts. Trust me, this is Swami Samarth."

Ram Bhau replied, "Baba give me some experience or proof, otherwise how will I be convinced?" Then Baba said, "You need proof, don't you? This morning I will give you *basundi* (flavoured, sweetened condensed milk) then will you believe me?" Ram Bhau told Baba that he would definitely believe him if he got proof, and came out of his meditative state.

Every morning around 8 a.m. Ram Bhau used to visit the Maruti Mandir. That day as soon as he entered the temple, an unknown person called out to him, and said, "I have prepared *basundi* as an offering today and I wanted to give it as *prasad* to some virtuous person and I remembered you. In this silver glass I have the *prasad*, so please have it." Ram Bhau didn't recognise the person and thought, "I speak to so many people and this must be one of them."

He accepted the *basundi* and took a sip; it was the most delectable *basundi* that he had ever tasted. Ram Bhau prostrated before Maruti and started circumambulating the idol. Just then, he remembered what Baba had told him, and it all fell into place. That unknown person was Baba, who had promised to give him proof. Immediately he ran out of the temple looking for him, but the person could not be traced.

Ref.: *Prasad*, Volume 33, No. 9, August 1979.

51

Baba Visits Charusheela

Charusheela Varadkar was devoted to Baba and had great reverence for all saints. Once she came to know that a great saint would be visiting the ashram (a home for a small religious community of Hindus) close to her home. Eagerly, she informed her sister about it and they both decided that they would go and visit that saint. Charusheela completed her chores and got ready to go. She waited, but her sister didn't turn up. After waiting for a pretty long time, she went to her sister's home and found out that her sister had left a long time ago. Charusheela was disappointed and hurt, as she felt betrayed. She returned home, sat before Baba's picture and cried her heart out. "Baba, she had promised to take me along and she went off by herself. She didn't keep her word, and I so wanted to meet that saint. Now I cannot help but feel betrayed." A short while later Charusheela fell asleep, and had this wonderful dream.

In the dream she saw a beautiful ashram, and a huge crowd gathered there. Charusheela found herself standing in a corner all by herself. Then she saw Sai Baba making his way through the crowd and walking towards her. He came and stood right in front of her and immediately Charusheela prostrated at his feet and clasped them tightly. She was sobbing, but this time it was out of elation and devotion. Then she stood up and joined her palms together. Baba placed his hand on her head and said, "Now are you satisfied?" and Charusheela awoke. Now she was in utter bliss.

At that moment, her sister returned from the ashram. Her sister told her, "It was good that you didn't come to the ashram. That saint didn't come today as he was not feeling well." Charusheela laughed and said, "Now I have no necessity to go there, as he came to my home and gave me a divine visitation." Then she narrated her dream to her sister, who apologised for leaving her in the lurch.

One day Charusheela's children were playing upstairs on the balcony of their house. They saw an old man entering the compound of their home. The man seemed rather old and he was walking with the aid of a stick. Charusheela's daughter ran downstairs and informed her mother, who was drying clothes on the clothesline. Immediately she went to the front door and opened it. By that time the rest of the children had gathered there. They found the old man seated comfortably resting against the front door. In disbelief, Charusheela murmured, "Are you Sai Baba?" He laughed.

Charusheela's eldest daughter, who about 12 years old at that time, states, "When my mother asked him if he was Sai Baba I looked at him intently. He resembled the picture that we worshipped. He had worn a white *kafni*, a cloth tied around his head, the only difference was that he had a stick in his hand. By then all our neighbours had gathered there. My mother asked him if he would like to drink some milk and he said, 'Yes'. My mother went inside and handed him a cup of piping hot milk, which he drank. Then he asked my mother for some oil and *dakshina*. My mother gave some oil in a bottle and 1 rupee 25 paise as *dakshina*. Then Baba got up to leave. He nodded at me and my sister to come near, and lovingly placed his hand on our heads and blessed us. He then walked out of the compound and we followed him to see where he was going, but after a short distance he just disappeared."

Ref.: *Prasad*, Volume 33, No. 9, August 1979.

52

Baba Blesses Bomborikar

It was exceedingly difficult for D. Bomborikar, a resident of Nagpur, to make both ends meet. He was a teacher by profession and had a large family of ten to feed and take care of. He was in a desperate situation and wondered if they would all soon have to face starvation.

Since 1957 Bomborikar had stared earnestly worshipping Baba. Along with the worship, he undertook performing many spiritual practices like singing devotional songs every Thursday in the Konda Bhuvan Baba Mandir. In fact, he never missed even a single Thursday. In December 1964, Bomborikar had diligently completed writing Dabolkar's *Shri Sai Satcharita* by hand on a Thursday. Now all he wanted to do was to offer it at Baba's feet the next Thursday. Bomborikar returned home around 1 a.m. after attending the *Sej Arati* and performing devotional songs, and lay on his bed.

In despair he said, "Baba with utmost devotion I have been offering my spiritual service to you for all these years. I have completely surrendered my life at your feet. Are you unaware of this? Now are you going to let us starve? Didn't you promise that there will be no dearth of food and clothing in my devotee's home? I have cast all my burdens on you, so are you going to give me some respite from it? Didn't you promise that you would stand beside anyone who sang or read your *Charita* with love and devotion? I wrote your entire *Charita* by hand and it took me three months to do so, and yet you are oblivious of it. I have heard that if a devotee seeks refuge in you, you never fail to fulfill his needs. Then why are you turning your back on me? Are all your promises just empty words? Are they all false? Are you a liar? I need some proof, or to get some experience confirming that you are not a liar. The next

131

Thursday I will go to your temple and offer the handwritten *Charita* at your feet. Following this I will sing your glories; at that time I need the proof and it should be evident to me. If not I will consider you a liar and a charlatan and believe that you are in the business of swindling innocent devotees. Then I will throw your photograph into the Vardha River, and forget that I ever prayed to you!" Having unburdened himself, he fell fast asleep.

Next Thursday, before going to the temple Bomborikar visited his friend's house. He then went to the temple along with his friend's family. First he worshipped Baba and kept the *Charita* at his feet, then offered *prasad* to him. About 60 to 70 devotees had gathered there. However that day he was the only devotee who was going to sing Baba's devotional songs. Bomborikar thought to himself, "I am not a professional singer, nor do I possess a good voice; the only thing I have is love and devotion. Besides, today the person who keeps the beat with the cymbals is also absent." Finally he told the rest of the orchestra that he would sing as best as he could and they could accompany him in any way they chose.

Exactly at 8 p.m. the devotional songs started, and it was a very spiritual environment. Bomborikar's legs were trembling and his mind was uneasy with anticipation. He kept wondering—would Baba give him any proof? Thereafter he sang his heart out, one song after another. Soon it was 10 p.m. and yet no sign of any proof! Now disappointment set in and he sang a heart wrenching song: "When I had the riches of *Kuber*, I destroyed my own home. When I embraced *fakiri* (poverty) I came begging at your door. Give me some crumbs, as your treasury is filled with divinity. To go empty handed from your *durbar* is agonising."

At the end of this song the priest asked everyone to assemble for the *arati*. Bomborikar looked at Baba's idol and said, "Tomorrow I shall definitely keep my promise and you will be submerged in the Vardha River." Then he stood with the rest of the devotees and joined his hand together. The *arati* proceeded and then Baba showered His grace on him. Bomborikar says,

"What occurred next left me enthralled. Baba's idol became huge, and in bliss it started laughing. Then it slid off the dais and roamed across the entire length and breadth of the temple. My eyes flew wide open as I looked at the idol with rapture, and tears of joy filled my eyes. I knew that I was wide awake, but what was happening here? Then the scene changed, and I found myself in the most beautiful garden, full of fragrant flowers and trees. On one huge tree there was a swing tied to it, and Baba in human form was sitting on it. His face was filled with bliss and he was swinging back and forth swiftly. Then he threw the flowers that he had with him on me and said, 'Here, take them. Indeed you are honest, remain like this your entire life.' This entire scene lasted for about three minutes, but Baba had given me an experience that was unforgettable." Following this experience, his financial condition slowly started improving.

Bomborikar states, "I haven't visited Shirdi yet, but the merciful Lord of Shirdi is present when I sing his songs. At one point in time, my family I and were on the brink of starvation, but gradually things started improving. Now I can assuredly say there will be no dearth of food and clothing in any of his devotee's homes. Baba does keep his promises."

Ref.: *Prasad,* Volume 33, No. 9, August 1979.

53

Baba Assigned a Mission to Balchandra Gondkar

The two following *leela*s were experienced by a devotee named Balchandra Gondkar, a resident of Baroda. It was the firm belief of Balchandra Gondkar that Baba guides his devotee's in three unique ways:

1. He gives *Sakshat Darshan* or a divine visitation in human form. For such an experience we have to have unshakable faith in him, like Prahlad or Dhruv. However, that kind of faith is nearly impossible.

2. A *Chamatkarik Darshan* or a miraculous visitation, which occurs when we are in a problematic situation and a third person comes to our aid at that crucial moment. Then we sigh with relief and say, "You turned up like God Himself and helped me."

3. *Appearance in dreams,* that is, when Baba appears in our dreams and provides guidance, or warns us of impending danger. We should pay heed to his words, and act accordingly. However, we don't always do so and thus we have to face the consequences.

Balchandra had a strange dream in 1998. "In the dream, I found myself in the Dwarka Mai and Baba was seated in his usual place near the railing. There were a number of devotees seated in front of him. Baba was assigning some work to each devotee seated there. Then I said, 'Baba please give me some work to do.' Baba replied, 'Distribute potato wafers to the devotees in the temple as prasad.' At that moment I woke up," says Balchandra. That morning he narrated his dream to his wife, who said, "On Thursday you can distribute the wafers to the devotees after the *arati*."

The following Thursday, Balchandra went to a Baba mandir close by, just prior to the *arati* service. At the time of the *arati* the priest sang only one *arati*, and the service was completed. Then Balchandra distributed the wafers to all the devotees assembled there. The next Thursday, Balchandra was present there and that day too a single *arati* was sung. The following Thursday, Balchandra took permission from the priest and sang four more *aratis*. Subsequently, every Thursday Balchandra would add a few more *aratis* till all the *aratis* were exactly like the *aratis* being held at Shirdi. Balchandra then took the next step and he taught the priest all the *aratis* of Baba and gave him an *arati* book to refer to.

After a period of time the members of the housing society that he lived in desired to build a temple for Baba in front of their building. They were aware that Balchandra had spent his time and energy in teaching Baba's *aratis* to the temple priest, so they requested him to supervise and get the temple built. Balchandra gladly agreed, and soon the entire responsibility of building the temple fell on his shoulders. Soon he got the temple built, and then he went to Jaipur and brought back a beautiful idol of Baba. That idol was housed in the temple with Vedic mantras and rituals, and life was infused into it. Following this, many temples sought his help in different ways and he got a chance to perform some service or the other for Baba. Thus he understood why Baba had asked him to distribute wafers. Then he was elected to be in charge of the *Sai Sagar* Magazine section in Baroda, and people started recognising him as the editor of the magazine.

A few years later, Balchandra was involved in an accident and fractured his leg; so for the next three months he was house-bound. Around this time many of his friends had visited Shirdi and he too had a keen desire to do so. Due to his fractured leg he was unable to go anywhere, and travelling to Shirdi was out of question. One afternoon he fell asleep and had this wonderful dream.

Balchandra found himself in Shirdi, and to his utter surprise it was not at all crowded. Balchandra wanted to enter the *Mukh Darshan* but the security personnel refused entry. Then Balchandra pleaded with him saying, "I will return within 5 minutes." After much pleading he was finally allowed to enter. However, Balchandra found himself standing in front of Baba's Samadhi and instead of the idol, Baba Himself was seated on the throne. He saw a few other devotees seated peacefully in front of Baba. In his dream, Balchandra ascended the steps of the Samadhi and prostrated before Baba. Baba blessed Balchandra and placed his hand on Balchandra's head. Balchandra then sat with the other devotees and looked at Baba to his heart's content. Then he exited the temple.

However, even after having such a long darshan of Baba he was not satisfied and a keen desire to have an auspicious viewing of Baba rose again. Balchandra again returned to the same security personnel and requested him to let him go inside again. This time the security personnel was really reluctant to allow him inside. Balchandra pleaded with all his heart and after much hesitation he was let inside again. This time, Balchandra saw Baba's idol on the throne. From this dream, Balchandra was satisfied to know that Baba, even after taking *Maha Samadhi* in 1918, is still there in Shirdi to fulfil all the wishes of his devotees.

At the end of that year Balchandra read the *Shri Sai Satcharita* and completed it in 7 days. At that time he was fully aware that Baba was near him, and could feel his presence. Baba solved his financial difficulties and took care of his mental state of mind. Thus Balchandra states, "If we hand over our life to Baba, and surrender our ego, pride, anger, passion, and jealousy to him, then we will definitely be able to experience his grace."

Ref.: *Shri Sai Sagar Magazine*, Dipavali issue, 2010.

54

Baba Extends Gondkar's Life

This is the story of how Baba gifted Balchandra Gondkar 12 years of life. Ever since, Gondkar's every heartbeat joyously sings "Sai Ram! Sai Ram!"

On 30th January 2009, Balchandra Gondkar along with nine of his friends set out to Shirdi on foot. The distance from Baroda, where they lived, to Shirdi is about 400 miles. The first two days they walked around 35 miles each, and thus they covered about 70 miles at the end of the second day. This was an unthinkable feat for Balchandra as he was 60 years old at that time. It was only Baba's grace that enabled him to walk that much. They walked in this manner for 6 days and reached a village called Satana in Nasik District where they halted for the night.

Around 10 p.m. when his friends were fast asleep, Balchandra felt a twinge of pain in his chest, which subsequently disappeared. Due to the pain Balchandra was restless and unable to sleep. He took a packet of *Udi* and applied it to his forehead. An hour later the pain recurred and soon it became unbearable. Along with this he also experienced shortness of breath. Balchandra thought of waking his friends and getting help, but they were all tired and sound asleep. For about 2 hours he endured this excruciating pain. It felt as if the funeral bells were tolling for him. Nevertheless he was still mentally chanting Baba's name. Along with that he mentally prostrated to all the Gurus, Gods and Goddesses and his parents. Then his thoughts turned to his friends who were devoted to Baba, and he wished them all well. Suddenly Balchandra remembered that his daughter and her husband were scheduled to leave Baroda that night and would soon be passing by Nasik. In the event that something serious did happen to him, they could

137

easily be contacted and they would come running to his aid.

Balchandra then happened to glance at his feet, and saw a dog lying next to his feet. At once the thought came to his mind, that when death approaches and the messengers of death come to take you away, dogs become aware of it and start whining loudly. However this dog was sleeping peacefully at his feet. Somehow this thought calmed him considerably and before long, he fell asleep. Balchandra had an exciting dream in which someone gave him Baba's *Udi* and said, "Tomorrow at this time I will definitely come to meet you." Upon receiving Baba's *Udi* he started feeling better, and he was assured that he would live another day. Balchandra awoke at 4 a.m. and he and his friends lit some incense sticks. Taking Baba's flag in his hand he set out.

Balchandra walked along with his friends and a short while later a dear friend named Indravadhan fell in pace with him. Balchandra was very fond of Indravadhan as he was utterly devoted to Baba. Indravadhan would meditate every day on Baba for 4 to 5 hours whenever he found the time and would often give Balchandra some interesting messages from Baba. Indravadhan now said, "Gondkar Kaka, last night when I was in deep meditation, Baba appeared to me and said, 'I have increased Gondkar Kaka's life span by 12 years. Now you take care of him.'" Balchandra was utterly amazed. He thought, "How kind and caring is Baba. I have now completed 60 years of my life and from this point on I will spend the rest of my life doing good deeds."

Balchandra then continued the walk to Shirdi, and then returned to Baroda. On his return he started the "Aum Sai Padyatra Bhajan Mandal" that meets every Thursday and sings devotional songs of Baba from 9 p.m. to 10.30 p.m. Along with this he participates in various religious activities. He also brings priests from various parts of Gujarat to Shirdi so that they can see firsthand how Baba is worshipped at Shirdi. At his expense he also brings poor devotes to Shirdi. Balchandra's only wish is that he passes away doing *seva* for his *Sadguru*.

Ref.: *Shri Sai Sagar Magazine*, Volume 3, No. 4, January–March 2013.

55

Manohar's Pilgrimage Experiences-I

The next two *leelas* describe the experiences that Manohar had while making pilgrimages on foot to various holy shrines.

Once, Manohar (his last name is not mentioned) was making a pilgrimage from Junagadh to Shirdi on foot. He had walked from Junagadh and had almost reached Porbandar. Just before reaching the city, he halted at a Ram Mandir, which was a short distance away from the main road. There he found a *Ramanandi* (followers of the medieval saint Ramanand) priest who was performing the worship, rituals and looking after the temple. The priest questioned him about the holy destination he was bound for. Manohar told him that he was walking to Shirdi. As soon as he mentioned Shirdi the priest's eyes twinkled with joy. He requested Manohar to stay overnight in the temple, and leave the next morning. Manohar gladly accepted his request as that was what he had intended to do. Then the priest served him a simple meal and they sat and chatted. The priest had a lot of questions about Shirdi, and asked, "Where in Maharashtra is Shirdi? How do I reach Shirdi from here? Is there a dharamshala for me to stay in?" Manohar gave him all the necessary information.

Then the priest recounted his experience. "A few days ago a fakir came here. I welcomed him, and inquired if he would like to have a meal. He refused the meal, but he accepted the glass of milk that I offered him. We chatted for a while but unfortunately his Hindi was very difficult for me to understand. The only sentence that I could understand was that he knew my Guru and then he had to leave. I requested him to stay but he refused. Just prior to that he handed me a book and asked me to read it. The book was a religious text as it was wrapped in an ochre coloured cloth. I accepted the book and put it away without opening it. The fakir then left and I stood at the entrance as I watched him stride away. He must have taken three steps when he disappeared. I was surprised to see this. I immediately turned around and opened the book he had given me. It was Sai Baba's *Charita*. I opened and looked at the photograph given in it. I was stunned to see that the fakir who sat here a short while ago was Sai Baba himself. The *pothi* was in Marathi so I was unable to understand it. Nevertheless I asked a number of people about the photograph and one of them told me about Baba. He told me that Baba was a great saint who lived in Maharashtra, and that he had taken Samadhi in 1918. Hearing this I was very astonished. So many years after his Samadhi Baba had appeared here. He had sat and talked to me. I am from Uttar Pradesh and Baba was from Maharashtra and yet he knew my Guru. I had seen him disappear before my very own eyes. All this left me spell bound and I wish to visit Shirdi at least once."

Ref.: *Prasad,* Volume 33, No. 9, August 1979.

56

Manohar's Pilgrimage Experiences–II

On another occasion, while on a pilgrimage to Rishikesh by foot, Manohar halted at Shankracharya Nagar, at the Ashram of Mahesh Yogi, called Swargh Ashram. This Ashram was situated on the banks of the Ganges River, and Manohar intended to stay there for a few days. The caretaker of the Ashram was Ramnesh, who was a Brahmachari (celibate) from the Gadhwal region. Ramnesh welcomed Manohar and gave him a room to stay in. What surprised Manohar the most was a picture of Baba hanging on the wall. He enquired about it from Ramnesh, who told him that a few years ago a Brahmachari from Maharashtra had stayed in the Ashram for a few days, and prior to his departure he had given the picture to Ramnesh. Ramnesh hadn't known anything about Baba at that time, but had accepted the picture happily. He had hung it in that room as he had thought that it would enhance the appearance of the room.

On one occasion Ramnesh had fallen quite sick, and all the treatment that he took proved futile. Soon he was confined to bed. As he lay on the bed in despair, his attention was drawn to the picture and he thought, "If I recover from this illness quickly I will start worshipping you." To his utter surprise he started feeling better from that very evening and soon regained his health. Thenceforth, he started worshipping the picture in his own way.

Ramnesh recalled, "I was doing yoga for a long time, and once I tried to do a very difficult asana but was unsuccessful. Time and again I tried without success, so I decided to forget it. A long while later I tried the asana again, but to no avail. Then I turned to Baba for help and said, "If you are a really great saint I will first take your name and try the asana, and if I succeed, then I will know for sure you are a *Sadguru*." Then he once again tried the asana and achieved it effortlessly, almost as if he had perfected it under the guidance of a Guru. Thus his faith and devotion in Baba grew even deeper. Ramnesh told many other celibates at the Ashram about it and they started ritualistic worship of Baba. Then he learned Baba's *aratis* and performed them daily. Although he does not know Marathi, he reads a chapter of the *Shri Sai Satcharita* daily, and in 1979 he went on a pilgrimage to Shirdi.

Ref.: *Prasad*, Volume 33, No. 9, August 1979

57

Baba Protects Telkar

This *leela* is about Dashrath R. Telkar. In 1963, Dashrath had diligently concentrated on his academics, and burned the midnight oil to appear for his Matriculation examination. After the examination, he was free to enjoy his vacation. Dashrath and his family lived in Mumbai and spent their vacation at their ancestral home in Khajni. He was glad to meet all his friends, and they spent all their time together. Early in the morning they would meet, go to the nearby forest, and eat mangoes, jackfruit and cashews that grew abundantly in the forest. At other times they would go rock-climbing or swim in the nearby lake. Life went on without a care in the world with Dashrath helping his parents in any way that he could. He would accompany his father to the fields and plough them when the need arose. Sometimes he would go to the village shops and bring a sack of onions or whatever grocery his mother required.

On May 13th, 1963 a frightening incident took place. Dashrath recalls: "That morning my father and I had decided to take the paddy to Murud (Janjira) to get it threshed. Both of us filled the paddy into sacks, stacked them on the bullock cart, and set out. Murud is about 8 miles away from Khajni, but the road to it is an unpaved dirt road. We reached the Murud threshing mill at 12 noon, I immediately went and got a number for our turn. According to the number we would receive the threshed paddy around 6 p.m. and that is exactly what happened. Quickly we stacked the sacks of rice on the bullock cart and took the road back to Khajni. After traversing about 2 miles, we were engulfed in pitch darkness. I lit the lantern that I had brought along, and started walking slightly ahead of the cart, hoping that the bullocks could see the dirt path ahead

143

of them. By then it was around 8 p.m. and I could hardly see anything around me. My father was urging and encouraging the bullocks to move faster. We must have walked another 3 miles, when the kerosene lantern that I was using flickered and extinguished. I realised that I didn't have a bottle of kerosene to refill it. It was around 10 p.m. at that time, and the night was filled with the chirping of crickets and other night creatures.

Now we were in trouble as there was no village nearby, and we were approaching the forest. The option of stopping for the night didn't arise. The tribal people who lived in the forest were known to waylay unsuspecting travellers and rob them. Moreover we had 5 sacks filled with rice, and I had the reins of the bullocks in my hand. The bullocks moved ahead very slowly and cautiously. The darkness was now denser as we were in the heart of the forest. I was scared. My mind stared playing tricks on me, and doubts and scary thoughts made my hair stand on end. I started praying to Baba and asked him to come to our aid.

The cart must have hardly travelled a mile when I heard some people approaching us. They were talking amongst themselves. I pulled hard to stop the bullocks from proceeding. My heart was in my mouth, and my father must have dozed off, as he asked me why I had halted. I was unable to speak from fear. Three hurly burly men with stout bamboo sticks came and stood before the cart. It was pointless trying to flee now as they were three of them and they knew the forest well. One of them shouted a barrage of questions, 'Who are you? Where are you going? What is in the cart?' In a quivering voice my father told them that that we lived in Khajni and had gone to Murud to get the paddy threshed. Then he asked us to get down from the cart and hand over all the money that we had. The only solution was to obey them; so we got down and I put my hand my pocket to give them the money when Baba came to our aid.

Four men with lanterns in their hands approached, loudly calling out my father's name. Now the thugs were outnumbered so they fled, and I started pelting stones at them. Our rescuers inquired about the attack, and two of them agreed to accompany us, while the other two went on. They accompanied us up to the village, but when my father requested them to come home, they refused. My father thanked them for saving our lives, and asked them who they were. One of them said, 'The four of us live together in the forest. We have neither a name nor a village to identify us by.' Saying this, they hurriedly left. My father and I were filled with awe at all this, so we bowed our heads and thanked Baba silently.

Finally we reached home at 1 a.m., unloaded the sacks and retired for the night. The next morning, we narrated everything that happened the previous night to everyone. Unanimously they all said, 'You are devoted to Baba and found yourself in a precarious situation so he came running to your aid and brought you home safely.'

We had no doubt in our minds that only Baba could have appeared as more than one person and saved us from those thugs."

Ref.: *Shri Sai Sagar*, Volume 11, July–August 2003.

58

Baba Performs Bani's Last Rites

Since childhood Hari P. Naik a devotee from Mumbai had heard stories of how Lord Krishna had stayed in the home of Eknath Maharaj and brought water from the river daily for his wife, performed the chores in his house, ground the wheat for Janabai and swept the compound for her. However, Baba did the unthinkable for him and his family which left them eternally indebted to him. As a matter of fact, Baba came and performed the last rites for his aunt.

With tears of gratitude Hari recalled the incident. His aunt Bani was ardently devoted to Baba and spent her entire time chanting Baba's name and reading the *Charita*. A few years ago, Bani fell ill and in spite of receiving the best medical care, her health started deteriorating. Finally the doctor suggested that perhaps a change of climate and peaceful surroundings would help her recuperate. Hari's father Pandurang and two of his uncles, Nilkant and Gajanan, decided to shift her to a suitable place in Nasik District. They went and scouted around in the surrounding villages and found a small village that had luscious greenery, unpolluted fresh air, and was peaceful. However, it was isolated and far from town. Bani was moved there and as her condition was unpredictable, Pandurang along with his brothers stayed there.

A week later Bani was at death's door, and at 11 p.m. she breathed her last. At that time Pandurang's and Nilkant's wives were also present, while Gajanan had returned home.

Now Pandurang and Nilkant were in a quandary, as they knew nobody there. Neither did they know where to purchase the wood and other supplies for the last rites. Finally they decided to go to the river bank to cremate the body. They cast their burden on Baba, and chanting his name they hesitantly set out. After going a short distance they heard a thunderous voice behind them saying, "Stop." They turned around and saw a tall, lean man dressed in a long white shirt with a white turban on his head wearing *khadaw*s (wooden footwear of ascetics). He continued, "I will take care of everything. You don't have worry about a thing. Now both of you return home, as the two women are alone there and at this time a man ought to be with them." Pandurang and Nilkant were astonished how this man knew that their wives were alone at home. Mesmerised by what he said, they quietly returned home without questioning him. But what they saw next left them speechless. Right in front of their house all the materials necessary for the last rites were there, right up to the garland and mud pot. They went inside the house and asked their wives to get Bani ready for her last journey, and finally placed her on the bier. The next problem was that there were only two men to carry the bier for cremation. Again they heard the same voice, saying, "Both of you shoulder the front of the bier and I will take care of the back." Simultaneously both turned around and saw that it was the same man who had helped them previously.

They reached the cremation ground and this man swiftly arranged the wood for the funeral pyre. He also guided them in the rituals to be followed, and Bani's body was laid on the funeral pyre. Now the question of who would light the pyre loomed ahead of them. But what happened next left them speechless. That man lit the pyre and disappeared. The pyre burned brightly and in the light of it they looked for that man, but found him nowhere.

Soon it was dawn and still that man could not be found. After lighting the fire of salvation for his ardent devotee, Baba returned to Shirdi that night.

Ref.: *Shri Sai Sagar*, Volume 13, No. 9, January 2005.

59

Sailesh's Blissful Experience

Once Sailesh, his wife Rajshri, and his mother set out from Pune on a pilgrimage to Nasik. His wife wanted to visit Shirdi first, and then go to Triambakeshwar and return home. However his mother had set her heart on going to Triambakeshwar first, so he agreed.

When they reached Shirdi they immediately got a room, and after they had a wash they went to the temple complex. Sailesh went to the Chavadi prior to going to the Samadhi Mandir. There he sat in front of Baba's photograph for some time and closed his eyes when he had a divine vision, wherein he saw Baba with serpents playing all over him. Baba loudly proclaimed, "I am Triambakeshwar and I will make you fragrant just before you leave."

Sailesh was at a loss to understand what Baba meant by his comment that he would make him fragrant. Then Sailesh and his family went to the Samadhi Mandir and found that it was crowded beyond expectation. As he slowly made his way to the Samadhi he wondered if he would be able to lay his head on Baba's *padukas*. Unexpectantly when his turn came there were only a few devotees around. Calmly he laid his head on Baba's *padukas* and a sweet aroma surrounded him. Surprisingly he could smell the aroma on his clothes, his body, and even on his wallet. Many years after his visit, his wallet still has the fragrance on it

In her prayer room, Rajshri, Sailesh's wife, had a beautiful idol of Baba that she had bought from Shirdi. Just like the idol in the Samadhi Mandir, she had adorned it with a golden crown, dressed it with a beautiful shawl and put a 'rudraksh' garland around its neck.

Around October 2004, Rajshri had this wonderful

experience. One morning she sat in front of the idol meditating when she saw Baba, who said, "My hair has become dirty and sticky. Every day you bathe me with milk then dress me in a shawl embroidered with threads of gold, and the threads of the shawl prick me. I want you to mend my torn *kafni* for me." In awe Rajshri inquired if she could take of his *shrivesh* (cloth covering the head) and Baba replied, "Yes take it off". Gently she removed the *shrivesh* and unbelievably long hair rolled down. The hair was so long that even if she had laid it on several reed mats placed side by side, they wouldn't suffice, as the hair would still lie on the floor. Amidst the tresses of hair she saw a green snake. Rajshri was taken aback and terribly afraid. Baba in a soothing voice said, "There is no need to be afraid." Then Rajshri washed Baba's hair for him, and tied the *shrivesh* on his head. Then she patched up his torn *kafni*.

As soon as this was done Baba held two *jholi*s (cloth bags for collecting alms) in front of Rajshri and said, "Take whatever you want." One bag was filled with gems and diamonds, while the other had food collected as alms. Immediately she said, "Baba give me some prasad from your alms." At that moment Rajshri came out of her meditation.

Some years ago, Rajshri's husband was displeased with her and said, "Rajshri get a container and put the *Udi* in it. The packets of Baba's *Udi* fall here and there and we are disrespecting the most sacred and sanctified gift from Baba." In her home the *Udi* was kept on a large piece of paper that was then folded into a packet. However, Rajshri completely forgot what her husband had told her to do.

After a few weeks she met an old friend of hers who invited her home and Rajshri went along. They chatted together over tea and snacks and had a great time. When Rajshri got up to leave, her friend gifted her a brass tin with a packet of *Udi* in it. Rajshri was delighted as the tin had a picture of Lord Ganesha etched on it. Rajshri then told her friend about the conversation she had had with her husband regarding storing the *Udi*. Then Rajshri said, "I had totally forgotten about it but Baba never forgets and in a trice he arranged our meeting. I accompanied you home and of all the gifts in the world, he aptly made you gift me this beautiful container with a packet of *Udi* in it, thus reminding me of what I had promised my husband to do. How compassionate my Baba is! I thank you for this gift from the bottom of my heart."

Ref.: *Shri Sai Sagar*, Volume 13, No. 9, January 2005.

60

Baba Takes Care of his Devotees

Maya A. Savant, a devotee, resided in Malvan in Sindhudurg district, but had recently moved to Kurla, Mumbai. A few years earlier, in the month of November, Maya's father-in-law passed away. That year, during the Deepavali vacation, Maya's six-year-old son Vaibhav visited his friend's home where they were making elaborate preparations for the forthcoming festival. He was thrilled to see his friend's home decorated with lamps and flower garlands.

Vaibhav returned home and inquired, "*Ayi* why are we not preparing for Deepavali? Are we not going to celebrate Deepavali like everyone else?" Maya told him that as his grandfather had gone to heaven, they would spend it without much pomp and show. However, Maya had decided that she would prepare some confectionery and offer it to Baba as *prasad* and buy some savouries from the market for the children.

A short while later, her eldest daughter Jyothi was preparing lunch and was unable to find the canister of rice. Maya told her that it was on the top shelf. Jyothi then climbed on the table and reached for the tin and brought it down. She opened it and screamed, "*Ayi*, come here." Maya ran as she thought her daughter had most probably slipped and fallen. But when Jyothi handed the tin to her mother, she saw that it was filled with different types of confectioneries and savouries. Surprisingly they were hot as if someone had just prepared them. Maya joined her hands together and said, "Jai Sai Baba!" Just at that moment Viju, her neighbour who was also a devotee of Baba, entered her kitchen and said, "Maya give me some of Baba's *prasad*."

A year later Maya moved back to her home in Malvan. One

day she got a telephone call from her daughter who was married and settled in Mumbai saying that her husband had had a severe attack of asthma. The next day Maya and her husband went to the station but were unable to get reservations, so they bought their tickets and boarded the unreserved bogie. The bogie was packed with passengers; however they managed to enter the bogie. Maya and her husband were senior citizens and the thought of standing for 12 hours loomed before them. Maya however knew that Baba would take care of them. As usual she was silently chanting Baba's name.

At the next station a tall man entered the bogie and made his way through the crowd. He stopped for a moment before them, then proceeded inside the bogie and looked around. He then went to a lady and her son who were seated next to the window and asked them if they had their tickets with them. They admitted that they hadn't purchased tickets, so he asked them to vacate their seats. He turned and came to Maya and said, "Both of you can sit on those seats. I am seated in the adjacent bogie, and if you have any difficulty let me know. I am there to help you, and I am all the way with you."

After some time the bogie became less crowded, so Maya's husband decided to go and thank the person who had been so kind to them. But he was not to be found in the adjacent bogie nor was he anywhere else on the train. Maya and her husband wondered how he could have possibly gotten off a moving train. When they realised it was Baba who had helped them, Maya was exceedingly pleased that Baba in the form of the tall man had said, "I am there to help you, and I am all the way with you."

Ref.: *Shri Sai Sagar Magazine*, January–March 2013.

61

Vijaykumar Experiences the Power of Udi

The next two *leelas* are about a devotee from Pune named V.D. Mule, alias P. Vijaykumar.

Vijaykumar's father was ardently devoted to Baba and spent most of his spare time in service to him. He was largely responsible for helping in the building of Shri Sai Baba Mandir in Bhivpuri which is near Kasara on the Nasik–Igatpuri Railway line. From him Vijaykumar had learned to participate and do service for Baba in any way that he could.

Bhau Sahib Lombar had always been very kind to Vijaykumar when he was a lad. Lombar was blessed by Baba and he had built the Shri Sai Baba *Mutt*, under Baba's guidance, which is on Satara Road in Pune. When Vijaykumar was a young lad, he and a few of his friends would visit Lombar's home prior to their examinations, and seek his blessings. When the kids turned up at his home, Lombar would chide them saying, "You seem to remember Baba only when your examinations are approaching. Don't you remember him the rest of the year?" Then turning to Vijaykumar he would laugh and say, "You are the leader of this gang. Are you also like them? Baba will see what he has to do. Here, take this *Udi prasad* and run home and study diligently." Then he would pat Vijaykumar on his head and he and his friends would go home.

Vijaykumar says, "In those days we didn't have electricity in our home so I would study in the light of a lantern till midnight and give my examination the next day. I followed this routine till all my papers were completed. I was confident as I had the *Udi* that Bhau Sahib had given me."

Once, Vijaykumar was feeling terribly unwell and exhausted.

Even though he was taking the treatment prescribed by the doctor, there was no improvement. He changed his doctors twice, but even after taking their treatment for over a month there was no significant improvement. One day Vijaykumar went to his doctor's clinic and the doctor gave him an injection and sent him home. He returned home, lay down and soon fell asleep. Then he heard Baba say, "Are you sleeping? Get up. I have kept my *Udi* on your prayer altar to pray to it. What are you waiting for? Go and get it." Vijaykumar saw Baba standing near his pillow. Immediately, he got up, brought the container of *Udi*, and held it before Baba. Baba took a pinch of *Udi*, and closed his eyes for a few moments. Then he put the pinch that he had held back into the container and mixed it about. Then he said, "Now this is alright. Allah Malik is there to look after everything. Every morning and evening mix it in water and take it internally and also apply some on your forehead." Vijaykumar then prostrated and placed his head on Baba's feet. And there ended the dream. Vijaykumar opened his eyes and looked around for Baba, who had disappeared. However, he had left the aroma of roses behind. Needless to say, Vijaykumar followed Baba's orders and soon recovered.

Ref.: *Shri Sai Sagar Magazine*, Volume 7, No. 2, April–May 2009.

62

Vijaykumar is Blessed with Baba's Grace

At one point of time in his life, Vijaykumar had to face a lot of adversities. Nothing seemed to work for him and he felt as if he was drowning in a sea of troubles. Everywhere he turned, he found nothing but disappointment. His family and friends turned their backs on him. Life was taking its toll on his physical and mental health, and he did not know what to do. Finally he took his horoscope to a renowned astrologist who went through it in great detail. But the astrologer couldn't tell him what exactly was wrong at that time, neither could he give him any solution for his inauspicious planetary configurations.

Finally he sought refuge in Baba, and mentally sought his blessings. Vijaykumar started learning about his own horoscope and along the way he learned a lot about astrology. He seriously studied astrology, and not content with this he learned the science of divination that was available at that time. Vijaykumar studied numerology, gemology, *Vastu Shastra* (science of architecture), and graphology (studying handwriting). During this period many people in this field guided him, but somehow he was not completely satisfied. Neither did he get peace of mind, but felt that something was lacking in his life.

Vijaykumar's job required him to visit Shirdi often, and he was glad about this. While in Shirdi, Vijaykumar first went to the Dwarka Mai, as Baba had stayed in the Dwarka Mai for 60 years, showering His Grace on his devotees via the infinite *leela*s. While in the Dwarka Mai, Vijaykumar would pray and chant Baba's name, and sit there for sometime as he found peace there. However because of his job he had to travel a lot, so whenever Vijaykumar had time he would do Baba's *seva*.

Then for a period of time Vijaykumar was unable to visit Shirdi as he concentrated on divination and his job. It so happened that one day he was exceptionally busy, so much so that he was unable to have lunch. Vijaykumar finally reached home totally exhausted, and he couldn't wait to get into his bed. However he first stood in front of Baba's picture, and prayed to him and placed a lighted incense stick in front of the picture, then fell upon his bed, and was soon fast asleep.

The next morning at around 4 a.m., Vijaykumar had a dream wherein he found himself in the Dwarka Mai which seemed like the Dwarka Mai of the bygone years. There was a huge stone wall on all four sides, and a flight of steps to go up, with an open courtyard in front of it. In the corner there was a mud hut and next to it were two rooms. Baba was seated on a seat in the courtyard and was reading a book.

Vijaykumar thought, "Baba is the 'Complete Supreme Divinity' who knows everything about everything. He does not need to read anything." His curiosity was aroused and he went near Baba to see what he was reading. As he drew nearer, Baba became aware of him, and for a moment Baba looked at Vijaykumar with love. Thereafter Baba shut the book and started walking towards the rooms, and Vijaykumar followed him. Baba entered a room and Vijaykumar tried to follow but saw that his entry was blocked by a stick that was placed at an angle against the sash of the door. Vijaykumar was reminded of Gangapur. In the temple of Narsing Saraswati's *Nirguna Padukas*, a stick is placed at an angle against the sash of the door during the *Kakad* and noon *arati*s and whenever *prasad* is offered to the deity. However Vijaykumar removed the stick and entered the room.

Baba was seated on an old wooden cot, on which an even older, worn out reed mat was spread. In the corner of that room there was an earthen pot filled with water. Now Vijaykumar was afraid and very hesitantly he went forward and joined his hands together in salutation. Baba looked at him and said, "Why have you come here? And what do you want?" With reverence Vijaykumar replied, "Baba you know everything and yet you are asking me?" Baba said, "Okay. Alright." Vijaykumar continued, "Baba please show me the right path so I don't stray and wander about. Then I can take the path that you want me to follow." Then Baba said, "It's alright. Now sweep this entire room and make it clean. Sweep each and every corner clean. Also sweep under this cot, and make this room spick and span. There is a broom in the corner."

Like a good, obedient child he swept the room. Finally, Baba looked satisfied and hesitatingly Vijaykumar placed his horoscope before Baba. Baba inquired what it was, picked it up and looked at it, then placed it under the reed mat that he sat on. Then Baba picked up an old tin container and placed some candied sugar crystals in Vijaykumar's hands. Vijaykumar paid obeisance to Baba and went out of the room, and at that moment he awoke.

After having a bath, Vijaykumar sat and chanted Baba's name for about an hour. Then he took the copy of his horoscope and went to the Sai Baba *Mutt* on the Satara Road, stood in front of Baba's idol with folded hands and from the bottom of his soul thanked Baba. Vijaykumar folded the copy of his horoscope that he had brought along with him and quietly slipped it under the silk shawl that Baba was seated on. Again he closed his eyes and prayed to Baba.

A young priest spoke to him saying, "After such a long time you have come to the *Mutt*. It seems Baba has shown you some *leela*." Vijaykumar nodded his head in acknowledgement. The priest gave him a coconut, a garland and some prasad of *pedas*. Vijaykumar went to the Dhuni Mai, and made a resolution that henceforth he would not show his horoscope to anyone. Now he was in a state of utter peace, and he went to work.

That evening Vijaykumar thought about the dream seriously and tried to decipher its meaning. "This human body is like a house, nonetheless it is dusty. The dust represents the unwanted six internal enemies like anger and pride. This dust ought to be swept away. We should consciously get rid of our bad tendencies. Then we are worthy of receiving the Guru's

Grace or candied sugar, and our life becomes sweet and we are able to take the right path which is the spiritual path, making our lives even sweeter." This experience gave him a lot of encouragement and hope and along with this his condition also started improving.

Vijaykumar became well known for his accurate astrological predictions and his friends and relatives came to him for advice. Due to Baba's Grace his financial condition improved beyond expectations. Later he bought a house, got married and lived happily.

Ref.: *Shri Sai Sagar Magazine*, Volume 7, No. 2, April–May 2009.

63

How Baba Fed Vivek's Family

As far as Vivek Majgavkar, a devotee from Mumbai, is concerned, nothing in life is of value if it is devoid of Baba's Grace. His life revolves around Baba, and at one point in his life Baba enabled him to overcome demeaning circumstances. Now with Baba's grace he is happy and contented.

Once, his relatives requested him to take them to Shirdi. The group consisted of a few women and children. He hired a large van and they comfortably reached Shirdi. They stayed overnight and early next morning attended the *Kakad Arati* and had a satisfying *darshan* of Baba. After having breakfast his relatives suggested that they would like to visit Akkalkot from there. So they packed their belongings and got ready to set out. At that time, it was about 11 a.m. Vivek was unaware that Akkalkot was far away from Shirdi. He asked the driver how long it would take to reach Akkalkot, and the driver told him that they would reach in about 2 hours. At that time he was unaware that the driver neither knew the route to Akkalkot, nor did he know how far away it was from Shirdi. They decided that they would have lunch at Akkalkot as they would reach there by 1 p.m.

After travelling for over 2 hours there was no sign of Akkalkot and Vivek hadn't the slightest clue where they had reached. The driver reassured them time and again saying, "Look we have nearly reached." With the help of the road signs the driver had finally taken the route via Sholapur after it had dawned on him that the road to Akkalkot was via Sholapur! Every now and then he would reassure his passengers that they would be reaching in a short while. Finally, they reached Akkalkot late at night, tired and hungry.

Akkalkot is a small remote village without facilities and

hotels. Vivek decided to first get a room where the women and children could rest while he could find some place to have a meal. The Sansthan's Bhakta Nivas was under construction, so it was out of the question. Every place around had closed for the night, and he could neither find a room nor a restaurant to eat something. The kids were clamouring for some food and their condition was pitiable. He told the driver to drive on the main road hoping he would find some place that provided something to eat. But everywhere it was dark and deserted. Finally he found one shack that sold betel leaves and next to it was a tin shack hotel which was closed. Hunger was gnawing at his stomach, so he asked the owner if they could have something to eat. The owner informed him that every place was closed and it was impossible to get any food, but in the morning he could get a meal. Intensely hungry, he had to find a place to eat, so they drove ahead and again they were disappointed, so they turned around. Again he stopped at the shop and pleaded with the owner, but what could the shop owner do? All he could do was provide him with a sympathetic ear.

Finally, Vivek decided to go further into the village hoping he would find some restaurant there. But again he was met with disappointment. When all else failed he called on Baba. "Baba what kind of a test are you putting me through? There are small children with me; and they are starving. It's unbearable for me to see their plight. Baba at least for their sake, provide us with some food." Vivek then asked the driver to drive slowly back to the shop they had stopped at first. What happened next left him speechless.

As they approached the shop, the owner came running, waving his hands asking them to stop. "Sahib! Stop! Come inside the hotel!" he said excitedly. Vivek didn't know what was happening, or what to expect. They all trooped into the hotel and saw four or five stainless steel buckets lined up, all filled with piping hot, delectable food. The food looked heavenly. One bucket had cashew pilaf, while the other buckets had potato curry, puri, rice and lentil gravy.

Astonished, Vivek inquired, "A short while ago you said that there was nothing in the restaurant to eat; then where did this come from?" Excitedly he replied, "Sahib, what can I tell you. You had hardly left this place when an old man hurriedly came here bringing all this food with him. He said, 'My children are terribly hungry. They will return in a short while. Feed them this food' and left."

Vivek instantly knew that nobody but Baba could have done such a compassionate thing. Then all of them sat down and ate the ambrosial *prasad*. With each morsel of food that Vivek put into his mouth, tears of gratitude rolled down his cheeks. Vivek and his relatives stayed at Akkalkot for two days, and on their way home they stopped at that betel leaf shop to thank the owner. The owner however told him that the old man hadn't returned to take his buckets back.

Ref.: *Shri Sai Sagar Magazine*, Volume 7, No. 2, April–May 2009.

64

How Baba Blessed Kadam's House

In Baba's *Manglacharan* (invocation of blessings) it is said that "Even the lame can climb a mountain". Certainly with Baba's grace nothing is impossible, even under adverse conditions.

Lakshman Ranjiv Kadam was bogged down by a mountain of difficulties. Kadam was employed as a menial worker in a factory. He was illiterate, so the scope for advancement was impossible. His pay was meagre and he had a large family to feed. Around 3 years prior a profound change had occurred in him—he had stopped eating meat, began wearing a *Tulsi mala*, and started living a spiritual life.

Then tragedy struck. One day, while at work, a piece of steel flew and got lodged in his left eye. Kadam was treated for it for a period of three months. However he completely lost sight in that eye and later that eye had to be enucleated. Through all these difficult times, Kadam didn't lose heart, but accepted his loss as destiny and went back to work.

During this time, Kadam built a bigger house at Vadval as his old house had become too small for his growing family. His family moved in, but not for long. They claimed that the house was haunted because when they slept at night some unknown person came and slapped them on their faces. Kadam reassured them that it was a new house so it couldn't be haunted. Nevertheless, no one was ready to sleep there. So Kadam went and slept there all by himself. That night he had a wonderful dream of Baba who walked a few steps towards him; at each step, beautiful red lotuses sprouted around his feet. And there ended the dream.

Kadam asked many of his friends to decipher the meaning of the dream but no one could give a satisfactory answer. So Kadam decided to build a small temple for Baba, so that he

162

could permanently reside in his home. Around that time the manager of the factory where he worked compensated Kadam with an amount of 32,000 Rupees for the damage caused to his eye. Immediately Kadam went to Mumbai, bought a 2 ft tall idol made of marble and installed it in the temple with due rituals. Following Baba's arrival in his home, his family members came and lived happily in that house as Baba was now there to take care of them.

Ref.: *Shri Sai Leela Magazine*, Volume 67, No. 8–9, Deepavali 1988.

65

Satyavan's Lunch Guest

Satyavan Devendra Panchal was an automobile mechanic and owned a small garage in Pune. He was devoted to Baba and he would do *seva* daily in the ISKCON temple near his home.

In the month of June 2008, around noon, Satyavan had returned home after doing *seva* at the temple. His wife asked him to be seated so that she could serve him lunch. Just then he heard someone at his door, so Satyavan went to see who it was. An old man, wearing a white cap, a long white shirt over a white *dhoti*, with a *jholi* slung over his shoulder, was standing at the door. The man had a short white beard and moustache, but his face shone with a spiritual glow. Satyavan looked at him and felt a cloud of peace descend on him.

The old man said, "Give me one rupee, one *chapatti*, and one *bhakri*." Satyavan invited him to have a meal as the food was about to be served by his wife. They both sat down and his wife served them lunch. While they were eating the following conversation took place.

Satyavan asked him, "Baba where are you from?" Baba said, "I'm from God's *gaon*." Satyavan couldn't understand what he meant, so Baba replied, "God's *gaon* means I have come from Shirdi."

As soon as Satyavan heard the word Shirdi, he eagerly asked, "Baba where exactly do you live in Shirdi? Who else lives with you at home? If I come to Shirdi where will I be able to meet you?" Baba replied, "I am in Shirdi, and I have two children and one of them is a physician."

Now Satyavan was puzzled. He thought if this man's son was a doctor then what was the need for him to wander about from house to house. However with such a highly educated son he must be having a bungalow in Shirdi. Satyavan asked, "But what exactly is your address?"

Baba said, "I stay in the temple. I eat there and sleep there." This didn't ring a bell, so Satyavan asked, "But where in the temple can I meet you?"

Then Baba gave the most incredible answer. "When you come to Shirdi I will meet you at the entrance door of the temple. I will call out to you, you don't have to worry about that."

Now Satyavan's mind was completely numb and he didn't know what to say. Baba saw the state that Satyavan was in and changed the subject. He kept looking intently at the picture of Lord Krishna that Satyavan had got from the temple. So Satyavan told him that he did *seva* daily at the temple and that he was a devotee of Lord Krishna. Then Baba cautioned him, "It is okay to say you do *seva* but don't say you are a devotee."

Satyavan asked, "Why?" Baba replied, "A person should follow the path of devotion. But he shouldn't proclaim that he is a devotee. What is the necessity of broadcasting the fact that you are a devotee? If you find a new devotee, talk to him humbly, show him the right path. Don't be proud that you are a seasoned devotee and you know more than him. **On the path of devotion you should be humble and not arrogant**. And what you have achieved on that path should be treasured in your heart. Act as if what you have achieved is nothing or a very meagre amount, and you have yet to achieve a vast expanse. This should be your attitude. Don't fight with your wife, talk to each other respectfully. There are two demons ever present at your door, and when you fight with your wife they immediately enter your home and drive the Lakshmi out of your home, turning your life into rack and ruin." In this manner Baba gave Satyavan a lot of advice.

As Baba had finished his meal he got up washed his hands. Then Baba said, "I had gone into the forest once and there I met two old people..." Then Satyavan told Baba that he was getting late for work and Baba said, "Okay, Okay. I will leave now." Then he reminded Satyavan of the one rupee he had asked for earlier, but he didn't have any change with him. So he asked his wife to get the money from the room above.

Satyavan asked him where he was bound for, and Baba replied that he was going to Pandharpur. His wife came with a ten rupee note as she couldn't find any change. Satyavan turned to take it from her, when Baba vanished. They looked for him all over but he couldn't be found.

With regret Satyavan recalls, "I don't have to tell the devotees that he definitely was Sai Baba of Shirdi. Usually I am a cautious person, but what happened to my brain that day is beyond my understanding. I regret not having given him *dakshina*, or touching his feet; for cutting him short while he was trying to tell me something in the form of a parable. Now that I have missed such a golden opportunity, I have only this desire and that is, 'Baba when will you come again and have a meal at our home?'"

Ref.: *Shri Sai Sagar Magazine*, Volume 8, No. 1, January–March 2010.

66

How Baba Protected Dinesh

It is the firm belief of Dinesh Mahlar Dhotre that if you concentrate your entire spiritual energy and have complete faith in Baba and Baba alone, no one can harm you in any way. This is his experience.

Dinesh resided in Pune and worked as an officer in the Bajaj Company. The supervisor of his department was a very strict man, but in a rather strange way. He wanted everyone to do the work allotted to them in his way and his way alone. If the work was completed satisfactorily but not done in the way he wanted, it wouldn't be accepted. The supervisor also had the irritating habit of talking about everything in the world other than the assignment of the day.

In 1996, Dinesh's supervisor asked him to accompany him, as he wanted to meet some saintly person. He said, "Come with me as I want to meet this Maharaj. I have heard he is a very powerful person." Dinesh refused, saying, "I have only one Maharaj and he is Shri Sai Baba of Shirdi so please excuse me as I don't go anywhere other than Shirdi." Everyday his supervisor would ask Dinesh to accompany him, and Dinesh would politely refuse. His refusal didn't sit well with the supervisor and he left.

A week later Dinesh's supervisor came and stood in front of his desk, and in his palm he had some sort of *vibhuti* (holy ash). He said, "You refused to meet my Maharaj. Now you can experience for yourself how powerful he is." And saying this he blew the *vibhuti* on Dinesh. Dinesh said, "Your Maharaj may be extremely powerful, but my Sai Baba reigns over him as Baba is the Supreme God."

However that incident had an adverse effect on his mental peace. Dinesh recalls, "I started feeling restless, and was quite

167

disturbed mentally. I didn't go to work, nor did I leave my house or go anywhere. All I did was lie in bed. I didn't tell my family about the incident and even stopped talking to my wife. My family was worried and wondered what had happened to me as my job was an important part of my life, and I had never missed going to work. I myself didn't know why I had become so lazy. However I knew one thing, that only Baba could rescue me from this predicament. The entire time that I stayed at home I constantly chanted his name and begged him to help me regain my mental stability. Thus a few days passed while I refrained from going to work.

One afternoon I felt exceedingly drowsy and lethargic, and I lay on the floor, and soon fell asleep. But just before I slept I asked Baba to show me some way to get out of this dilemma. I must have slept for a long while, and as I woke up I looked at the cot in front of me and clearly saw Baba seated on it. He was sitting exactly like the 'sitting on the stone posture'. He looked at me compassionately and said, 'Why are you worried? I am there to protect you, nothing adverse will happen to you. Now get up and go to work.' And before I could say anything, he disappeared. Hastily I got up, and it felt as if Baba had blown new life into me. All my laziness and lethargy vanished at that moment. I called my wife and narrated the entire episode to her.

My restless mind became peaceful; in fact, I was in bliss. I immediately thought that I would go to work, but it was long past our working hours. The next morning I enthusiastically returned to work and started working as usual. My supervisor looked at me in astonishment and some disappointment. The tantric spell that he had cast on me didn't last for a long period as he had expected. I, on the other hand, didn't say anything to him."

A few months later, Dinesh went to visit a friend and coincidently a renowned palmist also happened to be there. This palmist had shunned publicity and fame, but was an expert in predicting the future. Both his friend and the palmist requested Dinesh to have his palm read. But Dinesh's reply was the same, "My life is in Baba's hands. All the happenings in my life are controlled by Him, and He will do what is best for me. So why do I need to know what lies in my future?"

The astrologer was an aged man who requested him repeatedly. He seemed to be eager to tell him something, so respecting his age, Dinesh let him read his palm. Dinesh was firm that he had no question to ask. The astrologer looked intently at his palm for a rather long time. Then in a worried voice he said, "That man who went out of his way to trouble you will have to bear the consequences of it. He will stay for only one month and then go." Dinesh returned home with the thought, "Without my saying anything to the astrologer about that supervisor, how did he know that he had cast an evil spell on me? Now what will happen to him in one months' time? Only time will tell."

A month later Dinesh's company had an award ceremony for the most capable worker, from all the ranks. Dinesh's supervisor received the award in the supervisor's category. Dinesh thought "This is Baba's wish and I have nothing to say." But what happened next was beyond anyone's imagination. The supervisor had received an award in the morning, yet that evening his services were terminated. Now he was jobless; this indeed was Baba's *leela*. Dinesh remembered the prediction of the astrologer. The following month, Dinesh heard the shocking news that the supervisor had passed away after being sick for a short time.

"What you sow, you reap" is Baba's edict. Dinesh categorically believes that everyone has to face troubles in life, but there is no need to go to any Maharaj or Tantric. Baba is there to take care of you as promised: "I will carry your burdens forever, or this promise of mine is false."

Ref.: *Shri Sai Sagar Magazine*, Volume 1, No. 1, May–July 2010.

67

Baba Manifested from Thin Air

Sarojatai Kasturi, a fervent devotee, resided in Baroda. From the time she was a young girl she had complete faith in Baba, whom she considered as the Supreme God.

At one point in time Sarojatai was disheartened and dismayed by the fact that she had been married for 6 years but was unable to conceive. The couple yearned to have a child, and she prayed to Baba to grant her this wish. The couple then got themselves checked for infertility.

Sarojatai got admitted into Bina Clinic as she was scheduled to have a dilation and curettage. She endured a lot of pain during the procedure and she knew very well she would have to. So while the procedure was being done, Sarojatai closed her eyes and chanted Baba's name. Sarojatai kept repeating "Sai Ram, Sai Ram" softly under her breath. Finally the procedure was completed and a short while later she felt better. The doctor checked Sarojatai again and allowed her to go home that night. Her husband was waiting for her, and both of them left riding on a motorbike. They had hardly gone about 20 ft ahead when they saw something which looked like a bright white cloud which slowly took the form of a fakir. Both of them were stunned and couldn't believe their eyes. Her husband, Kasturi, had jammed the brakes and they waited and watched as Baba from his *Nirgun* state (formless) took *Sagun* appearance (with form) and gave them this divine vision. Baba with ingenuity showed that even in this day and age, a divine visitation was possible.

Baba looked compassionately at Sarojatai and asked, "Why were you calling out to me?" Sarojatai was so confused at seeing Baba actually manifest from thin air that she replied, "I was not calling you, Maharaj." Then Baba said, "Just now in the clinic you were calling me. Why?" Sarojatai replied, "Oh! I was calling my Shirdi Sai Baba. I didn't call you, Maharaj." Then Baba said, "I have come from Shirdi, my child. Don't worry, you will definitely give birth to a baby boy soon." Baba turned and looked at her husband and asked him to give him 2 rupees. Immediately he put his hand in his pocket. There was a single rupee coin which he gave the fakir. Baba wouldn't accept it and asked him again for 2 rupees.

To behold the manifestation of God in front of you is far beyond the comprehension of the human mind. The mind gets baffled, and it feels that brain has shut down. Hence you just mechanically answer questions even when the fakir gives you many hints and clues.

Shri Kasturi was worried about his wife's procedure and he said, "Maharaj, my wife is not feeling well. I am in a hurry to take her home. So please accept this coin." And he dropped the coin in Baba's *jholi*. Shri Kasturi started his motorbike and drove a short distance, when Baba loudly said, "You owe me 1 rupee. Give it to me when you come to Shirdi." And he disappeared gradually.

Shri Kasturi drove on and then he realised what he had actually seen. He was perspiring profusely although it was a chilly night. He stopped and turned to his wife and said, "Don't tell anyone what we just saw, as it is unbelievable. No one will ever believe us, they will think we are making up stories. But today we saw the divine manifestation of Baba. We should have prostrated at his feet. We made a terrible mistake."

With regret, he cried out to Baba, "Baba we invariably profess to have utmost faith in you. But in reality the truth is very different. As a matter of fact we don't have true faith in you. We just make a show of looking at you. However we are constantly looking at worthless objects with the hope that it will bring wealth and comfort in our lives. Thus we are constantly groping in the darkness of ignorance. Oh! Compassionate Lord, if only we had had unshakable faith in you and loved you from the bottom of our hearts; and given our lives in your hands, then no power on earth could have separated us from you. Baba by your grace this veil of *Maya* can be torn asunder. Then our lives can become pure and we can offer our lives into your hands so that you can guide us on to the right path of devotion. Baba the veil of *Maya* had enveloped me so completely that even after seeing you manifest I could not grasp it. I was more concerned about my wife's well being, hence I did not even make an earnest attempt to find and give you 2 rupees. Yet I claim to be your devotee. Baba please forgive me; and from this moment on I give my life into your hands."

Following this divine incident, Sarojatai and her husband's faith in Baba increased by leaps and bounds. Their faith grew stronger with every passing day, as they had witnessed Baba's omnipresence with their own eyes.

Ref.: *Shri Sai Sagar Magazine*, Volume 7, No. 2, April 2008.

68

Baba Removes Ramchandra's Doubts

In 1962, a tragedy occurred in Shirdi. A wall collapsed and 22 people lost their lives. The newspapers had described the tragedy very vividly and had given their opinion about it. Ramchandra Govind Koyande, a resident of Mumbai, had read this news with disbelief. The news had negatively affected him, and swayed his opinion about Baba's divinity, and humanity. Ramchandra had only one question and that was: "If Baba was God, then why didn't he save these people?" Like a man possessed, he repeatedly asked every devotee whom he met the same question. However, nobody's answer could satisfy him.

In 1965, Ramchandra went to Nasik, to be trained as an Assistant Police Inspector at the Police Training College. At that time some of his colleagues requested him to accompany them to Shirdi. However, he refused, as he could not accept Baba as God because he still felt upset that Baba hadn't saved the 22 people from death.

In 1972, Ramchandra's wife had booked a pilgrimage tour though a travel agency. The tour would take them to Alandi, Dehu Road, Nasik, Triambakshwar, Mukti Dham and Shirdi. The tour was for two days, so Ramchandra, his wife, their three children, his father and mother-in-law all set out on the tour. From Nasik they arrived at Shirdi in the afternoon, and since that day happened to be a Thursday, they had the opportunity to witness the 'Palkhi procession'. Ramchandra was immensely affected by the spiritual energy during the procession and before he could realise it, he was totally submerged in it. Early next morning they left for Pune to visit Alandi and Dehu Road, and soon they were back in Mumbai.

The next Thursday at around 5 a.m., Ramchandra had this interesting dream of Baba. He had a picture of Baba hanging

173

on the wall in front of him. From that picture Baba put out his right arm and stretched it far away to the opposite wall where his shirt hung. Then he reached into the top pocket of his shirt and took out a *bidi* (indigenous cigarette) and started smoking it. Ramchandra's mouth flew open in astonishment. He had never ever smoked a cigarette or a *bidi* in his life, then how could there be a *bidi* in his pocket?

Then the following conversation took place between them in which Ramchandra is being referred to as "He" and Baba as "Baba":

Baba: "You had a question and that is 'Why did those 22 people die in Shirdi' and why didn't I save them?"

He: "I still have the same question. I have asked this question to innumerable devotees of yours but no one has yet given me a satisfactory answer."

Baba: "Child, a coin has two sides to it; however you are looking at only one side of the coin."

He: "Baba I cannot understand what you are saying."

Baba: "Every person who takes birth is definitely going to die. Right?"

He: "Yes."

Baba: "So when his time comes, he is surely going to die no matter where he is, be it in his home or anywhere else, because death is unavoidable, and inevitable?"

He: "Yes."

Baba: "These 22 people were destined to die at the same time. They would have died exactly at that time whether they were inside their homes or elsewhere. Do you agree to this?"

He: "Yes."

Baba: "Then why are you not looking at the reverse side of the coin?"

He: "Baba I still haven't understood the meaning of the 'reverse side of the coin.'"

Baba: "Child, whoever is destined to die at a certain time will die exactly at that time, regardless of whether he is at home or on the road. If they come to Shirdi and die at my feet, that means that they will become free of the bondage of Karma, attain salvation and go to heaven. Can you accept this?"

At that moment, Ramchandra awoke. Now he fully understood what Baba meant by saying, look at the reverse side of the coin. But he was filled with wonder at how Baba took out a *bidi* from the pocket of his shirt. Ramchandra had never smoked a *bidi*. Baba's picture was on one wall and his shirt was on the opposite wall. Now how was it possible for Baba to do this? He decided that he would go to Shirdi the next Thursday and ask Baba about this.

The next Thursday he and his family reached Shirdi just prior to *Dhup Arati*. Ramchandra had bought a bundle of *bidi*s. Way back then there was a "show room" where the articles used by Baba were displayed on the right side of the hall in the Samadhi Mandir. Ramchandra went and stood near the glass encasing of the show room. He kept the bundle of *bidi*s in front of Baba's *padukas*, and closed his eyes for a moment. From the bottom of his soul Ramchandra said, "Baba you gave me darshan, and smoked a *bidi* in my home. Today I have brought you a bundle of *bidi*s and kept it at your feet. Please accept this bundle from me. Also please bless and look after the welfare of all the devotees gathered here." When Ramchandra opened his eyes and looked down, the bundle of *bidi*s had vanished! He knew that Baba had accepted his offering.

Ref.: *Shri Sai Sagar Magazine*, Volume 7, No. 3, July–September 2009.

69

Kishanrao's Miraculous Recovery

The human body is made up of the five basic elements, which are earth, water, air, fire and ether, but Baba had total control over them. It is an unspoken rule with Baba not to meddle with the laws of nature. Yet sometimes to grant the wish of a devotee his miracles seem to do just that, as it happened in the case of Kishanrao Sitaram Makamle.

In the year 2002, Kishanrao, a devotee from Satara, was on his way to work at Vadegaon. He worked as a building contractor and was driving a motorbike to Vadegaon. Kishanrao was cruising along on a fairly empty road when a three-wheeler appeared from nowhere driving at a terrific speed, and collided head on with him. The impact of the collision was so great that Kishanrao was thrown on the opposite side of the road. Soon some passersby came to his aid and got him admitted into Satara Civil Hospital. Immediately an X-ray of his right leg was taken as he had excruciating pain and was unable to bear any weight on it. The X-ray clearly revealed that his thigh bone was broken into two and the two pieces were slightly displaced. Krishanrao's doctor decided to perform a surgery on him the next day. From the moment the accident occurred, he earnestly kept praying to Baba, as Baba was his sole refuge. Furthermore, for the past 8 years, Kishanrao had been walking to Shirdi along with the *palkhi*. And the *palkhi* was to leave a month later. He worried how he would be able to walk with a fractured bone.

The next day the doctor gave him an anaesthetic injection and he was wheeled into the Operating Theatre. Kishanrao had a reaction to the anaesthesia and his entire body was drenched in perspiration. The doctor saw this and decided to defer the surgery, and so he was brought back to his room. The doctor told him that they would put his foot in traction and attach a weight to it. They told him that he would be immobilised for some time, but they failed to tell him for how long.

Thus two days went by, but Kishanrao was restless. He was eager to go home and make arrangements for the *palkhi*. His friends came to visit him and told him about all the preparations that were taking place for Baba's *palkhi*. Kishanrao couldn't help but think of the *palkhi*, and was exceedingly keen to join them. But he was haunted by the thought, could he walk with a bone that was broken into two? He wondered how the fracture would heal in such a short duration for him to walk along with the *palkhi*.

Thinking over the turn of events he fell asleep. Early in the morning, around 5 a.m., he dreamt of Baba. Baba had on a white *kafni*, and was standing calmly in front of him. Kishanrao was overwhelmed with love, and he joined his hands together in salutation. Emphatically Baba said, "Arre! Don't you want to walk in the *palkhi*? Come on, get up and start walking." Kishanrao heard Baba's command and got up with a start. He didn't give it a second thought, all he knew was that he had to follow Baba's orders. Kinshanrao's leg was in traction with a weight of about 30 kilograms attached to it. Despite the weight, he started walking, and walked up to the main gate of the hospital. The doctor and nurse came running to him aghast, and said, "You have fractured a major bone in your leg. How on earth did you walk so far?"

Kishanrao didn't hear a word of what they were saying, as Baba's words rang in his ears. All he knew was that Baba wanted him to walk to Shirdi and that Baba would take care of him. In utter consternation the doctor asked the nurse to remove the weight from his leg. Angrily the doctor told him that it was now totally his responsibility – he would have to bear the consequences of his rash action – and allowed him to leave.

Happily Krishanrao returned home, and participated in all the activities of organising Baba's *palkhi*. Subsequently he walked from Satara to Shirdi without difficulty. Surprisingly, he required no treatment on the way nor did anybody help him to walk. It is a medical mystery and marvel as to how his bone healed! It was all Baba's work. Thereafter Kishanrao has been walking yearly to Shirdi without any problems. So he claims that the basic elements that the human body is made of are like clay in Baba's hands!

Ref.: *Shri Sai Sagar Magazine*, Deepavali issue, Volume 8, No. 3, October–December 2008.

70

Baba Calls Nithu's Family
to Shirdi – I

The next two *leelas* are about Nithu P. Bhosle and her family.

The 22nd of March 2012 dawned bright and clear, and Nithu P. Bhosle was excited as she was taking her parents on a pilgrimage to Shirdi. Nithu had visited Shirdi several times, but it was the first visit for her parents, and there was a special reason for it. Over the past year her father had been very ill, and she had vowed that she would visit Shirdi along with her parents as soon as he recovered. Her father was suffering from hypertension and both his feet were swollen considerably. Her father Pandurang was taking the medications prescribed by their family physician, but to no avail. The swelling of his feet persisted and along with that he became exceedingly restless and irritable. Pandurang's doctor referred him to a cardiologist, who conducted a series of tests and a cardiac profile on him. Thus he was admitted into a hospital that had all the modern facilities. Nithu and her mother went with him and got him admitted there. Yet, Nithu was terribly concerned and frightened. Her mind was overwhelmed with doubts and questions. What will be the outcome of his investigations? What could be the reason for his swollen feet? Did he have a serious heart problem?

Nithu had unflinching faith in Baba and she vowed that if her father's tests revealed no serious disease, she would take her parents on a pilgrimage to Shirdi. Luckily for her, Baba answered all her prayers and now all that was left was for her to fulfil her vow. She soon realised that this was easier said than done. Whenever Nithu suggested some date or the other for their visit to Shirdi, her father would refuse right

179

away, and her mother was adamant that she wouldn't go to Shirdi unless her elder sister got married. Now she was in a dilemma as to how and when she would be able to fulfil her vow. Furthermore, Pandurang's swollen feet showed no signs of receding or improving. On the contrary, his feet seemed to swell even more, even though his tests were negative. Nithu continued her prayers for she knew only Baba could resolve this problem.

One night her mother dreamt of Baba. In the dream Baba hastily came to her and handed her a vessel containing some green substance. The substance was of a semi-sold consistency, like cream. Her mother inquired, "Shall I give this to Nithu?" Baba said, "No," and her mother awoke. That morning she excitedly narrated the dream to everyone. Now Nithu wondered what that green stuff could be. Possibly Baba had brought some paste that had to be applied by her father.

"Why don't you ask Baba what it is?" said Nithu. That night Nithu's mother again dreamt of Baba; whereupon Baba said, "That vessel had the leaves of my Neem tree. I want you to collect abundant Neem leaves, grind them into a paste, and put some of my *Udi* in it. Then apply that paste on your husband's lower extremities. His swelling will disappear."

Unhesitatingly Nithu did just that, as Baba's words were never untrue. Sure enough the swelling rapidly reduced and finally disappeared, and even his hypertension started reverting to normal. Now the question of visiting Shirdi and fulfilling her vow arose. Nithu suggested that they go during her vacation in May. However her mother was adamant that she would go only after her eldest daughter got married. Nithu wondered when she would be able to fulfil her vow. Baba resolved her dilemma by appearing in her mother's dream again. He smiled at her and said, "Shirdi welcomes you. Come to Shirdi immediately." Thus in 2012 they finally visited Shirdi.

Ref.: *Shri Sai Sagar Magazine*, Volume 3, No. 4, January–March 2013.

71

Baba Calls Nithu's family to Shirdi ~ II

Every human being enters into this world with a balance sheet, especially when it comes to spiritual awareness. We have no knowledge of what karmas we have done in our previous lives, or what our destiny is. Yet we glibly say, "Oh! But Baba has a soft corner for you, and appears in your dreams all the time." The fact is, Baba has equality of vision.

Nithu and her parents set out for Shirdi, and as Baba had appeared in her dream and asked her to come to Shirdi, they knew that their pilgrimage would be successful. The morning prior to leaving Pune, Nithu found two fragrant jasmine flowers in her garden. She plucked them immediately and put them in a plastic container, so that she could offer them to Baba. They went from home to the Shivaji Nagar Bus Station, and caught the bus without difficulty. Nithu was thrilled to see a picture of Baba in the bus and said, "Thank you Baba for coming with us." They easily found vacant seats and during the journey Nithu frequently opened the small plastic container to see if the flowers had wilted. They had hoped to reach prior to the noon *arati*, however this was not to be. They reached Shirdi around 1 p.m. and her mother bought a shawl and a platter of offerings, entered the temple complex, and stood in the queue. There was a milling crowd around them, and the queue seemed never-ending. They stood in the queue for three hours and finally her mother asked the inevitable question: "When will we reach the Samadhi Mandir? Baba has called us to Shirdi, now how will Baba see us in this crowd?"

But when Baba calls he definitely takes care of everything. Finally the queue moved ahead and they reached the entrance of the Samadhi Mandir. There the queue split into two—on the right the queue had *darshan* and exited the temple. However on the left the queue got a chance to go to the front of Baba's Samadhi and exit. Immediately her mother said, "Let us go in the queue on the left side so we can stand in front of Baba." They did so, and they ultimately stood in front of the Samadhi.

Her mother handed the shawl to the priest and asked him to lay it on the Samadhi and unhurriedly he did that and returned it to her. Then he received her platter and returned it with a garland of *Tulsi* that lay at Baba's feet. Then the priest said, "Mother, when you come again bring your son-in-law along with you." Her mother was thrilled and was sure that Baba had answered her prayers through that priest. Nithu gave the priest the jasmine flowers that she had carefully brought along and he placed them on Baba's feet. She also gave a packet of money that she had kept in a plastic bag, which was an offering to Baba upon completion of her *parayan*, and various rituals. He touched it to Baba's feet and returned it to her. Nithu felt happy that Baba had accepted her *parayan* and rituals, and she put it in the collection box. After looking at Baba to their heart's content and praying, they exited the temple.

Nithu and her parents then visited all the holy sites in Shirdi and finally at 5 p.m. they caught the bus and returned home. That night Nithu's mother again dreamt of Baba. He smiled at her and said, "I have been waiting for so long to see you in my Shirdi. Don't worry, I am right there near your home. I wait to get a whiff of the jasmines in your home. And did you get the answer to your question?"

With this Baba disappeared. The next morning Nithu's mother joyfully narrated her dream to everyone. Nithu on the other hand was content that she was able to fulfil her vow successfully. Then her thoughts turned to the jasmine flowers and how lucky they were to lie at Baba's feet, and envelope his feet in their aroma.

Ref.: *Shri Sai Sagar Magazine*, Volume 3, No. 4, January–March 2013.

72

Baba's Udi Cures Mr. Kulkarni's Eczema

This *leela* was narrated by Rekha Kulkarni. However, she has not mentioned the first names of her parents or her brother. Hence they will be referred to as Mr. and Mrs. Kulkarni.

Rekha Kulkarni's mother grew up in a very spiritual environment and had deep reverence towards all ascetics and saints. She bowed to them whether they were Hindu or Muslim. It was Mrs. Kulkarni's firm belief that the saints and ascetics had no caste or religion, as they came to spread universal love, and love had no caste or religion. On the other hand her father, though he performed ritualistic worship of the various Gods and Goddesses, didn't believe in ascetics and saints. Neither did he have any faith in *Udi* or *Vibhuti* and considered it as mere ash.

Once Mr. Kulkarni had a small boil on his foot, and he didn't pay any attention to it. A few days later a few more boils appeared, and they started spreading. Now he got concerned, and got it checked. The doctor examined him and told him that it was eczema, and gave him the necessary ointment and medications. Despite the treatment the eczema continued to spread, so the case was transferred to a senior doctor in the Railway Hospital, and he started treating it. Again there was no improvement; rather it got worse with every passing day. Soon the lesions had spread up to his knee, and a watery fluid started oozing out from it. Mr. Kulkarni's foot became very painful, so he again went to the doctor. After checking his foot the doctor informed him that now his case had become serious and was out of his control, so Mr. Kulkarni had better go to Mumbai and get it treated there. Mr. Kulkarni was in turmoil as going to Mumbai meant taking his wife and children along with him.

The next day, Rekha's elder brother, whom she called Dada, informed his teacher that he would be unable to attend school for a long time. The teacher sat him down and inquired about the reason for his missing school. Dada told him about his father's ill health. The teacher went into his prayer room, and gave him a packet of *Udi* and said, "This Sai Baba's *Udi*. Take Baba's name and apply some of it on your father's lesions, and give him some *Udi* mixed in water, orally. Also, make a vow that when your father recovers fully, you will send 5 rupees to Shirdi and all of you will visit Shirdi." Dada brought the *Udi* home and told his mother everything his teacher had said. Mr. Kulkarni heard the entire conversation and said, "When the doctors and specialists couldn't successfully treat the eczema, how on earth will the ash given by some Baba heal it? Don't apply that ash on my lesions. Keep it with you."

Mrs. Kulkarni patiently told him about Baba's divine *leelas*, and asked him not to scoff at Baba's divinity. However, Mr. Kulkarni was unconvinced, and forbade her from applying the *Udi*. Mrs. Kulkarni knew it was futile trying to convince him, so she sat quietly at the bedside. When her husband fell asleep, she stealthy applied some *Udi* on his eczema. Then Mrs. Kulkarni went into the prayer room and prayed to Baba to forgive her husband and to have compassion on him, and heal his foot. A while later Mr. Kulkarni called his wife and asked her to change the sheet as it was wet. Mrs. Kulkarni noticed that a large quantity of water had oozed out of the eczema, and the swelling of his foot had noticeably reduced. Along with the reduction of the swelling, the throbbing pain in his foot had also reduced. As a result Mr. Kulkarni was able to sleep peacefully after a very long time, without groaning.

Mrs. Kulkarni seized the moment and every time her husband slept she applied more *Udi* on the lesions. Thus the entire night the fluid kept oozing out of the eczema. Early next morning, after a restful night, Mr. Kulkarni got up and looked at his foot. In utter amazement he asked his wife what medicine she had applied on it. Mrs. Kulkarni said, "The *Udi* of that saint Sai Baba that you forbade me to apply." Then her husband asked to get some more *Udi* and he rubbed some on his forehead, and took some internally. The "*Udi* treatment" was continued daily for a week. On the 7th day the lesions disappeared completely, and the eczema healed. Thereafter only a dark patch of pigmentation remained.

A few days later Mr. Kulkarni met his physician, who was astonished to see his foot. He wanted to know which doctor had treated him and what medicines had he prescribed. Then Mr. Kulkarni told him that the doctor was none other than the saint named Sai Baba and the treatment was the panacea for all ills—Baba's *Udi*. Thereafter he became an ardent devotee and visited Shirdi. It is said that eczema is never totally cured or eradicated; however, due to the power of Baba's *Udi*, Kulkarni never had a recurrence of the disease again.

Ref.: *Shri Sai Leela Magazine*, Volume 59, No. 8–9, September 1985

73

How Baba Saved Ravenkar's Life

One particular day is etched in Shashikala's memory as the night Baba blew life into her husband. Whenever she remembers that terrifying night, her hair stands on end even to this day and she prays that no one, be it friend or foe, should ever have to face such a dreadful experience.

Shashikala's heart was steeped in *Shraddha* and *Saburi* and no power on earth could shake it. Because of her intense faith in Baba she bravely faced every adversity in life with a smile. Shashikala also always extended a helping hand to the less fortunate and wiped the tears from the eyes of friends who were in trouble. This is the *leela* of how Baba brought her husband back from the jaws of death.

Around 1984, Shashikala was going through the toughest patch in her life. At every turn there was some problematic situation waiting with open arms for her and her husband. She wondered if she would ever be able to come out of this quagmire.

Finally Shashikala decided to go to Ambarnath and stay with her aunt. Hardly a week had passed when this frightful incident happened. One night all the male members of the family were having dinner in the kitchen, so Shashikala went and sat in the open courtyard. A short while later she went to the bathroom that was a short distance away, when suddenly a black devilish form appeared and jumped on her. Frightened out of her wits she screamed "Sai," and that evil spirit vanished.

Hearing her scream, all the men rushed to see what had happened, but they couldn't see anything unusual. However Shashikala went into shock and couldn't speak, and she had no memory of this. The next day was *Amavasya* (new moon day) and only Shashikala and her husband Ravenkar were at home. Around 7 p.m. Shashikala was in the kitchen preparing dinner. Her husband was sleeping next to the prayer altar. Suddenly, she was overcome by fear, and she didn't know why. She glanced at the window and saw a black devilish form stealthily climbing the window and trying to enter the kitchen. She yelled, "Baba, help me!" and the evil spirit disappeared, and she was thrown on her sleeping husband. Immediately her husband asked her what had happened; but she was struck dumb with fright. All she could do was point to the window. Her husband applied *Udi* on her forehead at once. Later she told him about the terrifying scene that she had seen. With Baba's grace she regained her composure, and the terrifying event had no untoward effect on her.

The next day was a Thursday and Shashikala as usual conducted Baba's *arati* and offered him some fruits. Around 10 p.m. she and her husband went to sleep. Her aunt was awake till 11 p.m. and then she retired for the night. Shashikala hadn't fallen asleep at that time, and she heard her husband groaning in his sleep and saying, "*Ayi! Ayi!*" Shashikala thought maybe he was having a bad dream, so she didn't get up. As this groaning continued for about five to ten minutes, her aunt got up and tried to wake him. Ravenkar was motionless, and he didn't respond to them. Then her aunt sprinkled some cold water on his face but to no avail. Shashikala immediately got some *Udi* and rubbed it on his forehead and mixed it in water and tried to administer it to him. The *Udi* mixture came out of his mouth, his eyes remained closed, and his head fell off the pillow. Desperately Shashikala shook him vigorously but his body had become stiff and cold like a dead body, and he had no heart beat. Both she and her aunt kept screaming and trying to wake Ravenkar.

A lot of people gathered there and everyone tried in their own way to wake him up. This continued for about half an hour. Shashikala kept weeping and calling out to Sai. Finally she went and fetched the picture of Baba in his blessing posture and kept it next to her husband's pillow. Pitifully she cried, "Baba please don't make me a widow. Grant me the gift of my husband's life, only you can do this. Thus far I have uncomplainingly borne whatever trouble life threw at me, with *Saburi*. But now I have no time for *Saburi*. If you cannot grant my husband's life then take me along with him. If that is not possible, you will be maligned, as I have never doubted you, nor has my faith in you ever wavered. Baba thus far so many people have laughed at my faith in you, but I have defended it and continued praying to you. Now it is up to you to grant me my married life again."

Saying this, Shashikala took some *Udi* and forcefully rubbed it on Ravenkar's chest. Simultaneously her aunt took a few pods of garlic and chewed them and started blowing air near his nose. Slowly Ravenkar opened his eyes and sat up. Loudly he cried out, "Look! Those fiendish black guys were dragging me far away but after taking me some distance they shouted loudly and fled because an old man with a white beard appeared from nowhere, and threatened them. Then he gently carried me and brought me here."

Hearing this, everyone was thrilled. Shashikala's happiness knew no bounds, and she felt as if she had conquered the world. Silently she thanked Baba for his ultimate kindness, as she knew that nothing was impossible with Baba.

Ref.: *Shri Sai Leela Magazine*, Volume 59, No. 8–9, September 1985

74

The Sanctuary of Baba's Feet

A devotee named Neena P. Salvi resided in Vasai, Mumbai. Once she had developed Septicemia and was admitted to a hospital in a critical condition. Her condition worsened by the hour and she was hovering at death's door. Soon she became semi-comatose despite the best possible treatment. At that point, she had a dream of Baba.

Neena found herself in the Samadhi Mandir of Shirdi. In place of Baba's idol, Neena saw Baba himself. She saw herself climb on top of the Samadhi and place her head on Baba's feet and fall fast asleep at his feet. At this, Baba shook her forcefully and said sternly, "Neena listen to me carefully. No matter what happens, don't let go of my feet. Clutch on to them with all your might." After a while a humongous python slithered over her body. Even in that semi-comatose state Neena felt the cold touch of the snake as it slithered over her body, from the top to her toes. Although she was frightened out of her wits, she held on to Baba's feet tightly and kept screaming, "Sainath, Sainath, save me!" from the bottom of her heart.

Neena recalls that dreadful day, saying, "What would you call this nightmare of mine? The snake that slithered over my body, was it death? However I know one thing for certain and that whenever I have called out to Sainath for help, he has always come running and I am reminded of His promise.

Nithya mee jeevantha jaana haechi sathya
Nithya ghyia pracheeta anubhavae

Roughly translated it means, 'I am immortal know this truth. And forever get experiences of my immortality'. I always thank my Sainath for the gift of life that he has granted me. I always request him to enable me to use it in his service and help me to remain at his feet till the end of my life."

Neena's father, Naryan Tukaram Gavand, was ardently devoted to Baba. Because of him she and her family also became devotees. Every year during *Shravan* (holy month) Narayan would do the *parayan* of the *Shri Sai Satcharita* in his home; and during those 7 days while he would read the *Charitra*, the room was pervaded with the smell of smoke, burning tobacco. Then everyone would be aware of Baba's presence in the room as if smoking his chillum.

In Chapter 3, Ovi 12, of *Shri Sai Satcharita*, Dabolkar states, **Muge jo gayiene vadekode. Maje Charitra, maje pavada. Thyicheya me mage pude, choekhede ubhache**.

It means: "He who fondly sings my praises, or narrates the story of my life, in any which way or in any manner, will always find me standing in front of him, or behind him, and everywhere around him."

How true are Baba's words; that even in this day and age he comes to hear his *Charita* being read, and then gives proof of his presence.

Ref.: *Shri Sai Leela Magazine*, Volume 66, No. 8–9. November and December 1987.

75

Narhari Meets Baba

This is the story of a fortunate adolescent who by providence stayed with Baba for 21 days. His destiny had been unenviable and wretched and Baba acted against his inherent nature and changed it. This adolescent was Narhari Vasudev Raikar, who witnessed a mind boggling scene of death and heard Baba talking about the future of the human civilization and what a sorry state it would become from 1978 onwards. Baba predicted to him many facets of life that we now often experience in the "Kali Yuga" (the age of the demon Kali, or the age of vice). The life story is exceedingly long so it has been described as several *leela*s.

On a Monday of December 1912, Narhari Vasudev Raikar, aged 16 years, decided to visit Shirdi and seek refuge at Baba's feet as he was fed up of his wretched life. He took the long arduous journey from Mumbai, alone, and finally reached Shirdi at about 4 p.m.

The village was very rustic, and the dirt road was full of holes and pits. There was litter scattered everywhere. Narhari saw a village woman coming from the opposite direction and he asked her where he would find Baba. She silently pointed the direction to him. He walked ahead and came upon a hut where a woman was standing, who Narhari asked for a drink of water. In a very kind and caring way she asked Narhari, "Baba, where have you come from?" Narhari replied that he had come from Mumbai to meet Baba. Surprised she asked him to sit down and hurriedly brought him a plate filled with peanuts and small bits of jaggery, along with a glass filled with water. She then requested him to eat it while she sat in front of him asking Narhari about his life in Mumbai.

Narhari replied, "I am an orphan and I can't remember when

my parents passed away. My uncle who works in a textile mill took me home. My uncle would frequently visit Dabolkar's house and I often accompanied him. There I heard about Baba's Godliness, so I decided to ask Him to help me. My uncle remarried, my step-aunt had two children and she disliked the very sight of me. She made me work from morning till late at night, gave me leftovers to eat, and very little of it. Then she said I was a burden on the family as I ate food for free. This hurt me a great deal, so I decided to ask Baba what the future held for me, take his blessings, and start living on my own. With only 3 annas in my pocket I dared to come to Shirdi."

That kind lady said, "Arre! My child, hearing your story I feel very bad. May God bless you with a great future! In the evening come to my house for dinner. I am a poor woman but I will definitely feed you whatever I have. You can sleep on the platform in front of my home." Narhari's eyes filled with tears as he heard this. He couldn't help but compare the difference in behaviour between this unknown lady and his own aunt!

Narhari then went to the Dwarka Mai, where he saw a man sleeping with his face towards the wall. He was wearing a dirty, torn white *kafni* which was hardly white any longer. A dirty white cloth was tied around his head and he was about 6 ft tall; lean but fit and strong. Now Narhari had to wait for him to get up, so he sat on the steps and waited. Half an hour later, he woke up and said, "Abdulla, give me some water."

Narhari immediately stood up and as no one was around, he fetched him some water from a bucket kept nearby. He kept the water in front of him. That man was murmuring something, and looked at Narhari and asked, "Who are you?" Narhari said he had come from Mumbai to meet Sai Baba. And where could he be found? The man replied, "You ass, who do you see in front of you?" Hurriedly Narhari placed his head on Baba's feet.

This was what happened when Narhari first came to Shirdi and met Shri Sai Baba.

Ref.: *Tey Soneri 21 Divas*, written by Narhari Vasudev Raikar.

76

Narhari's Stay in Shirdi: The First 8 Days

Baba kept Narhari by his side for the 3 weeks of his stay in Shirdi. He got to see this incomprehensible scene on the 5th day of his stay in the Dwarka Mai. This is how Narhari recalls it:

That entire day Baba was very restless, and that night I saw a terrifying scene with my own eyes. Baba was in the Dwarka Mai till darkness fell. At first he asked everyone to go home. Then he asked Abdulla to leave and sternly said, "Today nobody should stay here, or come here during the night. Tomorrow you may come but only after sunrise." Next, he turned to me and said, "You sleep right here." Hearing this, the rest of the devotees glowered at me, and left reluctantly. After that, Baba made me sit near him and gave me some milk to drink.

Finally, he asked me to go to sleep. However, he categorically said, "Now listen to me carefully. Don't be the least bit afraid. Whatever you may see, you are not to get up. Lie quietly and watch. If you get up and stand then you will definitely die. Lie down calmly, don't make any noise or scream. Whatever comes, in whatever form, you are not to get up from your bed. Just lie still and watch. Is it clear?" Then he asked me to lie on my sack and drew a line by the side of the sack with his *Satka* and the milk from the vessel. Again Baba said, "Follow my instructions and don't move or get up." I lay down quietly, and after a long time I glanced at Baba. Baba was seated next to the wall with the Dhuni Mai in front of him. Next to him was the pot with water in it, and a small bowl of milk and a *rudraksh* rosary. He was calmly seated and chanting the name of Allah. Soon I was sound asleep.

At some time during the night I was awoken by a loud slithering sound. I woke up startled, but my ears were ringing with Baba's admonition so I lay still like a dead person. A humongous black python slithered near my foot, but did not dare to cross the line drawn by Baba next to where I lay. The snake then came and stood next to my face with the upper half of its body raised straight up with its hood spread in an attacking stance. Its hood was huge, about 3 to 4 ft long, and its eyes were like red beads. It kept staring angrily at Baba and trying to strike him, but it dared not because of the Dhuni Mai in front of Baba. In actuality it could have easily bitten Baba from where it was, but it was unable to do so, as much as it tried. I couldn't understand why. Baba was tranquilly seated there, chanting Allah's name. Behind his head I could see a brilliant halo. The halo became even more brilliant and the entire Dwarka Mai was lit up due to its brilliance. The python repeatedly tried to strike Baba, but in vain. Neither could it cross the Dhuni, so it kept thrashing its tail on the ground in frustration. This continued for quite a while.

Finally Baba came out of his meditation and the halo behind his head disappeared. From Baba's eyes a brilliant ray of light emanated and fell on the snake; and from the eyes of the snake a ray of light was emitted and met the ray of light from Baba's eyes about midway. At the meeting point, a beautiful scene was seen; a small miniature form of Baba that looked like a small doll appeared. This doll-like figure slowly moved forward, and engulfed the ray of light from the snake. Then the figure of Baba slowly disappeared into Baba himself. After this the snake slithered over my body and God knows where it went. By then I was shuddering with fright and I wet myself. I felt I was half dead and I don't remember when I fell asleep.

The next morning Baba shook me awake; at that time I was running a high fever. Baba took his *Satka* and tapped my head thrice with it and the fever vanished. He asked me to wash my face, my hands and feet and accompany him. Then Baba briskly walked into the village and I ran behind him. He stopped in front of a house and called out to a person called

Hari, and asked him to give us some tea. After drinking the tea and blessing Hari, we proceeded till we reached an elevated place, which had a tree on it. Right below the tree, the snake from last night's terrifying scene lay dead. Baba with tears in his eyes said, **"Child, there is no better deed in this world than giving your life for someone."**

Then Baba picked up a large stone and started digging a hole with it, I also did the same. Soon a large pit was created and Baba laid the snake in it. He then stood still for some time, then lifted his hands towards the sky and said, "Allah have mercy on this snake." Then he filled the hole with mud and placed a leaf from the tree on top of it. Suddenly a strong wind blew, creating a small whirlwind and both of us were covered with dust. This lasted for about 5 minutes followed by utter calm. I looked at the grave and on it was a heap of *Parijatak* flowers (night flowering jasmine; botanical name: nychanthes arbotristis). Baba then walked briskly back to Shirdi, after sternly warning me not to look back.

Upon reaching the Dwarka Mai, there was a crowd of villagers eager to know what had taken place the previous night. Many of them tried to bribe me with "goodies" hoping I would tell them something. However I said that I had slept soundly through the night. Then they wanted to know where we had gone that morning. Innocently, I said, "For a walk."

On the 8th day of his stay in Shirdi, Narhari heard Baba tell Tatya Kote Patil that he had been given a new life. Now he would live for another five to six years more, so Tatya need not worry. Narhari was puzzled as to why Baba said this, as the snake was unable to cross the Dhuni Mai and bite him. Who was to die that night? For whom did that snake give up his life? Thus Baba predicted his passing away.

He said, "Tatya you don't have to worry, I will be around till 1918. I have this brick with me. It is my life-line so I take good care of it. But if this brick should break I will not survive for long. A person who is born is surely going to die, so why should you grieve about it? God has a unique method of keeping the population at a constant level; this is why human beings die.

The cause of death is varied, some die of hunger, some due to illnesses, others die due to natural calamities like floods. But 80-90 years from now there will be a population explosion and unusual diseases will arrive throughout the world. Massive numbers of people will succumb to these diseases. There will be new diseases in different continents of the world and cure will be difficult to find. Human beings will lose empathy and sympathy towards others and people will be recognised only by the amount of wealth they possess. Dharma will be in great trouble and holy men will face diverse difficulties. Even the Government will have many problems and in the chaos it will be difficult to govern justly. This is going to be the dismal future of mankind."

(Whatever Baba predicted has come true in this day and age. There are diseases like HIV–AIDS, a multitude of new viruses that cause diseases like dengue, chikungunya, swine flu and the recent EBOLA virus.)

Then he told Narhari, "You are fortunate you will never go hungry. You will have a place to sleep and clothes to wear. This is my blessing to you." Thus Baba's blessings came to pass.

Ref.: *Tey Soneri 21 Divas*, written by Narhari Vasudev Raikar.

77

Narhari's Stay in Shirdi: Days 9–18

On the morning of the 9th day, Narhari's stomach was rumbling with hunger. Bayjabai came there with a basket of freshly prepared, hot *bhakri*s. Narhari without brushing his teeth fell upon the bhakri and ate them. Baba said, "Look how hunger makes a person desperate makes him lose his equanimity and presence of mind. He becomes blinded by the gnawing hunger pangs in his stomach. A rational person turns into a devil, and all he thinks of is how to fill his belly. Even if he has to snatch the food from a child's hand, he will not hesitate to do so. In the years to come, man will yearn for money, and he will have no regard for family and loved ones. When it comes to getting money, his actions will put even the devil to shame."

How true Baba's words have been proved today. There is rampant hunger and malnutrition in the world. There are plenty of organisations to relieve "world hunger". In India numerous devotees try to relieve hunger in their own way like contributing to "Sai Roti" and "Sai Bharosa". Other devotees do *Annadaan* in temples and Gurdwaras and feed people of all castes and creeds.

On the 11th day of Narhari Vasudev Raikar's stay in Shirdi with Baba, he was woken at the crack of dawn by Baba, who shook him and said, "Arre! Get up and come with me." Immediately Narhari woke up and followed Baba, who briskly walked to the small Maruti temple which was not far off. There was a peepal tree and under it was an idol of Maruti with ochre paste on it. Baba ordered him to do 11 *pradikshinas* (circumambulations) around it, and Narhari did as he was told. Thereafter Baba asked Narhari to keep a fistful of mud below the parapet and place the lighted lamp that was there on the mud. Next Baba asked him to place the fistful of mud back in its original place.

After that, they returned to the Chavadi and Baba asked him to have a bath. Then they both had tea that a villager had brought. After drinking the tea, Baba asked him not to return till it was evening. He said, "Go and spend the entire day in the village somewhere or the other. In the evening come and meet me in the Dwarka Mai." Narhari went away in accordance with Baba's orders. That evening, when Narhari returned to the Dwarka Mai, Baba called him, took a fistful of ash from the Dhuni Mai and sprinkled it on him, murmuring something the entire while. Then Baba asked Narhari to sit calmly near the Dhuni Mai. After a long period of time, both of them left Dwarka Mai and went to the Chavadi. Finally Baba said, "Now your work has started. Don't worry about anything." Narhari had been concerned about his future and had suspected that there was something in it that was not too good. Thus he felt this was probably Baba's remedy for it. Who can guess what Baba does and why?

On the 18th day of his stay in Shirdi, Baba took him to the place where they had buried the snake. At that time it was late afternoon. On reaching the place, Baba looked at the sky and raising both his hands said, "Oh, Master! Have mercy on this child and throughout his life provide him two square meals a day, and take care of his needs." Then Baba asked Narhari to close his eyes and sit calmly with his eyes shut. A short while later a supernatural phenomenon occurred wherein he felt as if a whirlwind was taking place in his head. Narhari then had the feeling of being shaken. The intensity of this sensation started increasing, and he was scared stiff. Then he felt as if he was being pulled down. The whole episode was eerie and he was exhausted. Narhari couldn't quite comprehend what was happening to him. As he had handed his life and future in Baba's hands, there was nothing more that he could do, so he lay down and went to sleep. It was dark when he finally got up, and he looked around for Baba, but he was nowhere to be found. So he hastily went to the Dwarka Mai and found Baba there. In a pleasant manner Baba spoke to him, saying, "Come, my child. Your life had started improving from today."

Baba had often told Narhari that his destiny was wretched, and what was written in the annals of his life was meagre. It was Baba's pledge that there would be no dearth of food and clothing in his devotee's life. Here was this lad who had come all by himself to Shirdi to seek refuge in him. Now Baba was determined to change it and he did change it, by the *leela* just described.

Ref.: *Tey Soneri 21 Divas*, written by Narhari Vasudev Raikar.

78

Narhari's Stay in Shirdi: Baba's Predictions

The palm that Baba drew   **Dr. Sashikant Javari's palm**

This *leela* is quite mystical and I can hardly find the words to describe it, because Baba predicts many things there.

On the 19th day of Narhari's stay with Baba, this episode took place. That entire day Baba was in a pleasant mood and at night he sent everyone away from the Dwarka Mai. Then he asked Narhari to go to sleep, and only get up when he asked him to. Sometimes during the night Baba woke Narhari and asked him to listen to him with utmost attention. Baba took a heap of *Udi* from his Dhuni and spread it in front of him, and drew a picture of a hand on it, with some line. Unequivocally Baba spoke, "This is the imprint of the right palm of a person. There are lines that form a fish next to the mount of Venus, that is, the fleshy portion at the base of the thumb. A straight line goes from it to the web between the index finger and the middle finger. Did you understand what I just showed you?"

Narhari shook his head negatively. Baba admonished him, and explained it again. "You ass, this is the identity of that person. So look at it carefully and keep rehearsing it in your mind till it becomes a part of you. This person is a friend of mine, and he will meet you when you are about to die. My friend will meet you in a hospital which is near an ocean. After checking his hand thoroughly, give him what I am going to give you now, without fail. Don't forget. Now listen to me carefully and attentively. This young man does not believe in God or the Supreme, so he will not be convinced by what you say. So tell him that he will be involved in a fight on the third day from that date and on the 4th day he will miss his lunch and remain hungry till night fall. If these two conditions are fulfilled, then give him what I will give you now."

In this manner Baba predicted Narhari's death and his own passing away or Maha Samadhi, and this is given below. It is exceedingly difficult for me to write this part of the story; and how it all finally came to pass, hence I will write it in Baba's words as he spoke, to the best of my ability. I hope the readers will forgive me.

Baba continued, "This boy will be born 20 years after I leave my mortal body. On his right palm you will see the lines that I showed you, this is his identification. He will meet you just prior to your death, and will perform your last rites. The last rites are very important because when a person dies, he is relieved of his burden of sorrows; and passes on to a period of happiness. He is very pure at that time because he takes nothing with him from this life. Even his body is burned to ashes, and even that is left here.

Hereafter, you are going to practise palmistry, and you will attain knowledge of it. You will gain only that much of knowledge that will enable you to get food and clothes till the day you die. This is because of my blessings; you will never go hungry."

Baba embraced Narhari and held him close to his heart, and stroked his head, and asked him to sit calmly for a while. Hurriedly Baba went off somewhere and returned after some time. He washed his feet and started circumambulating Dhuni Mai, for a total of 7 times. Then he tore the cloth that he had tied around his head into two, and laid it on a heap of *Udi*.

Thereafter he stood on the cloth for a short while. Thus an imprint of the soles of his feet got etched on it. He neatly folded it and enclosed it in the other piece of his *Sirvesh* (cloth tied around his head). He tied it securely and handed it to Narhari, who was to give it to that young man whom Baba called his dear friend.

Baba asked Narhari to tell that young man that Baba wanted him to prepare two sets of his *padukas* from that imprint. One set was for his devotees to have *darshan* of, while the other set was for *Abhishek* (holy bath). "These *padukas* will uplift my devotees, and fulfil their desires. According to their faith and the good deeds of their past lives they will be benefitted exponentially. The *tirth* (holy water) from the *abhishek* of my *padukas* is ambrosia; it will relieve unusual diseases, infertility, difficult labour and deliveries, and sanctify any place."

Then Baba said a mantra in Narhari's left ear and asked him to say it in the right ear of that young man. "This mantra should be conscientiously recited, once only at 1 a.m. at night for a period of 30 years. Only upon the completion of recitation of this mantra for 30 years, my *padukas* will be sanctified and will be 'alive' and potent. Thereafter they can be used for the benefit of my devotees. In that day and age civilization and society will be at its lowest. People will be measured by the wealth, that is money that they possess, and not by their humane qualities. There will be a population explosion and people will be like ants. People will not have empathy towards each other, and only 'money will talk'. Human beings will be recognised by the amount of money they possess, so to reassure my devotees, my *padukas* will be there as their refuge. Thus when the time is right give this bundle to my friend, he will definitely follow through, I assure you, as I am positive that he will. Narhari remember this well, do not ever repeat this mantra before anyone or tell anyone about it. While you are with me in Shirdi you will remember it, but once you leave here it will fade away. However, when you have to speak it in his right ear it will come back in your memory, and you will speak it clearly."

By early next morning, Narhari couldn't remember a word of

the mantra. Time was drawing near for Narhari to bid farewell to Baba, as Baba had decided that he would leave on the 21st day. On the 20th day Narhari tried in vain to remember the mantra. Then Baba made him sit close to him and said, "I told you that you will forget the mantra till the appropriate time. This is God's wish, don't worry about it. Let God do his work; this is his divine play, and we are unable to understand it. We are servants of God, and if we live the way he has planned it, we will be happy. We are all beggars as we ask him for numerous things. However, he knows what to give to whom, when to give it, and how much to give. I go for *bhiksha* every day and will do so till I pass away. This is to show devotees where they stand and how they stand in this drama of life. But if they help the less fortunate, and render some service to the downtrodden, this is true devotion to God. To wipe other people's tears, to talk to them lovingly, this is true service for the Guru. This is what my Guru taught me and this was the key to his treasury that he gave to me. And that I am handing over to you, this is a mantra for life."

On the last day, that is the 21st day, Narhari was exceedingly sad to leave Baba. Then Baba hugged him and said, "There always is happiness and sorrow in the journey of life. Whatever difficult situation you are faced with, if you tackle it calmly with courage you will overcome it. Keeping *Shraddha* and *Saburi* by your side, think over the situation or incident, and then you will definitely choose the right path. This is how every devotee of mine should live in this world and I want you to tell every devotee you meet, as this is the teaching of my Guru: that is, *Shraddha* and *Saburi*."

Narhari had to leave Shirdi that day as Baba had asked him to. There was a *tonga* waiting for the devotees going to Kopergaon. Baba brought him to the *tonga* and asked him to sit in it. Just prior to that Baba placed his hand on Narhari's head, caressed his face and blessed him. Baba also gave him 16 rupees and said, "Keep this Lakshmi with you and you will not lack food and money for expenditure."

And there ended Narhari's 21 golden days with Baba. Five

years later, Baba took Maha Samadhi, and Narhari was unable to visit Shirdi during that time. Narhari talked to everyone about *Shraddha* and *Saburi* and how to live life, as that is what Baba told him on the last day of his stay. Thereafter many people came to meet him and brought clothes, food items, groceries and fruits. Narhari felt awkward about it but this was Baba's blessing and he accepted it graciously

Ref.: *Tey Soneri 21 Divas*, written by Narhari Vasudev Raikar.

79

Baba's Predictions Come True

Dr. Sashikant G. Javeri

Years rolled by and in March 1961, Narhari V. Raikar was admitted in KEM Hospital Mumbai, for a stomach ailment. Dr. Sashikant G. Javeri worked in that hospital under Dr. B.N. Purandare. It was customary for Javeri and his friends to meet in the evening in the ward of whichever colleague was free at that time. They would sit and chat and one day, his friends told him that a patient named Raikar was an expert palmist and his predictions were faultless. One of his friends introduced Javeri to Raikar. Javeri liked Raikar who was simple and gentle and had the unusual quality of making one feel like an old friend. One evening, "just for the fun of it" Javeri decided to have his palm read, although he didn't believe in palmistry or in God for that matter and stayed away from all that.

Raikar looked at his palm for an unusually long time. From an old bag he took out a magnifying lens and looked at it again with a great deal of concentration. Then he exclaimed, "You are the one. O Lord Sainath, your doings are incomprehensible! O, at last I have met your friend!" Javeri didn't quite know why he said all this. Then Raikar took out an old diary of his and showed him a sketch of his palm that he had made in 1912. Now Javeri was utterly confused, but he vehemently opposed it by stating it was just a coincidence.

Then Raikar told Javeri that he must have been born in 1938 and said, "Baba had told me that you will be born 20 years after his Maha Samadhi." Javeri was puzzled and he left, thinking, "For heaven sakes, which Baba? What have I to do with any Baba? I had better put an end to all this gibberish." However his mind wouldn't let him be at peace.

The next day was Sunday and that evening he was free, so he went and sat with Raikar. Raikar smiled and said, "So your restless mind didn't allow you to sit quietly. I know you don't believe a word of what I said and now you have come to have a little fun, right?" Javeri just nodded his head in consent. Raikar continued, "Three days from today you will be involved in a fight. And the next day you will miss your lunch and be hungry till nightfall. If you cannot prevent these two events then you will follow Shri Sai Baba's orders. Do you agree to this?" Javeri agreed, thinking that all this was in jest, not knowing that he was being drawn into this drama by a superior force. Then Raikar asked him to promise that he would do as Baba had ordered, and he agreed.

Three days after Javeri promised Raikar, he and his friends were returning home to Shivadila. At that time he and five of his friends stayed at the residence of his friend's relative. It was around 12 noon and they caught a bus to return home. The bus was relatively empty, when a young lady with a small child came and sat in the seat in front of him. The lady bought her ticket; however her naughty child while playing with it, threw it out of the open window. At the next stop the Checker came to check the tickets, and Javeri and his friends showed him their tickets. Then the Checker asked the young lady for her ticket and she told him what had happened. Javeri and his friends also testified to it. He didn't say anything and left. However, the conductor of the bus came and shouted at her, using abusive language. At this, Javeri and his friends intervened and a terrible fight ensued. Finally they took the bus to the police station. Thus Baba's first prediction came true, and Javeri lost his peace of mind.

On the 4th day, Javeri and his friends went home around 2 p.m. to have lunch. To save money, he and his friends would order one meal and three of them would eat it. With the money they saved, they would go to see a movie. At that time they stayed in a Municipal Chawl (high rise building) that was adjacent to the main road. That day the pavement in front of their building was not crowded, so they put a cot on the pavement under a tin shed and started eating their lunch. Happily Jhaveri put the first morsel of food in his mouth, smugly thinking, "This part of the deal is untrue and so is all this palmistry."

In his building there were a lot of residents from Goa, and they had shops adjacent to the pavement. One Goan lady came running and said, "Doc come quickly this young man is behaving strangely and he needs your help." Immediately, they all left and ran to help. A young man around 20 years of age was frothing from his mouth and having a seizure. They immediately got a cab and took the young man to the hospital, where they admitted him and attended to him. The patient's condition took a serious turn and finally he breathed his last. By that time it was night and they were unable to have their lunch.

Now the doctor was in a quandary and had to admit defeat. That night he couldn't sleep a wink as there was a whirlwind of thoughts in his mind. "Who was this Sai Baba? How could he know the lines on his palm 20 years prior to his birth? How could he predict events that were to happen after his Maha Samadhi? How could he assure Raikar in 1912 that these two events would take place at this time? How did he know when I would be born?" Finally, Javeri had to bow down to this supreme power who had such infinite knowledge of the future.

The next day Javeri quietly went and stood before Raikar, and told him that everything he predicted was true. Thereafter he spent every spare moment with Raikar. Every night after Javeri completed his work he would sit with Raikar and ask him about Baba, and Raikar would tell him about Baba's divinity. One day, Raikar asked him to bring his trunk down from the shelf and gave him a small bundle. Raikar said, "I will pass away very soon and after I die, open this bundle and make two sets of *padukas* from the imprint in the bundle. One should be made of stone and the other of brass. After I die make a bundle of everything that I have and cremate it along with me." A short while later Raikar did indeed pass away and Javeri followed his instructions and immersed his ashes in Nasik.

After Raikar died, Javeri opened the bundle and in it he found an extremely old black cloth upon which was an even blacker imprint of the soles of Baba's feet. Javeri then got the *padukas* made and brought them home. He kept the black cloth over the *padukas*, lighted some incense sticks and closed his eyes and said the mantra that Baba had given him. When he opened his eyes, the cloth was nowhere to be found, although he searched for it everywhere. Finally he realised that the cloth had finally gone home; or the cloth had got immersed into the feet of the Lord. Thereafter, for the next 36 years, Javeri faithfully got up at 1 a.m. every night and said the mantra that Baba had given him and then went to sleep. Javeri didn't quite know why he should go to sleep immediately after saying the mantra, but he followed his Guru's command.

As this *leela* is very long it shall be continued in the next chapter.

Ref.: *Tey Soneri 21 Divas*, written by Narhari Vasudev Raikar.

80

Dr. Javeri and Baba's Magical Padukas

Dr. Javeri's mind was troubled by the thought of Guru *dakshina*. He decided that the best *dakshina* was to help the suffering humanity, as service to mankind was service to God, and Baba would have liked it. So for the next 30 years he did research and found a drug in Ayurveda that could bring relief to asthmatic patients. Thereafter he has treated more than 7000 patients successfully.

Even today, Dr. Javeri attends to patients and lives in Pune. Baba has blessed him abundantly, and so has Raikar. Every patient who is relieved of his breathing problems blesses him from the bottom of his heart. Thus he is living a peaceful and contented life. Dr. Javeri feels that God, the Supreme or Allah, or whatever name he is referred to by, is that supreme energy that makes this universe work. Thus one should have faith in the universe, as it bestows its bounty on everyone. Regardless of who the person is, it impartially gives sunlight, air to breathe, and rain for plants to grow and yield food, hence it is the biggest benefactor.

Thus, every devotee should have *Shraddha* and *Saburi*, little expectation, and minimise their needs; then they will lead a happy and contented life. Who is to die and when he will die is in God's hands. How wealthy a person will be, and when he will become wealthy is in the hands of God. Science in this respect is at a loss to predict these things. Devotees should bear this in mind and then their behaviour with each other will be more fruitful.

Dr. Javeri says, "Baba could foresee what awaited mankind in the future, and that was concern with health and wealth.

209

For health Baba said, *'Paav garam, pet naram, dimag thanda, rog ko maro danda.'* Roughly translated, it means 'Keep the feet warm, the abdomen soft, the mind cool, and then whip disease away.' These phrases were told to me by Raikar. To keep the feet warm is to be ever active, take long walks. Do your own chores and work hard; such a devotee will rarely fall ill. Keep the stomach soft, that is, do not to gorge yourself with food, so that your stomach becomes bloated. Have your meals on time and eat two morsels less than your satiety level. Keep your mind cool means be calm and have equanimity in all situations in life. Finally, don't be restless and make hasty decisions, in other words have *Saburi*. He who has *saburi* is always happy. Such a devotee will be able to whip disease away, or will be free of diseases and ill health."

Then Dr. Javeri talks about the two sets of *padukas*. A devotee can perform *abhishek* on the *padukas*, as this will increase his *punya* that is, the merit earned by virtuousness and good karma, and this wealth will keep on increasing.

This is the mantra that Baba gave Dr. Javeri:

Janm, Janmo, Janmi.
Shri, Charan, Shri Bhagya Sai

This mantra is unique, fruitful and encompasses the *pancha maha bhutas*.

Shri: The first life form came out of water, (*Jala*) so *Shri* is the water element.

Charan: Because of the earth (*Prithvi*) we are stable and centred, so this is for the earth element. The word *charan* signifies it.

Shri: This is the fire (*Agni*) element.

Bhagya: Luck or fate like the wind (*Vayu*) keeps changing, so this is for air element.

Sai: Means *Shakshat Ishwar* or the Supreme who encompasses the entire globe like the sky. Hence Sai is lovingly called the sky or *Akash*.

Dr. Javeri says, "The devotee's thoughts (*vichar*) mental makeup (*man*) and intelligence and discretion (*buddhi*) and the *Atman* (Self) all get activated and come together or work in unison. This is achieved by the auspicious energy and sacred vibrations that this mantra produces. This energy is from the *Atman* and reaches the Supreme. Similarly the Cosmic rays from the sky or Sai envelope the devotee reciting this mantra. As a result of this energy some devotees gain *Divya Drishti*. *Drishti* means the ability to see the visible and tangible, the *saguna*. But *Divya Drishti* means the ability to see the invisible and the intangible, the *nirguna*. They could see what no one else could see. Others attained *Divya Shakti* or supernatural power, and yet others gained *Divya Gyana* or deep spiritual knowledge. All these phenomena are achieved slowly and over a period of time. Along with this, many devotees are cured of unusual diseases, and a wretched fate. The devotee's mind, behaviour, and actions change for the better over time, and the devotee is drawn towards the Supreme Being, or Baba. So a devotee should constantly meditate on this unique mantra."

This *leela* gives us a glimpse of how effective the *abhishek* done to the *padukas* is.

This is a true account of Ganga, from Kolhapur.

In December 2004, Ganga, the daughter of Shri Balkrishna Ramchandra Bakre a resident of Kolhapur suddenly fell very ill. That night Ganga was quite alright, she cooked dinner and the family sat together and had the meal, then she did all the household chores and went to sleep. The next morning she awoke as usual at 6 a.m. However, she was unable to move her limbs. Her limbs were flaccid both in her upper and lower extremities. Her father realised the something was terribly wrong with her, and immediately took her to the hospital, where she was admitted in the ICU. After an intensive workup, she was kept there for a week and then discharged with the diagnosis of paralysis. Balkrishna was devastated to hear the diagnosis, and the doctors couldn't tell them if and when she would regain the strength in her paralysed muscles. With this bleak prognosis she was sent home.

Balkrishna then went from one doctor to the next hoping that his daughter would recover, and every possible mode of treatment was given to her. Ganga was treated by various specialists in neurology, by *Vaids* and *Hakims*. Thus for one and a half years, Ganga was given allopathic, homeopathic, and ayurvedic medicines. Balkrishna spent millions of rupees on her treatment, without any noticeable improvement. Ganga was confined to the bed, and Balkrishna hired a nurse to look after her daily needs.

One day, a devotee of Baba told Balkrishna about the "*Shri Bhagya – Sai Baba's mantra*", and the *padukas*. Immediately he went to Pune and on Ganga's name he got *abhishek* of the *padukas* performed, and repeated the mantra, "*Shri Charana Shri Bhagya Sai,*" ceaselessly. Balkrishna with utmost faith administered the *tirth* and *Udi* to Ganga. This was done for a year, with marvellous results. Now Ganga who was earlier confined to bed is doing all the household chores without any problem. Ganga also learned tailoring and now earns a living in her spare time. This was achieved by the blessings of Baba and his *Udi*, *tirth*, and mantra. Ganga and her family are eternally indebted to Baba.

Balkrishna recalls, "The total cost for this including transportation, flowers, and *abhishek* was only around 1800 rupees, compared to the million rupees I spent on the numerous doctors, medicines and hospitalisation. Now that I look at my daughter who is healthy, I thank Baba for giving Sai devotees this unique mantra, and *padukas.*"

Dr. Javeri gives some of the benefits derived by the devotees. He says, "The devotee with *Shraddha* and *Saburi* should recount his heart's desire before the *padukas* three times. Till his desire is fulfilled he should continue repeating his desire frequently. There are a host of difficulties we face in life, and these difficulties get resolved. Difficulties like dearth of money, infertility, litigations, matrimonial problems, difficulty in finding or keeping a job, ill health and diseases, problems in business and losses therein, and various worldly problems, even *Vastu dosha* (defects in the architecture of any building, and its effects on the inhabitants) are rectified."

81

Umamaheswara Rao's Unwavering Faith

This incredible *leela* is narrated by Dr. A Prahakarao, a civil surgeon in Hyderabad.

Shri B. Umamaheswara Rao, a resident of Hyderabad, worked as the editor of *Sai Prabha,* a journal that was printed and circulated every month. He was totally devoted to Baba. At that period of time he was suffering from a cardiac disease, which resulted in bouts of loss of consciousness. These bouts usually lasted for an hour or so; however, sometimes Umamaheswara Rao became unconscious for a day or two. In 1969, Umamaheswara Rao was admitted in Vijayawada Government Hospital, with such a severe attack of cardiac failure that the doctors taking care of him declared him to be dead. However, when they were taking the "body" home, he gradually came "to life".

In 1983, Umamaheswara Rao was seated in his prayer room in front of a picture of Baba and praying. The picture that Umamaheswara Rao had was a picture of Baba with his right hand raised in a "blessing posture". Incredibly, from the palm of Baba's hand a beam of light emitted, and settled on Umamaheswara Rao's left side, on the area of his heart. The beam of light was so intense that it left a round "burn mark" about 3 inches in diameter on the skin of his chest. From then on, Umamaheswara Rao didn't experience any chest pains. So he discontinued taking all his medicines; however, he never failed to take a pinch of *Udi*, twice a day. He took the *Udi* at exactly the time that he would normally take his medicines. Umamaheswara Rao resolutely believed that *Udi* was the panacea for every malady. This also cut his expenses for the medicines, besides giving him mental peace. Thereafter, Umamaheswara Rao often went into a trance, wherein Baba would appear and reassure him that nothing untoward would happen to him, and there was no need for fear, as there was no danger to his life. These trance-like states were common in his life in 1983.

On the 4th of January, 1987, Baba appeared in Umamaheswara Rao's dream at around 3:30 a.m. and warned him, "It is not a good day for you today. During the period between 10:30 and 11 a.m. your life will be in danger." Then Umamaheswara Rao saw his corpse laid on the floor; however Baba was seated near his head and Baba had placed his hand on Umamaheswara Rao's chest. Surprisingly, Umamaheswara Rao saw Sivaneshan Swami and Shri Ayodhya standing close by and looking down at him.

That morning, Umamaheswara Rao sent a message to his close relatives and dear friends stating that he would pass away that day. Thus his friends and relatives arrived at his home, and assured him that Baba was there to take care of him. Umamaheswara Rao said, "Baba has always reassured me in the past that nothing serious would happen to me, and that he was there to take care of me. However in this vision there was no such assurance." Upon hearing this, his friends and relatives started collectively praying for him. They also urged him to recite the *Vishnu Sahasranam* along with them. Others started chanting Baba's name, and praying in their own way. Then the crucial hour approached, and Umamaheswara Rao was seated on the couch reading a book. At 10.40 a.m. he complained of giddiness. Shortly thereafter, he jumped off the couch to the feet of Sai Baba, whose photograph was placed on a chair in front of him. Gradually he lapsed into a comatose state, and lay on the floor in front of Baba's photograph. However, this time Umamaheswara Rao was exhibiting unusual symptoms, as he was snoring loudly and his abdomen was literally "oscillating up and down" and this persisted for about an hour. During this time his pulse and heart rate were stable. Now everyone was in a quandary as Umamaheswara Rao had warned them not to seek any medical aid, and he didn't want to be hospitalised. Finally his son decided to place chits before Baba and to follow Baba's orders. The chit picked up by a small boy revealed "Yes," that is, Baba wished that Umamaheswara Rao be taken to the hospital, where he later recovered fully.

A year later, Umamaheswara Rao had a rather severe attack of unconsciousness. This time his respiration and heart stopped working and he was clinically dead, so his wife rushed him to the hospital much against his wishes. Umamaheswara Rao however had resumed breathing on the way to the hospital. There he was diagnosed to have cerebral haemorrhage and as a result he had total paralysis of his body. His vital signs were unstable and his organs seemed to be shutting down. Hence he was transferred to a major hospital that was well equipped with the latest technology. The doctor suggested that he have a brain scan and possibly invasive surgery to stop the cerebral haemorrhage. Umamaheswara Rao was thus admitted into the Army Medical College, and the best possible treatment was given to him. The doctor however was doubtful of his recovery, and also informed his relatives that he would have a whole host of complications. Umamaheswara Rao's family fully trusted Baba to do the best for him. Silently his wife placed a picture near his head and gave him a pinch of *Udi*. Two days later a miracle happened and Umamaheswara Rao regained consciousness, with Baba's name on his lips.

Dr. Prabhakarao recalls his ordeal saying, "Umamaheswara Rao was displeased to be in the hospital and he chided his wife for not respecting his wish. He then asked the doctors to discharge him, as the only medicine that was needed was Baba's *Udi*. The doctors tried to reason with him, but he didn't heed their advice and 'left against medical advice' and told them that his doctor was Baba and he knew what was best for him. After all these harrowing experiences I can only applaud Umamaheswara Rao for having unwavering faith in Baba and his *Udi*. And I only wish I had a quarter of the faith that he had."

Ref.: *Shri Sai Leela Magazine*, Volume 66, No. 8, November 1987.

82

How Baba Cured Ashvini's Children

The month of July 1985 was a very difficult month for Ashvini A. Chipker, a devotee residing in Mumbai. At the beginning of the month her eldest son, Atul, got a severe allergic reaction. Thereafter his face started swelling, and soon both his eyelids were swollen to such an extent that his eyes were mere slits. The skin of his face was red with hives and so was the white part (conjunctiva) of his eyes.

Ashvini was alarmed to see her child suffering and she immediately took him to an ophthalmologist, who examined him and prescribed some anti-allergy medicines. Ashvini prayed to Baba saying, "Lord if I have committed any mistake knowingly or unknowingly please forgive me. Give me Atul's pain and suffering, and make him alright." Ashvini gave the medicines prescribed to Atul, and soon the swelling started subsiding, and a few days later it disappeared.

Soon after Atul recovered from his allergy, Ashvini's younger daughter Shraddha had a severe bout of diarrhoea. The diarrhoea occurred a few days prior to Shraddha's first birthday, and lasted for 6 days. Then Shraddha was alright for about two weeks, and Ashvini sighed with relief because Shraddha was not dehydrated; and didn't require hospitalisation. However, the diarrhea recurred, with a vengeance. This time Shraddha had numerous loose stools, accompanied with vomiting. She lost weight and became listless. Ashvini had her checked by her pediatrician and gastroenterologist, and faithfully gave her the prescribed medicines. But instead of improving she started deteriorating, and started having fever, accompanied with listlessness. Ashvini's father-in-law suggested that Shraddha should be taken to Wadia Hospital. However her father was reluctant as he felt they would admit her there, and she would catch some other infection in the hospital.

That day was a Sunday, and Ashvini was concerned that the diarrhea had been continuing for the entire week. She decided to give her some indigenous medicine to stop the loose bowel movements. At that time Ashvini's younger brother came to the house and held Shraddha in his arms while Ashvini went to the kitchen to prepare the brew. Her younger brother had a *tulsi maala* (strand of beads made twigs of Ocimum Sanctum or holy basil) around his neck, and he took it off and put it around Shraddha's neck. And Lo! Shraddha recovered from her diarrhea and started playing.

Ashvini recalls the wonderful miracle of this *tulsi maala*. "Once, my younger sister came to our home for the delivery of her second child. It was her habit to apply *Udi* on the forehead of her son every morning. One day she took out the packet of *Udi* and opened it and to her amazement she found this *tulsi maala* in the packet along with the *Udi*. No one knew how that strand of beads happened to be in the packet. My sister gratefully accepted the strand of beads as a blessing from Baba and put it around the neck of her son. Later, our younger brother took the *maala* and when Shradha had the bout of diarrhea he put it around her neck. Only Baba knows the secret of this miraculous and magical *tulsi maala*."

The next day Shraddha was taken to Wadia Hospital, and Ashvini requested the doctor to hospitalise her. However the doctor reassured her that Shraddha had recovered sufficiently and didn't require hospitalisation. He prescribed some electrolyte fluids for the next couple of days and sent her home. Needless to say Shraddha soon became healthy.

While Shraddha had her attack of diarrhea Atul had gone to his uncle's home so that Ashvini's mother could take care of him. One morning Atul got up crying inconsolably. He said, "An old man with a white beard hit me. He had a box in his hand and he hit me with it. He said, 'I was eating mutton.'"

Ashvini's mother brought him home. Ashvini held him in her arms and consoled him. Then she asked him how the old saint looked, and showed him a picture of Baba. Atul started crying as soon as he saw Baba's picture and pointing to him said, "This is the saint that beat me. I never ate mutton, so why did he beat me?" Hearing this, Ashvini stopped all the medicines that Atul was taking, and soon he became robust and healthy.

Finally Ashvini says, "Through this period of trial and tribulation, it was our faith in Baba that helped us face all these problems. And Baba came running to our aid every time we prayed to him, and saved both my children from terrible pain and illness. Now thanks to him both my children are healthy."

Ref.: *Shri Sai Leela Magazine*, Volume 65, No. 8–9, November–December 1985.

83

Baba Changes Vazirbhai's Life

It was a miserable life for Vazirbhai. After toiling from early morning to late evening as a motor mechanic, he earned only half a rupee per day. That was just enough to buy some *bhel* (Indian savoury) to prevent him from starving. He wondered when he would be able to afford two square meals a day. Vazirbhai put his hand in his pocket and clasped the half rupee coin, and tried to remember which shop would give him a little more bhel for it. With these gloomy thoughts in his mind he slowly started crossing the bridge in front of him. He was about midway on the bridge when he saw a tall fakir coming from the opposite direction. But he paid no heed to him, as his stomach was growling with hunger. The fakir passed by Vazirbhai, and few seconds later started shouting, "Vazirbhai! Vazirbhai!" Instinctively, Vazirbhai turned around, and saw the fakir signaling to him. Stunned, he thought, "How does he know my name?"

The fakir came and stood in front of him and said, "Child why are you worrying so much? Don't worry, as your life will soon change for the better. Eight days from today a man will come to you on his own accord and change your life." The fakir passed his hand lovingly on Vazirbhai's head and said, "Allah will bless you." Vazirbhai put his hand in his pocket to give the fakir some money. "No I don't want your half rupee coin. Now go and have some *bhel* to eat. Allaha will make everything alright." Saying this, the fakir swiftly walked away. Vazirbhai was astounded by this incident. He thought about the photograph of Baba that he worshipped, and soon realised that the fakir was indeed Baba. Vazirbhai immediately turned around but he couldn't see the fakir anywhere. He walked the length and breadth of the bridge, but the fakir was nowhere to be found.

Vazirbhai was devoted to Baba, and he had often heard other devotees recount *leelas* where Baba had appeared and solved their problems. "Did I also get the same kind of experience just now? Although I have never seen that fakir previously, he certainly knew my name. He also knew how much money I had in my pocket, and that I was going to eat *bhel* with it. That only proves his omnipresence, so he was not an ordinary fakir. But was he actually Baba? Would Baba come to meet a poor person like me? I am no great devotee, I just pray to the photograph of Baba that is kept in Nana Sahib Rasne's home. I don't do any elaborate rituals or *aratis*, so why will Baba come to my aid. Now I am so confused." With these thoughts Vazirbhai slowly walked home.

Vazirbhai lived behind the Sai Das temple in Rasne chawl. Damodar Savalaram Rasne, alias Dammu Anna, who resided in Ahmednagar moved with his family to Pune. In the *Shri Sai Satcharita*, chapter 25, a detailed account is written about Dammu Anna, who had two wives but unfortunately didn't have any children. However Baba blessed him and gave him 4 mangoes, and said, "Give the mangoes to your younger wife. The marvel of these mangoes will bring forth 4 sons and 4 daughters." In Pune, Dammu Anna bought a multi-storeyed building (chawl) in Shivaji Nagar. Nana Sahib Rasne, his eldest son, bought two rooms in that building and converted it into a shrine in 1945. Devotees from far and near flocked there to attend the *aratis*. On Thursdays and festivals the shrine was overflowing with devotees. Nana Sahib realised that soon a temple would have to be built to accommodate the devotees. A small temple was thus built in front of the chawl, and Vazirbhai helped in whatever way he could. He also looked after the maintenance of the temple; moreover, he got up early in the morning and swept and swabbed the floors till they shone.

When Vazirbhai finally reached home that day, he was still confused, and with the thought of the fakir at the top of his mind, he fell asleep. Around 5 a.m. Baba appeared as the same fakir in his dream. "Arre! Why are you so confused? I am the same fakir that met you on the bridge. Don't worry, Allah will bless you and everything will be fine." Saying this, Baba disappeared.

Vazirbhai knew that Baba's words were never untrue, and he expectantly waited for the 8th day to dawn. He wondered what life changing event would occur that day. A gentleman named Mule came to the garage (repair workshop) that day and saw Vazirbhai hard at work. Mule was impressed by Vazirbhai's skill and asked him if he would like to work with him. Vazirbhai accepted. Mule had a large workshop and was well known in Pune. Soon, Vazirbhai was able to have two square meals a day and more. In some time, he was able to buy a workshop, and work for himself. Thus, Baba's blessings of "There are good days ahead" came true.

Ref.: *Shri Sai Sagar Magazine*, Volume 8, No. 3, May–June 2000.

84

Baba Visits Vazirbhai

After Vazirbhai bought his workshop, he constructed a house for himself behind the temple near the chawl, and brought his mother to stay with him. Thereafter, both of then spent their time in keeping the temple clean, and making all the necessary preparations for the *aratis*. Soon Nana Sahib Rasne handed over the management of the temple to him. During this period, Vazirbhai got married. At that time, the area was desolate and without any electricity. Nevertheless, Vazirbhai would get up around 4 a.m. and with a lantern in his hand go and open the temple. Then he would sweep and swab the temple and have it spick and span for the *Kakad Arati*.

One morning he got up as usual and opened the temple, and to his astonishment he saw a huge cobra lying curled up on the *padukas*. The cobra was unusually large, for the coiled up body was about three feet in diameter. Its raised hood was about 10" in length. However, the cobra was calm and didn't hiss at him. Vazirbhai was unafraid, and he sat cross-legged in front of it with folded hands. Solemnly he said, "Baba, was there any lapse in my service to you?" The cobra moved his hood sideways like a person would to say "No." The next question he asked was, "Baba is my service acceptable to you?" And the cobra moved his hood down as if to say "Yes." As Vazirbhai didn't know what else he should ask, he just sat there quietly. Sometime later the cobra slithered past him, and he could feel its cold touch. But it neither hissed, nor caused any injury to him.

Later, the devotee who assisted him arrived and Vazirbhai narrated what had happened some time ago. In wonder he said, "Vazirbhai you are truly blessed. I have been coming to this temple for the past so many years, yet Baba has never appeared before me in this form. How lucky you are."

One night, around 2 a.m. Vazirbhai heard someone knocking at his door. The person said, "Vazirbhai. O! Vazirbhai. Is Vazirbhai there?" Vazirbhai took his lantern and opened the door. He saw a tall fakir standing at his door. The fakir said, "I have come from far away. I have not eaten for many days so I am extremely hungry. Will you give me some food to eat?" Vazirbhai told his mother about the plight of the fakir and requested her to prepare a meal for him. His mother readily agreed and went to prepare the meal. Vazirbhai invited the fakir in and seated him. Then he went and helped his mother and both of them prepared a special meal, and fed him sumptuously. The fakir blessed them abundantly and left.

After the fakir left, Vazirbhai said, "I wonder if that fakir was Baba? But would Baba visit a poor person's house like mine?" His mother reassured him that he definitely was Baba. But Vazirbhai still had his doubts, and finally he fell asleep. Around 5 a.m. Baba appeared in his dream. He reassured Vazirbhai, "Vazirbhai that fakir was me. I wanted to know if you had forgotten me now that your financial condition had improved greatly." Vazirbhai replied, "Baba how can I ever forget you? Because of your grace I am here." Baba laughed and blessed him saying, "Allah will take care of you," and Vazirbhai woke up.

With utmost conviction Vazirbhai says, "After Baba's Maha Samadhi where is Baba? Is he in confined to Shirdi? Or is he in some temple? Or is he in a photograph? No! He resides in the heart of that devotee who has loving, steadfast faith in him." Hence Baba says, "Wherever you may be, when you spread your hand before me in supplication, with faith and devotion, there I stand before you, day and night, as steadfast as your faith and devotion is" (*Shri Sai Satcharita*, chapter 15, Ovi 67). This promise is true even today and devotees experience it all over the world to this day. If you want to become a true devotee, then you should cast aside these ostentatious external rituals and in solitude look inside yourself. Many devotees yearn to get the same experiences that Vazirbhai got. You can also get the same kind of experiences if you yearn for them and have steadfast faith in Baba. Baba is standing near you waiting to satisfy your craving; the only prerequisite is that your *jholi* to receive it should be woven on the loom of absolute faith.

Ref: *Shri Sai Sagar Magazine*, Volume 8, No. 3, May–June 2000.

85

Santosh Ghodke Experiences Baba's Grace

"Baba's merciful gaze (*Rahem Nazar*) constantly envelopes my son Sairaj. For which I am totally grateful to Baba," says Santosh Ghodke, a devotee from Pune. "Once, when Sairaj was a year and a half old he was playing on the floor, while I lay on the bed. Before long I fell asleep; then this astoundng phenomenon took place. A shadowy cloud entered the room through the window and took the form of a human being. The human being said, 'Arre! Are you sleeping? Get up. Don't you have to go to Shirdi?' I was jolted out of my sleep and I looked around, but no one was there. I then looked on the floor for Sairaj. He had crawled to the small table, on which a table-fan was on. Of course the face or blades of the fan were enclosed in grill casing. However, Sairaj had managed to put his tiny fingers through the grill. In alarm, I jumped out of bed and picked him up, and by Baba's grace his tiny fingers were alright. I dread to think of what would have happened if Baba had not woken me at that juncture. Baba's timely warning saved my son from losing the fingers of his right hand, or worse. All I can say is, 'Baba, always be like a shadow behind us, and envelop us in thy merciful grace.'

Recently I visited Shirdi and with great anticipation I went to the Samadhi Mandir. I hoped to lay my head on Baba's padukas, and touch his beatific Samadhi. However, in recent times the Sansthan puts up a glass screen or shield on three sides of the Samadhi. I can understand their objective—due to the ever increasing crowds the Sansthan has taken these protective measures. But I was sorely disappointed, as I felt my pilgrimage was incomplete without touching or having some physical contact with the Samadhi. I returned home with tears of disappointment in my eyes.

Crestfallen, I tried to return to my daily routine, but however much I tried, the thought that I was unable to touch the Samadhi because of the glass shield was at the top of my mind. I was obsessed by that one thought, that I was unable to touch the Samadhi. Morning, noon, and night I was haunted by this thought, and I was unable to concentrate on my work. So I started praying daily, 'Baba the next time I visit Shirdi please let me touch your Samadhi.'

Early one morning I had this wonderful dream. I saw a huge cave below Baba's Samadhi, and then I saw Baba coming out of this cave. Then right in front of me he went and sat upon his stone, and said, 'Now have my *darshan* to your heart's content.' I immediately seized the opportunity and lay my head on his feet for a long time. I sat in front of him and massaged his feet gently. 'Are content now? Every day you prayed for this; are you satisfied now?' Hearing these words I woke up startled. But my yearning to touch Baba's Samadhi and much more was fulfilled. What a wonderful God you are, that you fulfil even the tiniest wish of your devotees."

Years ago Santosh had brought some *Udi* from Shirdi. He kept it in a small box, and every day he and his family applied *Udi* from that box. Not only that, any devotee who came to his home would take some *Udi* from it. But by Baba's grace that box was always full. This *Udi* has the quality of multiplying, and due to this they are leading a contented life. If anyone is ill, the first line of treatment is the application of the *Udi*, and taking it internally.

In September of 2006, Sairaj who was 6 months old suddenly had a severe convulsion, and became unconscious. Santosh and his wife were at their wit's end and didn't know what to do. Then Santosh picked Sairaj and took him to Sidhanth Hospital that was close by. Dr. Lalwani, who was there, immediately examined him. However, during the examination Sairaj had another convulsion and he rolled up his eyes. Dr. Lalwani thus became aware of the seriousness of his condition and transferred him to a renowned hospital. He immediately took out his car, and asked them to get in. Then at break-neck speed he drove them there. Santosh was praying to Baba and from his pocket he took out some *Udi* and applied some on Sairaj's forehead and tongue. At that time Sairaj's breathing was quite erratic and irregular. Santosh was aghast that his breathing would stop for short periods of time and then continue again. However, after applying the *Udi* the respiration returned to normal, and Santosh breathed a sigh of relief.

At the hospital Sairaj was checked and admitted to the ICU. The doctor informed Santosh that Sairaj's condition was critical. Santosh sat outside and fervently prayed to Baba to save his child. Dr. Lalwani sat next to him and reassured him as best as he could. But Santosh knew that it was all in Baba's hands, and only Baba could turn Sairaj's condition around. So he surrendered completely to Baba, and said, "Thy will be done". The thought at the top of his mind was about the power of Baba's *Udi*. In the *Shri Sai Satcharita* he had read about the life bestowing power of the *Udi*.

With consternation, Santosh says, "I was told that visitors were not allowed inside for fear of contagion. But I was restless, and determined that I would apply *Udi* on Sairaj's forehead come what may. I knew that *Udi* was the only panacea and the only life giving elixir. Now I had to find a way to enter the ICU. I asked the security person there to let me in for a few minutes, but he curtly refused. Then I pleaded with him and told him that I wanted to apply some *Udi* on Sairaj's forehead. Hearing this he got even more furious, as he was of the opinion that diseases don't get better by these superstitious applications. However not paying any heed to him, I loudly called out to Baba and entered the ward. Swiftly I applied the *Udi* on his forehead and tongue, all the while begging him for the gift of Sairaj's life. Then I quickly came out and sat down and prayed.

After what seemed like infinity, the team of doctors again checked Sairaj. They stood in front of me and said, "Your child is responding to the treatment. We were very concerned as we were fighting a losing battle. We must admit that your faith has worked wonders." Hearing these words my eyes were filled with tears and I joined my palms together and thanked Baba for his mercy. A week later Sairaj was discharged and we brought him home.

The test of my faith was yet to come. A few days after we brought Sairaj home he again fell ill. Thereafter he had some problem or the other almost every day, and visits to the doctor became inevitable. Like Damocles' sword the fear of his getting another convulsion hung over our heads. I stood in front of Baba's picture and prayed earnestly, "Baba your *Udi* has given him a new life. Now please bring him out of these nagging illnesses, and make him healthy."

One day, Baba appeared in my dream. In the dream he was standing near Sairaj's head, while Sairaj was sleeping between me and my wife. Then Baba sat down next to his pillow, and picked Sairaj up and started playing with him. After playing with him for a short while, he said, "Why are you worrying so much? Don't you have faith in me? Don't you have faith in my *Udi*? Don't worry so much nothing is going to happen to your son. He will be alright soon." Then Baba put his hand inside his *jholi*, and with his palm laden with *Udi* placed it on Sairaj's forehead. His *jholi* must have been overflowing with *Udi* as Baba's palm was totally covered with *Udi*. At that moment, I got up. Since Sairaj returned home from the hospital, we slept with the light on as he might need something at night. I glanced at the clock and it was 4.30 a.m. I turned and looked at Sairaj who was sleeping peacefully.

What I saw next left me speechless with delight. Sairaj's entire forehead was covered with *Udi*, and the imprint of Baba's fingers was distinctly visible on his forehead. I immediately woke my wife and narrated the dream, and she also saw the imprint of Baba's beatific palm on Sairaj's forehead. Needless to say that Sairaj never fell ill after that, and now he is a delightfully mischievous three-year-old. But most importantly, he loves Baba."

Ref.: *Shri Sai Sagar Magazine*, Volume 7, No. 3, July–September 2009.

86

Ajit Mairalgwali Gets Baba's Sakshat Darshan

Ajit Mairalgwali, an ardent devotee, resided at Pune and visited Shirdi at every possible opportunity. Over the years Ajit Mairalgwali had heard countless devotees say that they had seen Baba in the Dwarka Mai for a fleeting moment, or they had seen Baba seated near the railing, or that Baba walked past them. Ajit hoped and prayed that Baba would bless him with such an experience, but what he experienced left him speechless.

Ajit's boss Basvaraj had never visited Shirdi prior to 3rd April 2004, nor did he know anything about the holy sites there. So Basvaraj requested Ajit to accompany him. Ajit seized this golden opportunity and readily consented to go along. The very next day Basvaraj, his wife and two sons arrived at his door early in the morning. They drove to Shirdi, and at Shirdi his wife bought a garland and a platter of offerings for Baba. After paying homage to Baba's Samadhi and praying to Baba, they went to the other holy sites. Finally Basvaraj's family went with Ajit to the Dwarka Mai. It was very crowded, but the devotees were patiently waiting their turn to climb up the hallowed steps of Baba's Masjid Mai.

Ajit relates what happened next: "Overcome with reverence, I thought, 'This is Baba's beloved Dwarka Mai where he gave succour and comfort to the downtrodden and distressed devotees. Where Baba gave his sacred *Udi* with his own hands and healed millions of people. This is happening even today, except that after his Maha Samadhi Baba is not here in his physical form.' But after what I, or rather we, saw next, I will never ever say that Baba is not here in his physical form.

We were slowly moving ahead waiting for our turn to enter the Dwarka Mai, when I looked at the steps of the Dwarka Mai and there I saw Baba standing. In fact all of us saw Baba, and Basvaraj and his wife were staring at him in awe. He was about 6 ft. tall, wearing a torn white *kafni* and white cloth tied tightly over his forehead. However he was younger, having a dark black beard, and his eyes glittered like stars. His arms were long and reached below his knees, and with his long fingers he beckoned us to enter the Dwarka Mai. Just like robots, we followed his orders, and one after the other we entered the Dwarka Mai. He was still standing on the steps and all of us entered the Dwarka Mai from those very steps. Upon entering the Dwarka Mai all of us turned to see him, but he had disappeared. In that fleeting moment it dawned on us that Baba had physically appeared before us. We looked at each other with a questioning look—had Baba really appeared before us? With a vacillating, dubious mind I asked the priest and his helper if they had seen anyone standing here wearing a *kafni* a few moments ago. Both of them shook their heads and said, 'No.' We then prayed to Baba's photograph and *padukas* to our hearts content. Prior to exiting the sanctum I carefully looked at every corner of the Sabha Mandap, but I couldn't see Baba anywhere.

We came out of the Dwarka Mai and returned the platter to the shopkeeper. Mrs. Basvaraj said, 'Shall we go again into the sanctum, as we may see Baba again?' I replied, 'This is once in a lifetime blessing from Baba. And we should savour it's sweetness till the end of our lives.'

I thought about the divine manifestation of Baba that I had seen. All I can say is that Baba's divine form was indescribably magnificent. Furthermore Baba can, at will, appear in his physical form even after his Maha Niryan. But the most mind boggling event for me was that Baba was calmly standing on the steps. If it was an ordinary human being standing there, we would have brushed past him and touched him. **However, we climbed up the steps one after the other and we actually passed through him. It was like passing through a cone of**

light.

From this incident I can vouch that Baba is eternally present in the Dwarka Mai but when we will be able to see his physical form is totally dependent on him. Whenever the need arises he will definitely appear before the devotee. Nonetheless every devotee should remember that this luminous form of his resides in our heart and soul. So a word of caution to those devotees who run after phoney god-men, and so called *avatars* of Baba; Sai Baba of Shirdi is the *Sat-Chit-Anand* and the Eternal Truth. For this *leela* that Baba performed at Shirdi for me I am everlastingly grateful."

Ref.: *Shri Sai Sagar Magazine*, Volume 12, Deepavali issue 2004.

87

Baba Appears to Bless the Shindes

The Shri Sai Das Temple at Shiviji Nagar, Pune, is a wish-fulfilling sanctuary, and Baba himself often comes there and reassures the devotees that everything will be alright.

This is exactly what happened to Samir Nivriti Shinde, a devotee residing in Pune. Samir was happily married, and he had two bright daughters, yet he and his wife yearned to have a son. After begging Baba to bless them, and taking a vow, their wish was fulfilled. On the 2nd of August 2006, their son Vedanth was born. Although he was slightly underweight at birth, he soon gained weight and before his first birthday he was like any other child of his age. The Shindes celebrated his first birthday in a grand fashion.

About two months later, Vedanth started running a fever and he was treated by their family physician. However he failed to improve despite the treatment, so his blood work-up was done. The blood test revealed that Vedanth had low haemoglobin, so he was admitted in hospital and a transfusion administered. With a sigh of relief the Shindes brought Vedanth home, as the ordeal of giving him a transfusion was over.

Vedanth returned for his post transfusion blood test, but the haemoglobin had not increased at all. So a haematologist was consulted and an extensive work up was done. The Shindes were told that Vedanth's red blood cells were being destroyed faster than they were produced (autoimmune hemolytic anemia) and that he would need to be transfused on a regular basis at regular intervals. As a consequence Vedanth was admitted monthly and transfused. His parents were at their wit's end and it became unbearable for them see their little boy's plight. Finally the haematologist suggested surgery, and the Shindes sought refuge in Baba. "Baba, Vedanth is a small child. We have agreed for the surgery to be performed, please be with the child during surgery. Please let it be successful."

The date for surgery was set, and prior to going to the hospital Samir's mother advised them to take Vedanth to the Sai Das Temple in Shivaji Nagar. Early that morning they drove to the temple. Just as they were about to enter the temple, a man resembling Baba suddenly appeared before them. "Don't worry, everything will be alright," he said, lifting his hands to bless Vedanth. Before they could mentally grasp what was happening, Baba disappeared. The Shindes took Vadanth into the temple and beseeched Baba's benevolence. The surgery was successfully performed that day, and Vedanth's sister donated her platelets for his surgery. He was then kept in isolation for a month, so that he would not contract common illnesses. At surgery Vedanth's doctor had inserted a Hickman's intravenous line for parenteral nutrition. The end of the line exited from his thorax. The Shindes were told that the Hickman would be in place till Vedanth recovered completely.

With Baba's grace, after surgery Vedanth started producing good red blood cells, and his haemoglobin was stable. After eight months post-surgery he became absolutely healthy. Then the doctor suggested that the Hickman line could now be removed, surgically.

The date for surgery was set and Vedanth was admitted again. As the time for his surgery drew near his parents were continuously praying to Baba. The nurse asked Mrs. Shinde to remove Vedanth's "street clothes" and put on the hospital clothes.

Mrs. Shinde recalls, "Chanting Baba's name, very cautiously I removed Vedanth's shirt. The Hickman's catheter got dislodged and fell down. My heart was in my mouth, and I yelled for the nurse. Hearing my terrified cries she came running, and both of us looked at Vedanth's chest. We couldn't believe our eyes, because the Hickman had come out intact. Moreover there was no bleeding, it was as if some unseen force had applied pressure on his large vein and stopped it from bleeding. Soon thereafter the doctor came and checked Vedanth. Flabbergasted he said,

'I can't believe that the Hickman came out without the surgical procedure. And there is not a drop of blood coming out of the vein. How is this possible? Now Vedanth does not require any surgery, and you can take him home.' Although the doctor couldn't comprehend how this happened, I knew for sure that this was Baba's leela."

Time rolled by and 4 years later Vedanth is a playful naughty child. By Baba's grace his red blood cells have a normal life span. He does have some minor side effect from the medicines that he took, like dry eyes and a dry mouth. But his mother is sure that when Baba cured him of such a major disease, he will definitely cure this too. Vedanth is now devoted to Baba and never misses going to the Shivaji Nagar Temple, as his saviour is there.

Ref.: *Shri Sai Sagar Magazine*, Volume 2, No. 4, January–March 2012.

88

Baba's Leela of Green Mangoes

April 3rd 1990 is etched in gold on Surendra G. Davle's mind, as that day Baba helped him through the most difficult phase of his life. That wonderful experience is described below.

At that time, Surendra resided in Dombivili, and he yearned to own a home. But his financial condition was in shambles. He had a large family to feed, and it was very hard to make both ends meet. However, he did have immense faith in Baba. Holding the hand of *Shraddha* and *Saburi* tightly, he lived life. Consistently he prayed to Baba, imploring him to give him a home of his own. Then his friend introduced him to the construction engineer of a high rise building, and Surendra registered his name for an apartment. Now the question of payment arose, and Surendra somehow managed to collect 70,000 rupees and gave it to him. But he still had a balance of 5,000 rupees to pay, and no matter what he did, Surendra was unable to collect that small amount. Impatiently the engineer informed him that if he didn't hurry up and pay the balance his name would be rejected. Surendra had no option but to seek Baba's help.

At the same time, tragedy struck, as his brother died. From his very soul Surendra thought of his late brother and prayed to Baba, "Baba I just have to pay the balance of 5,000 rupees for the apartment. My condition is like the elephant who managed to go through the eye of the needle but his tail got stuck. All my efforts to get the money have failed, but you can surely show me the way out of this predicament. Please help me."

The next day was a Thursday, the 3rd of April. Surendra had taken leave as his children had their annual examinations. It was around 9 a.m. and he was coaching them for the forthcoming

235

examination. Suddenly, a strong wind began blowing and it threatened to rain. His wife was in the kitchen cooking, when she said, "It has suddenly become so gusty, go to the yard and bring some green unripe mangoes for me." Surendra went to the yard and indeed found the ground covered with unripe mangoes that had fallen from the tree. He had worn a *lungi* (a sarong-like garment) and he quickly gathered a large number of unripe mangoes in the fold of his *lungi*. It started hailing and the sky became dark and overcast, with black clouds, so he decided to go home. Then from nowhere, a tall person wearing a white *kafni* stood before him. Surendra looked intently at his face, yet he was unable to see his face clearly due to the brilliance of his eyes. The brilliance was so radiant that he shut his eyes. That resplendent person said, "Child, give me the tender green mangoes that you have collected." Something about his voice made Surendra obey him, and like a robot he followed his command.

Surendra recalls, "From the fold of my *lungi* I started putting the mangoes into his *jholi*. But a strange phenomenon took place, as the mangoes actually leapt out one by one into his *jholi*, and left me quite baffled. And soon his *jholi* was full, he said, 'Child, just go a few yards forward and look.'

Again I obeyed him, and walked a few steps with my head bent. There I saw that a small puddle had been formed by the hail storm, and in it I saw a whole lot of rupee bills floating. The bills were of 50 and 100 rupee denominations. As I stared in disbelief, the bills changed to green mangoes and then again to rupee bills. I was utterly confused. This interchange happened about three times, till finally I bent down and picked up the unripe mangoes. I had no control over myself; I was under his influence, and mechanically I returned home. I went straight to the kitchen and threw the mangoes, which in fact were the bundles of rupee bills, on the floor. Then I felt giddy so I sat down for a while. My wife was concerned and she asked, 'What has happened to you? Aren't you feeling well?'

Then I heard my wife and my sister shout, 'What have you brought?' I replied, 'For heaven's sake, I have brought a whole lot of green unripe mangoes that you asked for.' By that time I had regained my normal composure, or rather the influence that I was under left me. So I went to the kitchen to see what all this uproar was about. There on the floor lay bundles of soaked rupee bills. Then I narrated the entire experience that had just taken place. Finally, my wife and I went back to the place near the mango tree where I had found the money. We thought that if someone had lost their money, they would be looking for it there. However, no one was there. We waited there for about two hours and as nobody turned up we returned home. We dried the bills and counted them, and the amount was exactly 5,000 rupees. We also enquired if any of the residents in our building had lost any money, but no one claimed the money. It was then that I realised that Baba had come to my aid. So I decided to pay the balance to the engineer.

The very next day I went to the engineer's office to make the payment. The engineer said, 'I heard that your brother has recently passed away. I am not in hurry to get the balance; neither will I reject your name from the client list.' I asked how he had come to know about the demise of my brother. He told me he had found out from my office.

It all seemed unbelievable to me that after meeting Baba near the mango tree, favourable things were happening to me. Baba in his unique way had provided me with the balance amount that I was short of. The attitude of the construction engineer had changed, and now he was empathetic towards me. I got a good apartment in central Bombay. I had some knowledge of astrology and palmistry, so I seriously studied it, and with Baba's blessings my predictions turned out correct. Soon I started getting a lot of clients, and gradually my financial condition improved. All this happened after that golden day when Baba came to my aide. However due to my ignorance I was unable to recognize him, this anguish will stay with me till the day I die. How I wish I had placed my head on his feet, now all I can do is hope that Baba will come again and I have the internal vision to recognise him."

Ref .: Sai Prasad Magazine Deepavali issue 1995.

89

Baba Gives Shiva Darshan to Vasantrao

The Goddess Durga was Vasantrao Samel's chosen deity. At that time he knew nothing about Baba and Shirdi. Once, his best friend casually told Vasantrao that he ought to visit Shirdi at least once in his lifetime, as Baba of Shirdi was the incarnation of Lord Shiva. Vasantrao was rather surprised as his friend was also devoted to the Goddess Durga. Vasantrao had a great deal of regard for his friend, so he decided to visit Shirdi at the earliest.

It was in the year 1947 that Vasantrao set out for Shirdi. He boarded the train at Mumbai and reached Kopergaon at midnight. The station was a small one without any facilities. A short walk of about 3 minutes from the station brought him to the State Transport station. However the street was desolate, with dense vegetation growing everywhere. Vasantrao reached the bus station and learned that the last bus had left at 9 p.m. The entire bus station was deserted and dark. Vasantrao waited there for a short while hoping that some bus or vehicle would come that way. He looked around and found three or four alleys leading to the bus station. He scouted those allies hoping that some bullock cart might pass that way. After diligently searching all the alleys without success, he returned to the bus station.

A short distance away, he saw a lamp flickering, so he went there. There he found a villager sleeping on a bed of leaves. He asked Vasantrao where he was going. When he said that he was going to Shirdi, the villager cautioned him. He said, "You better go back to the bus station and rest there. The next bus will arrive just prior to the *Kakad Arati* and you will reach in

238

time for it. No bullock cart will come this way till tomorrow morning. Don't wait here or walk about, as the thugs will rob you. It was my duty to inform you and that I did. Now it's up to you to decide."

Vasantrao turned in the direction that Shirdi lay and closed his eyes. He said, "Baba to come to your *durbar* one has to fear being looted by thugs. Your kingdom is full of thieves. Henceforth I will not come to your Shirdi." Just as he turned to walk back, he heard the tinkling of cow bells, and right in front stood 12 bullock carts with 24 bullocks. The driver said, "One anna for a ride to Shirdi. Sahib, where do you want to go? To Shirdi?"

Vasantrao was now on his way to Shirdi, he told the driver that he wanted to go to Das Ganu's House. The driver was aware of where Das Ganu resided and he told Vasantrao that he would drop him at Das Ganu's doorstep. And indeed that is what he did. Vasantrao happily gave him a 4 anna coin. But the driver refused to accept it saying, "Baba has decided that the fare is one anna, and that is what I will take. If I accept more, Baba won't be happy." So Vasantrao took the change back.

Vasantrao knocked at the door and Das Ganu himself opened the door. Surprised to see him, he asked how he came to Shirdi so very late. So he told him the whole story. Hearing this Das Ganu was overcome with emotion. He said, "You are fortunate, as Baba himself became the driver and brought you here. He has accepted you as a favoured child. And I am sure you were unable to recognise the driver. Right?" Vasantrao was astounded to hear what Das Ganu said, but he accepted it as a blessing from Baba. Das Ganu asked his mother to prepare a meal for his guest, and after the meal Vasantrao retired for the night.

Early next morning, Vasantrao accompanied Das Ganu for the *Kakad Arati*. There were about 25 devotees in the Samadhi Mandir and the *arati* started. A short while later Vasantrao heard the *arati*, "*Aisa yei Ba. Sai Digambara......*" This *arati* is sung at noon and evening, but he clearly heard it at *Kakad*. At that time some superior energy enveloped him and he was

239

drawn into it, he had no control over it. He thought, "Is Baba a Shiva avatar or a Datta avatar? But my friend said that he was a Shiva avatar." Vasantrao then saw a Lord Shiva in the place of Sai Baba, and a bright light appeared before him. The intensity of the light was tremendous, and he fell to the ground. Someone heard him fall and yelled that he had fallen. The *arati* stopped for a second; however Das Ganu asked them to continue, so he lay there in a semiconscious state.

"In that state I could clearly hear the *arati*, as I had the blessed *darshan* of Lord Shiva. In total awe I gazed at Lord Shiva. Then I heard a loud noise and the Samadhi opened, and next to it I saw a mud hut, that was exactly like Das Ganu's hut. However Das Ganu's hut was seen next to it. Everything that was happening was way beyond my control, and I couldn't make any sense of it, so I just lay there accepting it. When I finally came out of that state, I found myself close to Baba's Samadhi and my head was on Das Ganu's lap. He immediately put some *tirth* in my mouth, and I became my normal self thereafter."

This is how he narrated that wonderful experience to Das Ganu. Das Ganu was exceedingly thrilled, and holding Vasantrao by the hand, Das Ganu took him to the Dwarka Mai. From the *Dhuni*, Das Ganu took out a fistful of *Udi* and applied it on Vasantrao's entire body.

Ref.: *Sai Prasad Magazine*, Deepavali issue, 1999.

90

Vasantrao's Gurus

Sitaram Baba was Vasantrao Samel's Guru. Way back in 1934, his Guru had asked him to give discourses on the *Dnyaneshwari*. At that time Vasantrao said, "What can I talk on this wonderful *pothi*?" His Guru remained silent, then again in 1936 on an auspicious day, he called Vasantrao and patting his back said, "You hold discourses on the *Dnyaneshwari*, and I will speak through you."

In the Dwarka Mai, Vasantrao sat in front of the Dhuni and read the 11th chapter of the *Dnyaneshwari* aloud. In that chapter the *virat roopa* (cosmic form) of Lord Krishna is described. At that moment he thought, "*Baal Krishna* is Sai Krishna. I wonder if I will be able to see that form in this sacred place." Lo! He saw a young lad of about 5 years playing on top of the Dhuni, and simultaneously he read the *ovi* describing Lord Krishna's *virat roopa*. Seeing this wonderful scene, Vasantrao was overcome with love and devotion. Then the young lad signalled to him and said, "Keep on reading. I am listening to you." During the time that Vasantrao was reading the *Dnyaneshwari*, Das Ganu came to the Dwarka Mai twice looking for Vasantrao, but was unable to see him, although Vasantrao saw Das Ganu.

In the afternoon, Vasantrao met Das Ganu, and he asked Vasantrao where he was all this while. Then Vasantrao told him everything that had happened in the Dwarka Mai, and fell at Das Ganu's feet, sobbing. Das Ganu lifted him and patting his back said, "I want to hear your discourse on the *Dnyaneshwari*. I will give you a place in the Samadhi Mandir, where you can sit and read it. Let Baba also hear the *Dnyaneshwari*." Vasantrao was delighted as Das Ganu himself had asked him to give a discourse on the Dnyaneshwari and felt that it was Baba's orders coming from the mouth of Das Ganu.

Vasantrao gave his discourse on the *Dnyaneshwari* that evening in Baba's *durbar* before a fairly large audience. While the discourse was in progress, someone from the audience said, "Many *Babas* have I heard giving discourses. But there is only one Sai Baba and he is the Supreme." He said this in a belittling manner, and Vasantrao looked angrily at him. Das Ganu saw this and asked that person not to say such things. After the discourse was over, both Das Ganu and Vasantrao went home.

Around midnight that same man came searching for Vasantrao, and said, "I have come to apologise to you, as Baba beat me twice with his *satka*." Then he lifted his shirt and showed Vasantrao and Das Ganu two welts on his back. However Vasantrao said, "You didn't ridicule me, but it must have been an offence to Baba, hence you received his wrath. Now why are you asking me for forgiveness?"

The next day Vasantrao wished to return home and he asked Das Ganu's permission. Das Ganu asked him to go to Baba's Samadhi and ask Baba to grant him permission. Vasantrao then went and placed a coconut and 2 rupees *dakshina* on the Samadhi. He turned around to leave, when he distinctly heard Baba say, "Why did you come? Now leave this place." Vasantrao was terribly frightened hearing this and he immediately clasped Das Ganu's feet and told him everything. Das Ganu comforted him saying, "Baba has blessed you and given you permission to leave."

Upon reaching home, he learned that his Guru, Sitaram Baba, was seated in his Guru-sister's home. Vasantrao had asked a friend of his to let him know that he had returned from Shirdi. Prior to meeting Vasantrao, his Guru had met his mother, and had taken a white piece of cloth from her. That piece of cloth he had tied around his head, and was seated on the chair that Vasantrao used. However, from the next room Vasantrao was unable to recognise the gentleman seated in his chair. So he asked his mother who had come to visit them, and she casually answered, "No one." Then Vasantrao entered the room and his Guru shouted, "You cannot recognise your

Guru?"

But Vasantrao saw Sai Baba seated there, and he shouted, "Sai Baba has come. Look Sai Baba is here, with a white cloth tied around his head." Vasantrao ran and clasped his feet, and his Guru patted him on his back and lifted him up. Then Sitaram Baba said, "Why did you come? Now leave this place. Go back there." These were the same words that Baba had shouted in the Samadhi Mandir. Then his Guru said, "Both of us are the same." That was the turning point for him, and from then on, his every pore was filled with devotion to Baba. Every breath that he took was drenched in love and devotion and he surrendered completely to Baba. Now it is over 50 years, and he is ardently devoted to Baba.

Ref.: *Sai Prasad Magazine*, Deepavali issue, 1999.

91

Baba Removes Malti's Fears

Sometimes a sceptic meets a saint and turns into a staunch devotee, and this is what happened to Sudhir Kulkarni. He went to meet Sadanand Maharaj at his Chunabhatti ashram and was thoroughly impressed by his humble approach and equanimity. Gradually he experienced his spirituality and his faith in saints grew thereafter. Sudhir's wife Malti was devoted to Sai Baba, and a few years later Sudhir also accepted Baba as his Sadguru and God.

After they got married, the Kulkarnis lived in a multi-storeyed building in Thana. The apartment was large and every morning when Sudhir went to work, Malti was all alone in the apartment. Being rather timid, she was scared of being alone, and it was her habit to sit before Baba's picture and pray, "Baba take away my fear." Once during the monsoons, she sat praying before Baba's picture, when it became dark and overcast with black clouds. Suddenly she felt someone's presence behind her and was frightened out of her wits. But because Baba's picture was in front of her, she calmly said, "Baba is it you?"

Malti recalls, "Strangely enough, I became very calm, as I was sure the person standing behind me was Baba. His shadow was huge and it reached the sky, and slowly it enclosed me in it. Soon I was in utter peace and bliss. Finally I turned around and I saw this bright light. The light was exceedingly bright and had tiny whirls of incandescent colours in it. The whirls were predominantly blue, red and gold, along with the rest of the colours of the rainbow. The glow and luminescence was so great that I could hardly keep my eyes open. Instinctively, I knew that it was his cosmic form and he had blessed me. Thankfully, I knelt right there. Thereafter my irrational fear had totally disappeared. Now I am not paralysed with fear as I know my Baba is with me."

During the auspicious month of December (Margashish), Malti used to perform an elaborate ritual for goddess Mahalakshmi. She would fast during that period and recite hymns. On the last day of the ritual she asked Sudhir to tell the watchman on duty to bring a branch of a mango tree. She said, "On your way out, please tell the watchman to get a branch of a mango tree so I can complete my fast. I want to hang a garland of its leaves above the front door." However the watchman didn't come to her apartment with the branch; so she went downstairs. Then the watchman handed her a rather stout branch. Malti said, "I don't need such a big branch, what will I do with all these leaves?" The watchman told her to hang them all over her apartment. As usual she spoke to Sudhir that morning and thanked him for not forgetting about the mango leaves. However, Sudhir told her that he was unable to find the watchman at the door so he didn't tell him about it. A while later Malti went downstairs as she thought that the watchman might have inadvertently given her some other person's mango branch. However, the watchman said, "This morning a tall person with a charismatic personality came and stood before me. He had worn a long white shirt, and a white *dhoti*. On his head he had a white turban. Handing the branch to me he said, "On the fourth floor of this building a lady is performing my worship. Go and give her this branch, and ask her to put garlands of the mango leaves all over her home."

Hearing this, Malti ran home and stood in front of Baba's picture, crying. "Baba you came all the way to the building. You gave the watchman the branch so that I could successfully complete my ritual. However, if you had come home, how happy I would have been. But Baba if you really did come, give me some proof. If the garland from your photograph falls down then I will have positive proof that you did come." No sooner had she said this, than the garland adorning Baba's picture fell down. With tears of joy in her eyes she said, "Baba I have now realised that you are the embodiment of all the Gods, Goddesses, and the Sadgurus. With compassion for your devotees you come running to help them." Soon after Malti had completed her ritual she was blessed with a baby boy.

Sudhir had this wonderful experience a few days later. Early one morning he dreamt of Sadanand Maharaj, who gave him a mantra. Simultaneously, Baba appeared in Malti's dream and gave her the same mantra. Now both of then chant the mantra and find infinite peace and solace in it. Sudhir says, "Now I am no more a sceptic and I believe that Sadanand Maharaj and Sai Baba are the same. Although both the saints have taken Samadhi, yet they come running to help and guide their devotees both materialistically and spiritually. Indeed we are fortunate to have found a Sadguru."

Ref.: *Sai Prasad*, Ram Navami issue, 1997.

92

Baba Visits Vayjanthimala

It was a difficult period in the life of Vayjanthimala, a resident of Vasai. But she faced life armed with a great deal of faith in Baba. To put food on the table and educate her children she taught in a school nearby. Then in the late afternoon she coached some kids so that she could increase her meagre income. Vayjanthimala had an earnest desire to read the *Guru Charitra* during that trying time. She remembered how Baba had asked a number of devotees to read it on a daily basis, and had asked some to listen to it while it was being read. Vayjanthimala told her friends about her desire, but they said, "Women should not read the *Guru Charitra*." She was not convinced, so she sought the advice of a very knowledgeable and spiritual person. He told her that it was alright for her to do the *parayan*.

Her daily routine was to complete all her household chores and reach school around 7 a.m., and return home at 12 o'clock. At that time her children were at school. After a quick shower, Vayjanthimala would go to the Maruti Mandir across the street from her home. There she would lay her head at Maruti's feet and tell him all her woes, and ask his guidance. An hour later she would return home and coach the students at home. Then she read the assigned chapters of the *Guru Charitra*.

On the 3rd day of the *parayan* as usual she went to the Maruti Mandir, and laid her head at his feet. When she finally opened her eyes and turned around, just 2 ft behind there was a huge vulture. Vayjanthimala was scared out of her wits; however, she controlled herself and thought that God may appear in any form. Collecting all the courage that she had, she started doing *pradikshinas* (circumambulations) of the sanctum. The vulture also followed her. Vayjanthimala could hear the sound of his claws as he walked behind her. When she completed the *pradikshinas*, her students came looking for her. Seeing the vulture, they started yelling, "Come and see, a vulture is following our teacher." Soon a huge crowd had gathered there with sticks. Calmly Vayjanthimala asked them not to kill the bird as it was a sin. "Please don't crowd around the door as you are blocking it. The bird will leave the same way it came here. I am sure it will not harm anyone if you don't harm it." Unexpectedly, they moved away and the vulture flew away.

Vayjanthimala and her students returned home and she started coaching them. Just as she had completed her tutoring, she saw an old man about 75 years of age entering the compound. He had on a white *dhoti*, and a long white shirt, a *jholi* slung on his shoulder. In one hand he had a wooden bowl, and in the other a thin branch of a Neem tree. Vayjanthimala was surprised as no beggar, sadhu or saint ever entered the compound. However Baba did, and entered her home reciting the same mantra that she recited every day. She got up prostrated at his feet, and looked up, as his face shone with divine glow. Vayjanthimala then gave him a four anna coin. He said, "I want a rupee coin from you." Immediately she went inside and searched for the coin and gave it to him.

Baba accepted it and said, "You are in grave trouble. But don't give up, have faith and patience. I am there to take care of you, and everything will be alright." Saying this he applied sandalwood paste on her forehead, and sprinkled some *tirth* all over the room. Vayjanthimala seized the opportunity and asked her students to prostrate before him. Then he applied sandalwood paste on their foreheads, and left. Immediately Vayjanthimala asked her students to follow him and see where he went. They returned saying, "Madam, after taking a few steps he vanished into thin air." Vayjanthimala now knew without a doubt that Baba had come to her home to bless her and in his characteristic way, take care of her. Indeed as the years rolled by her financial situation improved, her children received their education and were happily married.

Then the Ganesh festival came around and her entire family

had gathered at her home to participate in the festivities and have a feast thereafter. Vayjanthimala was in the kitchen helping her daughter prepare the meal. Finally everything was completed to her satisfaction and everyone sat for their meal. However Vayjanthimala was surprised to find that there was an extra plate. She served everyone, including the extra plate, then took it and offered it to Lord Ganesha. Just as they were about to put the first morsel of food in the mouth, someone came to her door. "*Mai*, I am hungry. Will you feed me?"

Vayjanthimala went to the door and found a sadhu standing there. She was about to take the food from the extra plate and give him *bhiksha* when he said, "You have kept my seat and plate for me, right? I told you I could come and have a meal with you, so I come today." Filled with joy, Vayjanthimala went and held his hand and brought him into the room. Instinctively Vayjanthimala knew he was Baba, but where was she to seat him? Her relatives might frown at her action, so she wisely went to her prayer room. Next to Lord Ganesha's idol she placed a chair and a small table and placed the extra plate of food on it. Then she brought a large glass of water and entreated him to have his meal. Baba had a satisfying meal. Vayjanthimala prostrated at Baba's feet and gave him *dakshina*. Baba blessed her, "When you hold the hand of *shraddha* and *saburi* you will be successful in life and in everything that you do." Saying this, he left. Vayjanthimala says, "Baba's words are never false, I gradually achieved all my aspirations. And I was quite content and happy. Even my husband who had deserted me and the children returned home. Finally my entire family who scoffed at Baba turned into ardent devotees."

Ref.: *Sai Prasad Magazine*, Deepavali issue, 1995.

93

Mrs. Pandit's Dilemma Resolved

For the past 50 years or so, Usha Pandit, a devotee residing in Mumbai, was drawn to Nana Maharaj Tharnarkar. This saint resided in Indore, and Usha was blessed by him.

Usha says, "In my heart I knew that it was only through Baba's blessing that I met Nana. However, I was in a dilemma as I had many questions and doubts. I looked at the two saints as two separate identities. I was angry with myself and I felt guilty. Maybe I had committed a grave mistake. Time and again, I remembered Baba's words, 'Our father (i.e., Guru) is ultimately our father.' This *ovi* is given in the *Shri Sai Satcharita* chapter 45, and the *ovi* is 119. I lost my peace of mind. But Baba in his compassion showed me that all the great saints are one and the same. And this is how he did it.

On 21st January 1990, while watching a programme on the television, I got a heart attack. I was rushed to the hospital, and clutching Baba's picture to my heart, I answered all the doctor's questions. Slowly and steadily the intensity of the pain started diminishing, and with treatment I was able to perform my spiritual practices. It was my practice to do *parayan* of the *Shri Sai Satcharita* and complete it on Guru Purnima. With difficulty I started reading the *Charita*, and Baba enabled me to complete it on Guru Purnima.

That month, on the 25th of July, I had this wonderful dream. I saw myself in the Dwarka Mai and Baba was seated on his stone. Nana was seated on the right side of Baba. Nana placed a small round ball of *Udi* that was the size of a beetle nut, on my left palm. Nana said, 'With this *Udi* draw an "Aum" on your tongue.' At that moment I woke up in utter delight.

The next Thursday I again dreamt of Baba. In this dream I was seated in front of Baba and Nana, but I was sobbing because my spiritual practice was not on target, and it was not going well.

I narrated both my dreams to my husband, and told him of my desire to visit Shirdi. My husband said, 'You will not be able travel by the rickety state transport bus, so I will hire a private car and then we can go.' But when Baba wants to see you he arranges everything for you. A few days later, my nephew called me and said, 'Aunty I am going to Shirdi with my wife in our car. I hoped you and uncle would accompany us, as there is plenty of room in the car.' Immediately I thanked Baba for making it so easy for me.

My nephew Ujjval Babre had booked a room in the Sai International Hotel, which has an idol of Baba in the lobby. The priest gave us *tirth* and *prasad* and then we went to our room. Later, we visited all the holy sites. The next morning, after the *Kakad Arati*, I went and sat next to Dhuni Mai, and closing my eyes started chanting Baba's name. After a long time I heard a loud noise coming from the Dhuni. The devotees around there said, 'A coconut has exploded in the Dhuni.' I looked around and indeed charred pieces of the coconut were strewn all over the floor. A short while later an attendant was sweeping the debris towards where I sat. I looked towards him and was enchanted to see a small round ball of *Udi* amongst the debris. The small ball of *Udi* was exactly like the ball that Nana had given me in my dream. I jumped up and with reverence picked up the ball of *Udi*. Then I got a clean piece of paper and packed the ball in it. Now tears were streaming down my cheeks as I placed the sacred *Udi* next to my chest. Then I went and lay my head on the feet of Baba's portrait, thinking, 'O! Thank you, Baba. You with your infinite compassion have given me proof that you and Nana are not separate identities. And that you are not displeased with me.'

That evening all of us set out for Baba's *darshan*, but midway I had terrible back pain due to the spondylitis of the vertebrae. I asked my family to go ahead and have *darshan*, and I decided to go back to the room. Taking the aid of the devotees going my way, I reached the hotel. I sat in front of Baba's idol in the lobby and cried my heart out. The priest there was concerned about me, so he came up to me and we started chatting. I was pleasantly surprised to learn that he was Prabhakar Deshpande, Shama's nephew. I told him that I belonged to Anna Chinchinikar's (Babre) family. Another surprise awaited me, as Prabhakar was Nana's favourite student. And when Nana visits Shirdi, he stays with him. I felt that Baba had in his unique way, brought all the devotees of Nana together. In fact, Baba had pulled all of us into one large family. Now I am not restless anymore and my faith in Baba had increased by leaps and bounds."

Ref.: *Sai Prasad Magazine*, Deepavali issue, 1991.

94

Baba Rewards Arati's Devotion

It was over a year ago that Arati Kambli, a resident of Mumbai, had put her vacant plot up for sale. She was concerned that not a single realtor had contacted her to purchase it. Finally she turned to Baba for help. Arati said, "Baba I desperately need your help. I will start reading one chapter of your *Charita* everyday and within 53 days I must get a realtor who will buy my plot."

The very next day she started reading the *Charita* with devotion. On the day she was reading the 40th chapter, a builder came to her home. Seeing her read the *Charita,* he readily agreed to her terms, and was eager to buy her plot. Within a week the deal was finalised and he even gave her the deposit. Arati was ecstatic, as that day she had completed her reading. To mark the completion of the *Charita,* she had decided to perform a *Sai Satya Naryana Puja* in her home; so she invited all her friends and neighbours.

After the ritualistic worship was performed, she requested her guests to be seated for the meal. Her mother-in-law had offered a platter of food to Baba, and had kept aside a platter to feed a cow. She told Arati, "Now that all the guests are seated, close the door and start serving them. The cow can be fed later; as the kids are hungry, let them eat first." Arati served all her guests, and they were about to start the meal when she heard someone knocking at her door. Adjacent to her home there was a slum area, and the children from there frequently bothered the residents of her building. Arati presumed that they were knocking, so she didn't pay attention to it. A short while later again she heard the knocking. This time she opened the door and there stood a snow white cow. Her big brown eyes were full of compassion, as she looked at Arati. Arati was unable to take her eyes off her. Just like a human being she knocked at the door twice. By then all her guests also came to the door to look at this beautiful cow. Arati's mother-in-law came out with a *lota* (copper jug) of water and both of them performed ritualistic worship. Serenely the cow allowed her worship to be carried out. To Arati's utter amazement for a fleeting moment she saw Baba standing there. Arati rubbed her eyes and then she saw Lord Dattatreya there.

Her mother-in-law went in and immediately brought the plate of food that she had kept aside for the cow and placed it in front of her. The cow ate everything that was served to her. Arati then asked if she was satisfied or if she wanted another serving. The cow nodded her head and another plate of food was served to her. The cow then cast a glance at everyone assembled there as if to bless them. Then she turned and left. Arati and her mother-in-law followed her, but she walked about 30 steps and disappeared.

Arati says, "One never knows in what form Baba will come and bless you. Nevertheless I searched for that cow in our neighborhood, but was unable to find her. I can't help but wonder who that cow was. Where did she come from? And where did she go? It is said that all the Gods and Goddesses reside inside the cow, so I am extremely happy that by feeding her, I also served the meal to all the Gods and Goddesses, and that all the deities came to my home and had a meal."

Ref.: *Sai Prasad Magazine*, Deepavali issue, 1991.

95

Baba Heals the Bendres

Dr. Bendre, a medical practitioner, had his clinic in Ghatkopar, Mumbai. Once his mother was critically ill, and was almost at death's door.

One morning she had this vivid dream, wherein she saw a tall fakir dressed in a *kafni*, with a white cloth tied around his head. With utmost compassion in his eyes he said, "Now I will take away all your illnesses, and you will be alright. Thereafter come and have my darshan." The fakir then disappeared and his mother recovered completely.

One evening his parents visited a friend's home, when Mrs. Bendre saw a picture of Baba hanging on the wall and enquired about him. The friend gave a glorious description of Baba divinity and *leelas*. Immediately Mrs. Bendre said, "This is the saint who appeared in my dream and brought me back from death's door. He also took away all my illnesses, as I am fine now."

A few days later the entire Bendre family went on a pilgrimage to Shirdi. At that time, the doctor was only 10 years old. Since then he became devoted to Baba, and every year without fail the family would visit Shirdi. Years rolled by and their son graduated from medical college and set up his clinic in Ghatkopar. However, just like a '*warkari*' he would visit Shirdi every year. Whenever he treated patients he would first give them Baba's *Udi* and then prescribe the medicines.

When Dr. Bendre's son was about 2 years old he would tie a white towel around his head and sit with right leg across his left knee exactly in the "sitting on the stone posture". Then he would tell his friends, "I used to take care of Baba's treasury. And now he has sent me here." During his infancy, his health was very bad, and he frequently fell ill. The child was born with a congenital defect of the heart and had dextro-cardia (his heart was on the right side of the body). In 1970, the famous British cardiologist Chris Lincoln performed surgical correction of his heart. Prior to surgery he said, "This is an exceedingly rare congenital abnormality of the heart. It is the first time this operation is being performed in India. There are only 4 or 5 cases recorded in the world. I pray to God that the surgery will be successful, as only God's grace can save this child."

Indeed, Baba was there to oversee the surgery and it was performed successfully. Dr. Bendre's son's recovered fully and went on to study medicine and become a doctor. Both the father and son feel Baba's presence in their lives and know that Baba is there to take care of them.

Ref.: *Sai Prasad Magazine*, New Year's issue, 2000.

96

How Baba Deflected His Devotees' Death

Once a devotee named Chandralekha Bhosle, a resident of Pune, had gone to visit her sister in Gwalior and was returning to Pune by train. She was apprehensive about the journey as she was travelling alone. The train was at that time passing through the Chambal valley, which was notorious for dacoits who forcefully entered the train and beat and robbed the passengers of all their belongings, and even the clothes that they wore. The train stopped at a small village and the bogie got filled with a rowdy and rambunctious crowd. They sat wherever they found place, regardless of whose berth it was. Along the way, fights broke out between them and the passengers. Chandralekha was petrified, so she started chanting Baba's name as a mantle of protection against the rowdy crowd. An hour later, the crowd disembarked at a small station and Chandralekha breathed a sigh of relief. At that time it was around 9 p.m., so she thanked Baba for protecting her and soon fell asleep.

Around 6 a.m., Chandralekha heard the *Kakad Arati*. At first she thought that she was dreaming, and then she thought maybe someone was listening to a tape recorder or radio. However the *arati* was not accompanied by any musical instrument, so she got up and looked around. There on the top berth in front of her was a young man around 25 years of age singing the *arati* in a very melodious voice. Chandralekha was thrilled to find a Sai devotee in her bogie, so she signaled to him to come down, and they started chatting. Chandralekha was curious to hear how this young man became devoted to Baba. She asked him if he was on his way to Shirdi and he said,

"Yes."

The young man named Pankaj Sharma narrated this *leela* to her. Pankaj said, "A few years ago, I got married, and two years later I was blessed with a baby boy. Life was wonderful, and I didn't have a care in the world. Two years ago I bought a new car, and that very night we decided to take it to Shirdi. It was my idea to travel at night. I thought we would reach Shirdi early the next morning; then we could attend the *Kakad Arati*, and visit all the holy sites and we could return to Hoshangabad that very day. From Hoshangabad to Shirdi is around 600 kms, so I could easily reach Shirdi within 10 hours in my new car. I asked my friend to accompany us as he was a good driver and we could share the task of driving between us. Thus, my friend's wife, my wife and son all set out from Hoshangabad around 10 p.m. Along the way we chatted and had a lot of fun, as all of us were exceedingly happy to go to Shirdi. After all we were going to Shirdi to meet our Sadguru and God. Between me and my friend, the driving was quite effortless, and free from strain.

I had then taken the highway and was driving along, when I saw a huge buffalo standing like death itself in the middle of the road. Indeed he was death waiting for us. I was driving at a great deal of speed, and I tried to control the car. I pressed the horn with all my might. The headlights of my car fell into the eyes of the buffalo, and he froze in place, mesmerized by the headlights. He didn't move an inch, and possibly didn't hear the blaring of my horn. His glinting eyes came closer and closer to my car and the inevitable happened.

I was scared out of my wits, and I just called out to Baba and closed my eyes. There was a terrible thud and I could hear the buffalo scream with pain. My car flipped over four times, but came to stand upright. At that point in time I didn't know where I was; whether I was alive or dead. For a fleeting moment I saw Baba standing in front of the windscreen, however he was wearing a dark, black *kafni*. His face was grave, and soon his face turned jet black.

I heard my son call out to me. I looked around and everyone

was in shock, and there was silence. I called out to everyone, and asked them to get out of the car. I was wonderstruck that except for a few scratches, there were no serious injuries; even the car was in working condition. However, everyone was numb with fear. I gave them some water to drink, then I drove the car to the highway and parked it by the side of the road. I assured everyone that we were on our way to Shirdi, then how would he let us die? I then stopped a vehicle that was passing by and requested them to inform the police of the accident.

A short while later I remembered the male buffalo. I was sure that he had died as I had crashed into him at a tremendous speed. His body was lying on the road, so I got a crane to haul him away. By then it was daybreak, and everyone had settled down after the initial shock. I got into the car and looked at the dashboard. I had a small statue of Baba fixed on it, but it was nowhere to be found. Desperately I searched for it, but it had been smashed to tiny bits by the impact. I realised that Baba in his mercy had taken upon himself the death of all of us, and as a result his idol had broken into tiny bits, while we escaped with minor injuries. Baba had defeated Yama, the god of death and his messenger, and had slain their vehicle which was the male buffalo.

I picked the pieces of the broken idol and tears of gratitude gushed down my cheeks and bathed the pieces that I held in my hand. I cried because I knew that in every tiny piece of that idol, Baba was present, and every atom of my being was enveloped by Baba's grace. After that dreadful incident, I visit Shirdi at every opportunity I get. My entire life is now devoted to Baba, and I can assure you that he comes to the aid of all his devotees."

Ref.: *Shri Sai Sagar*, Deepavali issue, 2013.

97

Baba Saves Shruti from the Evil Spirit

This *leela* is narrated by Sudhir R. Apte, a devotee residing in Pune. He says, "I am very fortunate that my maternal grandfather, Naryanrao Vinayak Shakdev, was ardently devoted to Baba since 1915. Hence everyone in our household worshipped Baba and Baba has looked after us through thick and thin. This *leela* pertains to my maternal aunt, who had unwavering faith in Baba."

When Shankarao Naryan Shakdev retired from his official duties, he decided to reside in Kharapur near Sangli. He scouted the area for a house and found a wada in Damle alley. The wada was large and the price was right, so they bought it. After performing *vastu shanti* (worship to remove evil influences), the Shakdevs moved in. They also performed elaborate rituals all night long (*jagran* and *gondhal*) to seek the blessings of Tulja Bhavani and other Gods and Goddesses. Shankarao and his wife Indumati performed Baba's *arati* every day, and also did *parayan* of the *Charita* on a regular basis.

In 1993, their son Anil left his former job and took the job of a manager in a firm in Belgaon. Anil, along with his wife Shruti, their two sons Satish and Tushar, came to reside with Shankarao and Indumati. A short while later Shruti fell ill. She was given the best possible treatment, but without much effect. Her health started deteriorating with every passing day. The doctors were unable to diagnose her disease. Shruti was unable to talk, and she was now reduced to skin and bones. When all possible human aid failed, Indumati turned to Baba for help.

One night as usual Indumati applied *Udi* to Shruti's entire body and went to sleep. Around midnight, Indumati was awoken by Shruti's screams, and she rushed into her room.

Fear was written all over Shruti's face, and with her own two hands she was strangling her own neck. With all her strength, Indumati freed her from the grip of her hands, simultaneously yelling to Shankarao to help. Shruti woke up, shuddering in fear. After she had calmed down, she said, "*Ayi* after I had fallen asleep, a woman wearing a traditional 9 yard sari came close to me and said, 'I am feeling very hungry so I am going to take you away with me,' and she started throttling me. I couldn't breathe. And in agony I started shouting. I don't know what happened thereafter." Indumati told her everything. Then Shruti said, "You saved my life, or I would have killed myself. I don't want to stay here anymore; please let me go to my parents."

Indumati was aware that an evil spirit had come there in the form of that woman. She consoled her saying, "Don't worry anymore. My Baba is capable of driving away such evil spirits. By his grace everything will be alright."

The next morning, Indumati asked her husband to find Damle, who had sold the wada to them, and inquire about its history. Damle said, "Ages ago, the Kathe family resided in the wada. They fell on hard times, and his wife Rhukmabai was desperate as she had 6 young children and her husband to feed. There was no source of income, and her husband quarrelled with her and beat her frequently. To Rhukmabai's utter dismay she realised that she was pregnant; soon there would be another mouth to feed. She lost her mental balance and that night Rhukmabai jumped into a well and took her life. Within the next 6 years her husband and 6 children all died from some reason or the other. It was rumoured that the mother of seven children sacrificed 7 members of her family. Before long, Rhukmabai started torturing my family also. Fed up with this, I sought refuge in a saint. He advised me to sell the wada at a reasonable price to a spiritual person who conducted worship and religious practices daily. I knew that you were devoted to Baba and Tulja Bhavani, so I sold it to you."

Indumati heard the story and immediately prayed to Baba,

"Baba prior to purchasing the wada we got your approval through 'chits'. We have devotedly prayed to you, and done your *aratis*. Now that my daughter-in-law has come to reside with us, why have you piled all these troubles on her? Now only you can resolve all these problems."

That very night Baba appeared in Indumati's dream and said, "Bai, you are very stubborn. Now for your sake I have to look into this. That pregnant mother of those 7 children is very hungry. So she wants the mother who has borne two children. But I will not let this take place. However, you have to without fail on every *amavaysa* place a plate full of food near that well, for that woman. Then break a coconut there and prostrate. Then everything will be alright. Don't forget this."

This is practised to this day. Needless to say, Shruti recovered her health completely, and her sons are now grown up. The entire family is leading a happy, contented life.

Ref.: *Shri Sai Sagar Magazine*, Deepavali issue, 2013.

98

Mahendrabhai's Wonderful Experiences

Mahendrabhai Joshi, a resident of Baroda, was intensely devoted to Baba. Often he thought, "If ever Baba appears before me in human form I will clasp his feet and lay my head on it."

On 22nd February 1979, he and his family set out on a pilgrimage to Shirdi. They visited all the holy sites at Nasik and around 3.30 p.m. they arrived at the bus stand for their onward journey to Shirdi. His wife and son also accompanied him. Mahendrabhai was looking out for the bus that would take them to Shirdi, when all of a sudden Baba appeared before him. Mahendrabhai was startled out of his wits. His devotion was rewarded, and he thought he would lay his head on Baba's feet.

However, he was still anxious as to which bus would take them to Shirdi and he eagerly kept a watch on the buses that were scheduled to leave the station. Baba then said, "Are you going to Shirdi? Don't worry, that bus in front of you will leave in an hour." And indeed that was the bus that took then to Shirdi.

Baba then asked Mahendrabhai to give him some tea to drink. Mahendrabhai immediately got tea for him and his family. He had still not prostrated at Baba's feet yet. Just as he moved forward to do so, a bus swiftly passed in between both of them and Baba disappeared. Mahendrabhai then searched for Baba everywhere, but was unable to find him. Like child who was lost and was searching for his mother, he sobbed uncontrollably. The passengers waiting there wondered if he had lost his mind. Yet his tears flowed on, and he realised that devotion should be accompanied with patience.

Later they reached Shirdi, but Mahendrabhai was dejected, as he regretted not having prostrated at Baba's feet. He pined for Baba and yearned to see him again. He repented for what he had done. Mahendrabhai resolutely made up his mind that if Baba ever appeared before him again, he would not take his eyes off him.

The next morning the entire family went to a shack to have tea, and Baba appeared before him again and asked for tea. Mahendrabhai ordered the tea without taking his eyes off Baba, and they all started drinking the tea. He waited for Baba to finish his tea, thinking that then he would prostrate. Just as Mahendrabhai took a step forward, a vehicle passed by at great speed and he ran and caught hold of his son's hand. When he turned and looked at the chair that Baba sat on, it was empty. Mahendrabhai learned a valuable lesson from this—you have to have complete detachment to find God.

On the last day of his stay in Shirdi, Baba gave him this wonderful experience. Mahendrabhai took his family to the Dwarka Mai. He said, "Baba stayed here for 60 years, and is still here even to this day. He gives some lucky devotees evidence of his eternal existence. Here is the stone on which Baba had his bath. Everyday, Baba used to go for *bhiksha*, and all the food he collected he placed in this *kolomba*. Then mixing it all together (*kaala*), he allowed all the stray dogs and cats of Shirdi to eat first, and then he would eat a few morsels. We are not that fortunate to have his *prasad* today, but we can definitely venerate the *kolomba* by touching it to our forehead." With great devotion Mahendrabhai picked up that blessed *kolomba* and touched it to his forehead. And lo! The *kolomba* that was empty a few moments ago, now had piping hot chapattis, smeared with butter and a dry curry on it. With utter devotion Mahendrabhai took the prasad and distributed it to his family. With tears of joy in his eyes, he thanked Baba for his divine *prasad*.

Ref.: *Shri Sai Sagar Magazine*, Deepavali issue, 2012.

99

Udi Cures All Ailments

Often, it is a problem that draws a person to Baba's feet, and that is precisely how the Davles started worshipping Baba.

Suhasani Chandrashekar Chowdhari, a devotee residing in Pune says, "My elder brother Sudhir was born in 1954; it was an easy and normal delivery. As soon as he was born the doctor noticed that his anterior fontanel (soft spot) was exceptionally large, and it was covered with a thin membrane. The membrane was so thin that his brain could be seen through it. The doctor, along with my parents, was very concerned about it, and the doctor advised my patients to be cautious and vigilant, and protect the area from any knocks and bumps. He also prescribed some ointments and medicines so that the area would close quickly. Along with this the doctor also made a steel helmet so that the area would be protected. But even with all these extraordinary modes of treatment, there was no sign of it closing. My parents were very anxious about this.

"One day my father's friend visited us, and hearing about Sudhir's problem he immediately gave us some *Udi*. Up until that time we had never heard about Sai Baba or Shirdi. Nor were we aware of the power of Baba's *Udi*. He narrated some of Baba's *leelas* and told them that Baba's *Udi* was a 'cure all'. He told my mother to make a paste of the *Udi* and apply it on Sudhir's soft spot. My parents decided that as all modes of treatment had proved ineffectual, they would try this saint's *Udi*. My mother then made a paste of the *Udi* and applied it on Sudhir's scalp. Lo and behold, on the 5th day his fontanel had closed completely and the scalp of his head became normal. From that moment on, all of us became devoted to Baba and were indebted to him for life. This incident was so extraordinary that it challenged science and medicine and left the doctor dumbfounded.

Thereafter, *Udi* became the first line of treatment for all illness, and all incidents of life. Everyone ingested *Udi* and applied it to their foreheads twice a day. Without applying *Udi* no one stepped out of the house; and for any interview or examination *Udi* went with them. If children got scared, it was *Udi* to the rescue. In case of bad dreams, apply *Udi*; can't sleep, use *Udi*. But most importantly, each one of us carries a packet of *Udi* with us at all times, because it assures us that Baba is present with us in the form of his *Udi*."

Ref.: *Shri Sai Sagar Magazine*, May–June issue, Volume 3, No. 3, 2012.

100

Sushma's Grandson

It was a difficult time for Jayashri Ghokle. She was pregnant with her first baby, which was a breech baby and that too a footling delivery (where the feet come out first).

Even after receiving the best treatment, the gynaecologist was unable to correct the position of the foetus. Furthermore, the foetus was causing an obstruction; hence the gynecologist told Jayashri that she would have to perform a cesarean delivery and admitted her in the hospital. Full of remorse, Jayashri asked her mother-in-law (Sushma), "You regularly read Baba's *Charita*. Without fail you perform his *arati*, while I never go to the temple, nor do I prostrate before Baba. Is this retribution for my errant behaviour?"

Sushma pacified her, saying, "Baba is an ocean of mercy and forgiveness. Now that you have realised your mistake, seek refuge in him and he will never desert you." Shushma applied some *Udi* on her forehead, and went outside the hospital room to chant Baba's name. Her gynaecologist asked the nurse to prepare Jayashri for surgery, and summoned two more surgeons for the cesarean. Sushma then sat on a bench and read the 11th chapter of the *Shri Sai Satcharita*. At 6.38 p.m. the time that Sushma usually performed Baba's *arati* at home, the entire hospital was filled with the aroma of frankincense (*loban*). The air became pure and filled with good energy. Sushma was sure that by Baba's grace the child was born. A short time later a doctor came and informed Sushma that at 6.38 p.m. Jayashri had delivered a baby boy. In amazement, the doctor said, "It's a miracle that your grandson, a breech baby who was obstructing his own progress, was delivered normally."

Sushma was overcome with happiness, and tears of gratitude

flowed from her eyes. She was unable to say a single word. On the 11th day after the delivery, Sushma went to Shirdi. In the Samadhi Mandir she sat for a while in front of Baba's idol and closed her eyes. Sushma says, "A short while later I opened my eyes and looked at Baba's idol. And in the place of Baba's left foot I saw a baby's foot. I remembered that my grandson came into this world feet-first. Baba indicated to me that my grandson was his gift to me. I joined my palms together and surrendered to him."

After Sushma returned from Shirdi they had the christening ceremony, and her grandson was named Akshay. With delight she noted that on the left side of his hip he had a birthmark that resembled a Neem leaf. Right from infancy Akshay loved Baba. He would run and stand in front of Baba and laugh merrily. He also played peek-a-boo in front of his picture. During the *arati* he played the small cymbals. When he was two years old he would sit exactly like Baba, as seen in the 'sitting on the stone pose'. Akshay never went to sleep until he heard his grandmother sing Baba's *aratis*.

On the Ram Navami day after Akshay was born, Sushma remembered that on that day devotees carried water from the Godavari so that Baba could be bathed with it after Kakad Arati the next day. She joined her palms together in front of Baba picture and went to bed. That night she dreamt of a huge five-hooded serpent (*Sesh Nag*) and that Akshay was playing with it. The next day around noon a small cobra was found in her home. Sushma immediately worshipped it and asked her husband not to harm it. Slowly the snake slithered away.

Akshay grew up into a delightful child who was very devoted to Baba. Sushma repeatedly says, "I am ever grateful to Baba, for blessing us with a child like Akshay."

Ref.: *Sai Prasad Magazine*, Deepavali issue, 1992.

101

How Baba Protected Dapthdar

The seed of faith, however small it may be in the beginning, yields a huge luscious tree in the future. Saroj Dapthdar learned this from her experiences at a tender age, and this is how it came about.

In 1940, when she was 9 years old, she resided in a building in Dadar. Every morning around 6 a.m. she had to go alone to her school in Mahim. Saroj says, "As I walked in the alley alone, the street dogs would bark loudly at me. Then the pack of dogs would follow me till I reached the main road. At that age I felt that a pride of lions were after me, so in desperation I started saying, 'Sainath, Sainath'. At that time I realised that if I chanted Baba's name my troubles would flee. After all, 'nath' literally means 'Lord, protector and refuge.' During the course of my life I had to face many trials and tribulations, but whenever I called out to Sainath he came to my aid. I would like to narrate a grave experience in my life.

In 1962, I lived in a chawl in Goregaon. My husband worked as a clerk in a government office. I had three children all below the age of eleven. I could hardly make ends meet, but I was content with my lot. One night around 2 a.m., my husband got severe chest pain, and he was drenched in perspiration. I awoke my neighbour and requested her to get a doctor. But the doctor didn't turn up. I thought that maybe he had abdominal gas and colic due to it, so I gave him some baking powder with a little water. Then I applied a balm to his chest. I gave him some *Udi* mixed in water, and applied it to his entire body. All the while, I was continuously chanting Baba's name. Around 5 a.m., the severity of the pain lessened and finally he fell asleep. The next morning a neighbour was passing by on his way to work, and I stopped him and asked for help. He suspected some serious problem and immediately rushed me and my husband to the hospital. In GT Hospital my husband was diagnosed to have had a heart attack and was admitted. He stayed in the hospital for 2 months and was treated there. Finally he got discharged, so along with my sister and brother-in-law, we went to bring him home. When the ward boy was wheeling him out to the waiting car, a couple a stopped me and gave me some *prasad* from Shirdi. In my heart I felt that this was a good omen. Prior to leaving for the hospital, after locking my house I had left the key with my neighbour. I was in for another surprise, as upon opening the door I was astounded to see an idol of Baba seated on the table, as if he was waiting for me. Now how did this idol come there? Who could have kept it inside my house? After making a few inquires I learned that there was a person in my building who sold idols of Baba. For some reason, on that day he brought that idol and left it on my window sill; my neighbour saw it and placed the idol on my table.

My husband was asked to take bed rest, so he lay on the bed and listened to the speeches given at that time by Jawharlal Nehru. Early that morning at 4 a.m. he started shouting in his sleep. Like a man possessed, he made frantic actions with his hands, and yelled in frenzy. I shook him and asked him what had happened. He told me not to worry, as he had a nightmare. After some time, he fell asleep.

The next morning I asked him about the dream. Vividly he described his dream, "Yesterday two huge hideous looking black men with bloodshot eyes caught hold of me. This occurred near the gate of the Goregaon cemetery. Then they kicked and beat me mercilessly. I asked them what had I done and why were they beating me? At that moment a man resembling Nehru wearing a white shirt and white pants, came to my rescue. He said, "Arre! Why are you beating this poor man? If his family hears about it they will severely punish you." Hearing this, those satanic looking men fled and at that moment you woke me up." I pacified him saying, "Yesterday you heard Nehru give his speech and so you had this dream."

Around 4 p.m. that day, my elder sister Vimlatai came to

meet my husband, and inquire about his health. We had a pleasant time chatting over a cup of tea, and I told her about my husband's dream. Vimlatai is also devoted to Baba, so she said, "Saroj don't worry so much; after all Baba sent his *prasad* through that couple. I am sure nothing untoward will happen to him." At that time a person from my husband's office named Joshi came to our house. This gentleman was an ardent devotee of Lord Dattatreya, who visited the Datta temple atop the Giranar Mountain every year without fail. He was a renowned astrologer, but was quite eccentric by nature, as he hardly spoke to anyone. So I wondered how he came to visit us. Nevertheless I invited him in. As soon as he sat down he turned to my husband and said, "Arre! Dapthdar, don't say a word, first tell me, who is devoted to Lord Datta in your home?" My husband said, "Lord Datta? My wife is devoted to Sai Baba of Shirdi." Then Joshi said, "That is why your sudden death was prevented last night. So I came after searching all over for your house to tell you this." I asked him to explain why he said this. Joshi replied, "Last night at 4 a.m. I dreamt that I was climbing the Girnar Mountain with both of my young sons. There near the entrance gate I saw two people beating up some man. So leaving my sons there I went ahead to see what this was all about. There I found two men beating your husband mercilessly. At that very moment a Brahmin appeared there and said, 'Arre! Why are you beating this poor man? If Lord Datta finds out about this he will severely punish you and you will regret it forever.' Hearing this, those two fled from there." I was stunned that the same night, at precisely the same time, two different people from different places had the same dream. However, I thanked Baba for saving my husband's life, and giving him a second chance at life. Thus my husband lived for thirteen more years, and passed away in his sleep. With Baba's grace my children have grown up and are settled in life. I lead a comfortable life and my entire day is spent with Baba, who came home in the form of an idol.

Ref.: *Sai Prasad Magazine*, Ram Navami issue, 1994

102

Baba Is Lord Datta

Shankarao Baivalli resided in Santa Cruz, Mumbai and was ardently devoted to Lord Datta. He did not know anything about Baba, and had little interest in finding out anything about him. But all this changed in 1936. Shankarao's sister requested him to accompany her to Shirdi that year, and he refused her invitation.

A short while later while worshipping Lord Datta, he lovingly gazed at the photograph, and to his amazement it gradually changed to the figure of a fakir wearing a torn white *kafni* with a white cloth tied around his head.

Shankarao got up and wiped the photograph with the same result. He diligently wiped the photograph thrice but every time his favorite deity was transformed into this fakir. Shankarao had never seen a photograph of Baba; hence he didn't know who it was.

That evening Shankarao went to Dr. Thakkar's home and saw Baba's photograph and recognized him as the fakir that Lord Datta's picture had transformeyd into. Eagerly he asked Thakkar who the fakir was and received a lot of information on Baba. Shankarao told his sister that he would like gladly accompany her to Shirdi. Thus they set out to Shirdi, there he experienced a lot of peace and serenity that he had never experienced before.

Again and again Shankarao visited Shirdi; the effect of Baba's divinity on him was so great that he visited Shirdi nine times in a span of 6 months. On one of his visits he read the Guru Charitra in 7 days. On the night of the completion Shankarao slept in the courtyard in front of the Samadhi Mandir. At midnight he heard footsteps nearby and woke up. He looked up and saw Baba gazing at him his eyes filled with compassion.

Baba had walked from the Dwarka Mai to the Samadhi Mandir and Shankarao was overwhelmed by the love and compassion in Baba's eyes. Shankarao knew that he had found Lord Datta.

Ref.: *Shri Sai Sudha Magazine,* Vol 5, No. 8, June 1945.

103

How Sai Baba Blessed Daskisan Baba

Innumerable saints have been born in Maharastra, and left their legacy behind. One such saint was Daskisan Baba, who had a great influence on the people of Pune and Mumbai. He was born on *Shravan Vad Astami* in *Shake* 1829 at midnight by the Hindu calendar, and the month of September in the year 1904 by the English calendar. His parents, Lakshmanrao Naik and Jamunabai, resided in Pune and were exceedingly poor. When Daskisan was but a few months old his father passed away and his mother faced countless hardships and struggles. One day, in utter desperation his mother took little Daskisan and threw him in a garbage heap. However, a Muslim lady named Chandani who lived nearby rescued him and gave him back to his mother. Around the age of eighteen, Daskisan left home and wandered about, and finally came to Aurangabad. There he sought refuge in a *dargah* that had a lot of fakirs living there. Upon entering the *dargah* Sai Baba appeared before him and blessed him: "The Almighty god will take care of everything. Child, work honestly for an anna or two, so that you can fill your stomach, and perform service for the needy."

At that time Daskisan didn't have even a rag to cover his body, and Baba gave him a *kafni*. When he was 22 years old he married a pious and devout lady named Radhabai. Unexpectedly, his wife passed away a few months after their marriage. Daskisan was devastated and anguished by this, and felt life was not worth living. One day, he decided to end his life by jumping into the Mula Mutha river. So he went to *Lakdi Pul* (the name of the bridge) and was about to jump into the river, when Alishah Baba, a Sufi saint, prevented him from doing so.

Alishah Baba spoke to him compassionately and calmed his troubled mind.

About a year later, a devout lady named Lakshmibai introduced Daskisan to Sadguru Krishanath alias Khusha Bhau Mirajker. From the very first meeting, a deep friendship developed between the two. Following this, Khusha Bhau through Professor Narke gave Daskisan a "Guru Mantra" and initiated him into "Guru Bhakti". At that time Lord Dattatreya manifested before him and blessed him. As Khusha Bhau was ardently devoted to Sai Baba, it was but natural that he was greatly responsible for influencing Daskisan to worship Sai Baba. Once Khusha Bhau made Daskisan sit in front of a picture of Sai Baba and meditate and worship him intensely. And Lo! Baba appeared before him and blessed him. Thereafter Daskisan became devoted to Baba and inculcated Baba's teachings in his life. Khusha Bhau passed away on 19th February 1944, and thereafter Daskisan started performing Baba's *aratis* and preaching about Baba's divinity.

Finally Daskishan settled in Girgaon, Mumbai, where he built a beautiful Sai Baba temple, which houses a marble idol of him. This temple is popularly known as "Mangal Sai Dham". Here all the festivals that are celebrated in Shirdi are celebrated on a grand scale, along with *aratis* of Baba exactly as they are performed in Shirdi. On a regular basis there are talks and discourses on Baba's teachings, along with *kirtans* and devotional songs. The focal point of this temple is to make its congregation aware of Baba's teachings and help them incorporate it into their daily lives. The unique feature of this temple is that it is not just a place of worship, but it is foremost in doing "Sai Seva". They provide food on a daily basis to the slums and poor neighbourhoods. A dispensary is open and takes care of the poor and needy people. There is special care given to needy children, and a doctor is available to examine them free of cost, and provide free treatment to them. There is an orphanage that provides for all their needs, like meals, clothes and education. Besides this, numerous social services are provided, and this temple is one of its kind.

On 14th December 1931, Daskisan Baba breathed his last. However, the wonderful legacy he left behind continues to this day.

Ref.: *Shri Sai Leela Magazine*, Volume 66, No. 10, January 1988.

104

Madhavi's Raksha Bandhan Gift

Some devotees consider and treat Baba like a dear friend. Others treat him like a father, a mother, a Guru or Sadguru, but a few devotees treat him like a loving brother. Indeed Baba reciprocates the devotee's love with the same intensity and feelings.

Madhavi Rajshree Nanal resided in Baroda, Gujarat, and from the innermost recess of her heart regarded Baba as her elder brother. Thus, every year at Raksha Bandhan, Madhavi bought a silver *rakhi* to offer to Baba. Raksha Bandhan is the festival where a sister ties a sacred thread around the brother's wrist and the brother pledges to protect her till his last breath.

A day prior to Raksha Bandhan, in the year 2011, she bought a beautiful silver *rakhi* for Baba. Around noon a fakir came to her door and said, "My child I am very thirsty. Could you give me some water to drink?" Madhavi ran inside and brought him a large glass full of water. The fakir drank the water and gave Madhavi a silver coin. On one side of the coin was embossed a picture of Shri Sai Baba, and on the reverse was a picture of Baba's *padukas* and *satka*. The fakir said, "My child, offer turmeric powder (haldi) and vermilion powder (*kumkum*) to this coin every Thursday. This is for the good health and longevity of your husband." The fakir asked Madhavi to offer five coconuts (*Shri Phal*) and some incense sticks to Baba. He then turned towards her husband and gave him two coins of one rupee denomination and a small photograph of Baba. Then the fakir left.

Madhavi recounts, "I was thrilled as Baba came to my home a day before Raksha Bandhan. I am convinced that, that fakir was indeed Baba, as I never ever saw that fakir again anywhere."

Baba accepts our love for him in the manner we offer and

reciprocates with the same intensity. Like a brother, Baba gave Madhavi a gift of good health and longevity of her husband. What better gift could any brother give?

Ref.: *Shri Sai Sagar,* Volume 1, January–March 2011,

105

The Importance of Faith

In 1960 Kalavati Bhajirao Dhule was suffering from tuberculosis. She was given the best possible treatment; however, there was no visible improvement. Finally, the physician advised surgery.

Kalavati's daughter Kusum was devoted to Baba, so she sought refuge in him. Kusum prayed to Baba and started reading the *Shri Sai Satcharita* and completed it in 7 days. Early one morning Kusum had a vivid dream of Baba. Sternly he said, "Do not get your mother operated and if you do, do not come to me." Kusum couldn't understand a word of what Baba said. However she prayed to Baba and said, "Baba if you cure my mother of this terrible disease, I will bring her to Shirdi and stay there for two weeks, and attend all your *aratis*." Soon after Kusum had taken this vow her mother's health started improving. Her mother Kalavati started walking around the house without huffing and puffing. In due course of time she was able to climb the stairs with ease. Kusum fulfilled her vow and took her mother to Shirdi. At Shirdi, Kalavati visited all the holy sites with ease, and her health improved beyond her expectation.

Then doubt raised its ugly head in Kalavati's husband's mind. He wondered if his wife was really well as she claimed. He forced her to go to the doctor. Kalavati had herself checked and again the doctor suggested surgery. That day Kalavati was admitted, and surgery was to be performed two days later. Immediately Kusum and her husband rushed to the hospital, and vehemently opposed the surgery. But her father paid no heed to what they said. Then Kusum related her dream and what Baba had said in great detail, but to no avail. Kalavati had the surgery two days later and the same night she passed away.

In the dream, Baba had given them an indication of the calamity that was to occur. He said, "**Do not** get your mother operated and if you do, do not come to me." If only her father had faith in Baba's words, as Kusum and her husband had, her mother would surely have been alive today.

Ref.: *Prasad*, Volume 33, No. 9, August 1979.

106

Baba's Leela of the Drunk Man

For many years Vivek Magagaonkar, a devotee from Mumbai, never failed to attend all the major festivals at Shirdi. The reason behind this was that on the 1st day of the festival there was a *parayan* of the *Shri Sai Satcharita* for which the names of the devotees were selected by a lottery system. The fortunate devotee whose name was picked got to read a chapter of the *Charita*. Over the years, Vivek had always given in his name, but his name had never been selected. However, he never felt disheartened, accepting it as Baba's will, and happily participated in all the other festivities.

Sanjay was Vivek's friend. Once his mother said, "Vivek you regularly go to Shirdi, why don't you take Sanjay along with you? You can influence him to be devoted to Baba." Vivek replied, "Aunty it is not in my hands to make him a devotee. It is Baba who pulls the person towards himself. How can I make him a devotee?"

On the festival of Guru Purnima, Sanjay's mother forced Vivek to take him along. Although Sanjay was Vivek's friend, he was not in the least bit devoted to Baba, nor was he interested in knowing anything about Baba. Vivek didn't relish the thought of forcing his faith on anyone. Besides, Sanjay was addicted to alcohol, and he seemed to have more faith in alcohol than in any God, Guru or anything else. Hence Vivek was reluctant to tell him about Baba's divinity or *leelas*. Sanjay's mother hoped that her son's behaviour would change for the better if he went to Shirdi. Vivek respected his friend's mother and took Sanjay along.

Upon reaching Shirdi, Vivek went to the office to submit his name for the *parayan*. Sanjay who had accompanied him also submitted his name. Surprisingly, Sanjay's name was chosen on his very first visit, while Vivek's name was not chosen yet again. It was characteristic of Baba to oblige those who didn't believe in him and then turn towards his children who were already devoted to him. Sanjay sat down to read the chapter around 1 a.m. The arrangement for the *parayan* was in the verandah adjacent to the railing on which Baba used to rest his arm. Therefore the devotees could have darshan of the portrait kept for *parayan*, and then go into the Dwarka Mai and worship the *padukas* and Baba's Dwarka Mai portrait. Sanjay had started reading his chapter for a short while, and there were a few devotees around at that time. They would enter the Dwarka Mai and place their head on the *padukas*, and Sanjay could see this. Then again the Dwarka Mai would become empty.

At that time an old man climbed the steps of the Dwarka Mai with great difficulty. He was wearing a white *dhoti* and shirt, and he entered the Dwarka Mai staggering and reeling. Sanjay glanced at him and thought he had some neurological problem. But the man was inebriated with alcohol, and somehow he managed to stand before Baba's portrait. Angrily he said, "You have never done anything good for me. You have done nothing at all for me yet I have come to have your darshan. Answer me. Why are you not blessing me with anything good? Answer me." Hearing this, Sanjay lost his cool. The man was in a rage and Sanjay was shocked at this unexpected turn of events. He wondered if that man would turn on him next. At that time, the Dwarka Mai was completely deserted.

Finally the drunk kneeled at Baba's *padukas* and lay his head on them. Sanjay heard a "*Dhad...Dhum*," and the drunkard literally flew and fell against the door of Dhuni Mai. Baba had kicked him hard, as if he was a football. The drunkard cried out, "Kick me, kick me again and again! It's my mistake; I know you disapprove of my drinking. Yet I come in a drunken state. But I will not let go of your feet. You can kick me all you want, I will return again and again. I won't leave you because you kicked me." Then he staggered out of the Dwarka Mai.

Now Sanjay was drenched in sweat. He wondered if Baba

would give him the same treatment. From that moment Sanjay stopped drinking and never touched liquor again. The Dwarka Mai is alive with Baba's presence even today. It is not just a temple with Baba's photograph and *padukas* in it! This experience brought home this truth to Sanjay.

Ref.: *Shri Sai Sagar Magazine*, Volume 8, No. 3, July–September 2013.

107

How Muranjan Gained Faith in Baba

The power of prayer is mindboggling. Around 1963, Shri B.H. Muranjan, a resident of Mumbai, visited Shirdi. In actuality he didn't have much faith in Baba, nor did he know anything about this incredible God. Muranjan just went Shirdi for entertainment and enjoyment; his friends were going there, so he accompanied them.

Upon reaching Shirdi they went to Samadhi Mandir; it happened to be less crowded that day. Muranjan stood before the Samadhi and joined his hands together and prayed, "Baba, I don't know anything about you, nor do I have the necessary faith in you. I just came along with my friends for fun, but you must know all this because you are God Almighty. However, I wish that my father who has been suffering from asthma for the past ten years feels better. Baba, my father is plagued with repeated attacks of this disease, and he is incapacitated by it. He coughs all night and thus he cannot sleep, nor can he enjoy a full meal as he fears that he will be unable to breathe. Because of the shortness of breath he cannot even hold a conversation for a long time with his friends. If he walks even a short distance he gets out of breath, thus he is bedridden. Baba, I have but one earnest desire and that is to see my father fully recovered, and walking about in the verandah of our home. But I know that this is wishful thinking and it will never come to fruition."

After having said this, Muranjan visited the other holy sites. That entire day the thought of his father's illness didn't leave him. Muranjan's father had sought treatment from numerous pulmonary specialists. He had taken ayurvedic and homeopathic medicines for years, but to no avail.

Two days later, Muranjan returned home, and what he saw left him spellbound. His father was walking about in the verandah of his home. He couldn't believe his eyes. Immediately, he recalled standing before Baba's Samadhi and telling Baba of his wishful thinking. To his amazement, it did indeed come to fruition and that too without delay. Muranjan couldn't help but join his hands together and thank Baba, "Baba even though I did not have too much faith in you, you performed this incredible miracle. You indeed made the impossible possible and showed supreme power and compassion. Thus I am indebted to you for many lives. Lord! Give me the good sense to be devoted to thee my entire life, and not to stray away from thy feet ever. This is the only *bhiksha* (alms) I want from you."

Ref.: *Shri Sai Leela Magazine*, Volume 63, No. 8–9, November and December 1984.

108

Magical Healing Powers of Baba's Udi-Tirth

Right from childhood, Anuradha Adikari, a resident of Aurangabad, was devoted to Baba. In fact, Baba was the only God that she worshipped. Anuradha states, "As luck would have it, when I reached a marriageable age, I got married to a Sai devotee. At that time I didn't know that he and his family were ardently devoted to Baba. I was delighted when I stepped into my new home, because I was greeted by a huge picture of Baba in the Dwarka Mai pose that hung on the wall in front of me. I couldn't control my emotions and tears of joy filled my eyes. My mother-in-law escorted me into the house and asked me to prostrate in front of Baba. At that moment I knew that everything would be fine as Baba was already there to take care of me."

About a year later, her husband was transferred to Kolhapur, and Anuradha accompanied him. Then the following year, Baba blessed her with a baby girl. For some reason her christening ceremony was postponed. Anuradha states, "When my daughter Sandhya was around a month old, she had an ear infection. A foul smelling whitish discharge came out of both her ears. Sometimes the discharge was blood-tinged. She was checked by a specialist in E.N.T. who prescribed some ear drops. Religiously I put the drops in Sandhya's ears and cleaned them gently. However, the serous discharge didn't stop."

One day, Anuradha's father-in-law came to visit them, and he suggested that Sandhya be checked by his dear friend, Dr. Deshpande. Dr. Deshpande was a renowned E.N.T. surgeon who had done his post graduation from Berlin. Sandhya was then checked by Dr. Deshpande who gave them a bleak prognosis; he said that both her ear drums were perforated and the chances of Sandhya suffering from severe hearing loss or even deafness were high. Anuradha was in total despair about her child's future. Upon returning home she placed the bottle of ear drops in front of Baba's picture and fervently prayed to him. "Baba, if my daughter becomes deaf then her entire life will be ruined. Please do not nip the flower in the bud, but allow it to bloom. From this very moment I will stop putting the ear drops, and will put your *tirth* (sanctified water) in her ears. Please heal her ears. Her christening ceremony has not been performed yet. When her ears heal because of your *tirth*, I will christen her with a name that starts with the letter 'S', so that she may never forget your grace her entire life." Then Anuradha took a little *tirth* and mixed some *Udi* in it. After shaking it vigorously, she put two drops in each ear. Anuradha also started a fast for three days, praying to Baba to heal her ears.

The next day Anuradha was standing on the balcony of her apartment and looking at the street below, when she saw a fakir standing in front of her calling out to her, "*Mai*, come down." Anuradha went down with some rice, which she put in the fakir's *jholi* (bag for receiving alms). The fakir accepted it and said, "*Mai* you seem to be distressed. Don't worry, Sai Baba is with you and everything will be alright." Anuradha was perplexed as it was unusual to find a fakir who spoke Hindi in Kolhapur. The fakir continued, "*Mai* I have just returned from Rameshwaram and I am on my way to Shirdi. Won't you give me some *dakshina* (offering of money)?" Anuradha was impressed by the bright aura around him, and his compassionate eyes. She went inside and brought 1 Rupee 25 *anna*s and handed it to him.

The decision to stop the ear drops was entirely Anuradha's, and she didn't tell anyone about it. Every day she would put three drops of the *Udi-tirth* mixture, three times a day in both her daughter's ears. A few days later both the ears healed and there was no more discharge. When she took Sandhya for a checkup, the doctor was astounded to see that the ear drums were completely healed without the least bit of scarring. It was then that Anuradha told her family what she had done. She said, "Baba is the father of Dhanvantri (Lord of medicine). This is proof that his *Udi-tirth* is a panacea for every illness. The only prerequisite is that one should have intense faith in Him and his *Udi* and *tirth*."

Finally as per her promise to Baba, she named her daughter Sandhya.

Ref.: *Prasad*, Volume 33, No. 9, August 1979.

Conclusion

It is nearly a hundred years since Baba took Maha Niryan or left his physical body and yet he comes running to the aide of his devotees, and instructs them, provides them succour and comfort. It is mind boggling that Baba has kept his promise and that promise is *"Zari hae sharira gelo mee takuna. Tari mee dhavena bhaktan sathi".* It means "Even if I cast off this mortal body I will come running to the aid of my devotees."

In this promise Baba says, "Even if I shed this physical body." This promise is in part a statement that one day this physical body will not be there. But it also has a deeper meaning that is he has shed the physical body by his own will. And if and when the need arises he will assume that very same body again and again. Baba says, "Whether I am *Sagun* (with form) or I am *Nirgun* (without form), I will appear before the devotees and fulfil their spiritual needs. I am not bound by time, space and physical limitations; where there is intense devotion and I am needed I will be present in my physical form at once."

Prior to 1918 the devotees saw Baba in his physical form day in and day out. After Baba took *Niryan,* his physical form was not there, so does that mean that Baba is gone forever? Baba was there then and is there today and will be there tomorrow and eternally.

In chapter 15 of the Shri Sai Satcharita Baba says, "Wherever you may be, when you spread your hand before me in supplication, with faith and devotion, there I stand behind you, day and night, as steadfast as your faith and devotion is. I may be here in my physical body, and you may be beyond the seven seas. Yet, whatever you do there, I know it here instantly". This was Baba's assurance and commitment to Cholkar, however it is a promise to every Sai devotee. Hence another promise that Baba made is unquestionably true even to this day, and that promise is:

"Nithya mee jeevantha jaana haechi sathya
Nithya ghya pracheeta anubhavae."

Roughly translated it means, "I am immortal. Know this truth and forever get the experience of my immortality."